The A-Z of Management Concepts and Models

Bengt Karlöf and Fredrik Helin Lövingsson

THOROgood

Published by Thorogood Publishing
10-12 Rivington Street, London EC2A 3DU

Telephone: 020 7749 4748
Fax: 020 7729 6110
Email: info@thorogood.ws
Web: www.thorogood.ws

Books Network International Inc
3 Front Street, Suite 331
Rollinsford, NH 30869, USA

Telephone: +603 749 9171
Fax: +603 749 6155
Email: bizbks@aol.com

A CIP catalogue record for this book is available
from the British Library.

ISBN HB: 1 85418 385 0
ISBN PB: 1 85418 390 7

Book designed and typeset in the UK
by Driftdesign.

Printed in India by Replika Press.

Contents

Preface

In the world today, there has been a sharp rise in the number of executive positions requiring knowledge of management. As greater demands are being made on our intellectual abilities, the capacity to manage and develop a business is at a premium.

Semantic confusion is notable within management circles, where there exists an abundance of concepts and expressions lacking generally known or accepted definitions.

Other specialist vocabularies – in for example, medicine or the law – have expressions for facilitating and simplifying communication, thus leading to greater efficiency in their particular discipline. If in the field of medicine we were to speak of arthritis or, in the law, of an obligation to offer for redemption, we would be understood without the need of additional language. Things are not as well ordered in management. Terms such as business concept, vertical integration level, benchmarking or Boston matrix may be bandied about, but how many of them are really fully understood? Semantics (meaning and understanding) in business could be improved considerably.

A book called *Business Strategy* came out at the end of the 1980s. Its title could have been improved, for the contents were simply explanations and examples of terminology in management and business life generally. Little by little the book was developed, being published in English in 1993 under the title of *Key Business Concepts*. It has since been published in no less than 17 languages, including Russian and Chinese. The need for conceptual clarity and concise information is thus global, and not by any means limited to one language only.

This book includes ideas expressed previously, but it has been modified and elaborated considerably. In fact it is virtually a new book, with the ambition of giving the reader an insight into essential concepts and models as applied in management, not only in commerce but also in non-profit organizations and the public sector. We hope and believe that it will satisfy a need for many years to come.

During the writing phase we found *The Ultimate Business Library* by Stuart Crainer, and *Management* by Robert Kreitner, to be very useful. We have been inspired by a number of thinkers, among them Gary Hamel, Henry Mintzberg and Michael Porter. In addition, we have benefited from the creative input and experience of our colleagues within Karlöf Consulting.

The book is based on a number of concepts in management. If you feel that you can make a contribution to its contents, or would like to comment on it in any way, please contact the authors at: management@karlofconsulting.se.

Bengt Karlöf, Fredrik Helin Lövingsson

Introduction: Management

The need for management in society today

We have already intimated that semantics in management is in a parlous state. The definition, content and application of management terms are poorly understood, being only taught to a limited extent at universities and colleges. The function of specialist terminology in a particular discipline is normally to facilitate communication by preventing misunderstanding and obviating the need for lengthy explanation. We gave medicine and the law as two examples of disciplines which fulfil this function admirably.

Clearly, specialist terminology did not arise to obfuscate, or confuse people through the use of complicated language, but as an aid to communication. In this respect, language as it is used in management leaves much to be desired. The absence of systematic training in management, together with the use by consultants and professional managers of loose and vague terminology, make the language of management a rich source of parody and amusement.

Scott Adams' Dilbert character, among others, must have entertained millions by the use of similar jargon. While specialist terminology in other disciplines is there to clarify, management language is seen as ambiguous and confusing. The terms differentiation and diversification are often confused for instance, and for many people, the significance of other terms such as business concept, entry barriers, or benchmarking, is doubtful – even for the few who profess to know what they are talking about.

The Economist of 26 February 1994 expressed the view that "the only thing worse than to slavishly follow management theory is to completely ignore it." Given the enormous complexity and difficulty that there is in running a business, it is no surprise that management tends to follow current trends and fashions. After all, heads of department have to look for ways of solving their problems. The trouble is – there are so many!

While run-of the-mill managers tend to slavishly follow trends, the more talented will look at new theories and ideas to see whether they can build on earlier experiences and ever-present reality.

From now on in this book, we will hold to the premise that there are three different facets to management: leading, controlling and developing a business. To put it simply we can say that a manager has three different roles:

- The coach – motivating and leading people
- The controller – checking that the business is efficient
- The strategist – taking decisions and acting in the present to ensure future success

In the rest of this book, anyone carrying some kind of management responsibility will be called a manager. Managers are generally delegated from above, while leaders are normally accorded that distinction by those who are led. The leadership of people, together with knowledge of psychology and group dynamics, is a fundamental part of management.

This book, however, lays stress primarily on those areas that deal with the control and development of businesses. Some of the most important aspects of each of these areas are given in the three lists, below.

DEVELOPMENT	CONTROLLING	LEADING
• The leader as an individual	• How to work with strategy questions?	• How do you know that your business is efficient?
• The leader in a group	• Tools and methods for operational development	• Financial terms and their significance
• The leader as coach		• Quality control
• The performance review	• Competence development and educating organization	• Objectives management
• Entrepreneurship		• Process control
• Progress work	• Vision/ambition	• Benchmarking
	• Business concept	

The word 'management' comes from the Latin *manus*, which means hand, and *agere*, meaning to act. In modern Italian we find the closely related word *maneggiare*, which has dictionary meanings of to handle, wield, treat, cultivate, deal with, administer and run. According to Webster's, management is "The act, art or manner of managing, handling, controlling, directing etc."

Management thus has to do with all forms of organized business that are to be led, controlled and developed. During the industrial revolution, roughly one hundred and fifty years ago, there were few people who held responsibility for a business. Perhaps 0.5 per cent of the gainfully employed population would lead and control a business, while 99.5 per cent carried out more or less repetitive work. The situation today has changed radically. With the advent of decentralized responsibility and automation, the number of the gainfully occupied with a management responsibility has virtually taken off. Areas of responsibility may vary, from the handling of a business portfolio to project management, but the main functions of leading, controlling and developing are nevertheless common to all management responsibility.

The complexity of large-scale enterprises today has led to the organizational pie being cut in a number of ways, leading to a wealth of new work arenas, all of them calling for management competence. This applies to all of the functions, processes and projects, as well as competence centres and sales companies of a great variety of businesses.

Then there is the range of activities outside purely business operations. Under the pressure of government budgets, there is an ever-increasing need for management competence in the public sector. The same applies to non-profit activities, whether of religious bodies or the many professional and industrial organizations that exist. The demand for management has thus grown dramatically and continues to do so.

Due to the amorphous nature of the subject, this need has been relatively well represented in the number of books published in recent years, although the same cannot be said for what is taught at business schools and faculties of applied economics. There has been a boom in the number of published titles in the last 25 years. The trendsetter in the field can, with some justification, be said to be the book *In Search of Excellence* by Thomas Peters and Robert Watermans (1982), and others, such as the well-known authors Michael Porter, Henry Mintzberg and Gary Hamel have followed in their footsteps. The general level of awareness of published material among active managers seems to be increasing, and they tend to be less mindful of trends nowadays. Good managers will have their own approach and probably read books which they hope will throw up new ideas in their areas of responsibility. The tendency to package and standardize on the other hand, can sometimes lead to an approach that has not been thought through.

Management plays a meaningful role in the debate on innovation, which in most cases is understood to be synonymous with products and seldom as encompassing the whole business concept with all its commercial ramifications. Regardless of how we look at it, any debate on innovation must to a great extent include commercial competence, or in other words, management. The basis of all organized business is actually to create a value that is higher than the cost of producing this value. Value should not be understood here as mere commercial value, but as consisting of all the components built into an offering of goods or services. This is true for all types of business, whether they are religious, state-owned, or municipal organizations.

There is less need of management competence at times and in situations where a business is guaranteed its survival. But the more pressure there is, the more important its management competence becomes. An illustration of this is given by the tight budgets which during the last ten years have led to a greater demand for management competence in the public sector.

This introduction to the subject of management is intended to put into relief the rest of our account of the subject, which in condensed form will attempt to define, explain and give examples of concepts and models. We naturally had to be selective as to material, basing our choice primarily on personal experience of the usefulness and frequency of the terms included. Readers are cordially invited to make suggestions for improvements, changes or additions.

Activity-based costing (ABC)

In 1987, the book *Relevance Lost – The Rise and Fall of Management Accounting,* was published. The authors, Thomas Johnson and Robert Kaplan, criticized existing models for costing and presented the fundamentals of their ABC model. Kaplan developed his ideas further with his Harvard colleague Robin Cooper in the article *Measure Cost Right: Make the Right Decisions,* which was published in the *Harvard Business Review* in 1988. The ABC model made its breakthrough through this article.

One important aspect of the background to ABC is that the growing complexity of industrial systems has gradually led to a situation where joint costs constitute an increasingly larger part of the total cost mass. Other factors that have given greater importance to indirect costs are diversification, a greater degree of customization, and shorter product life cycles. In the days when direct materials and labour accounted for the lion's share of a product's costs, it was acceptable to make a routine allocation of joint costs in proportion to variable separable costs. The present situation however, requires more sophisticated and equitable methods for cost allocation. ABC was applied from the beginning in the manufacturing industry, but latterly has been used in the service industry to an increasing degree.

ABC is a method for the systematic allocation of common costs to products, services and/or customers on the basis of their consumption of resources activity by activity.

The principles of cost allocation are as follows:

- Products, services and customers generate a need for activities.
- These activities create a need for resources and themselves generate costs.

ABC is usually introduced in firms to create a better basis for pricing, profitability analyzes and product evaluations, as well as to prioritize marketing efforts. To all of this can be added a better control over expenditure, providing opportunities for cutting costs.

The concept of a *cost driver* is fundamental to an understanding of ABC. Cost drivers represent the key links to a company's total costs. A cost driver is the quantity that links activities to the object (a product, for example), which is the target of the ABC model. Let us suppose that the cost of delivery work (the activity) is to be allocated to a particular product (the cost object). The more deliveries there are, the more time (the resource) will be needed to deal with deliveries. The result is that incremental costs will be attributed to the product. In this case, the *number of deliveries* is a cost driver.

The allocation of costs through cost drivers is an effect of the *cost causality principle*, in accordance with which the cost object is attributed costs equivalent to the resources it has used. When they are allocated, all costs are regarded as variable, therefore any decisions made on the basis of an analysis should be regarded as relatively long-term ones. Short-term decisions may need to be supplemented by a measure such as variable costing.

How ABC is employed by a business will largely depend on the reason for its introduction. Generally speaking, ABC can be introduced in the four stages described below.

1. Activity analysis

The first step is to analyze and specify activities which, directly or indirectly, are connected to the analysis object. Businesses often have documented procedures which can be used as a basis for an activity analysis.

2. Use of resources

The resources employed in activities can now be examined. These may be direct costs in the form of materials and labour, or indirect costs such as administration or sales costs.

3. Specification of cost drivers

The next step is to identify the cost drivers that can be used to describe the connection between activities and the analysis object. Cost drivers should be chosen with great care.

4. Costing of the cost object

Costs are finally allocated to the object, and here the cost drivers are used. These will indicate the extent of activities under scrutiny and thus the resources consumed by the cost object.

Many of those who have used ABC in practice have done so on the basis of the theory that it is better to be roughly right than exactly wrong. It should be evident from our account that ABC is not an exact science. Good results will, by and large, depend on careful assessment. It may therefore be a good idea to apply the 80-20 rule when we make a decision on whether to introduce the ABC model. Getting the final 20 per cent right may require input that is not on a par with the value of the result.

A close relation to ABC is ABM, which stands for Activity Based Management. ABM not only looks at the consumption of resources by activities, but also at how they contribute to value creation by satisfying customers' utility functions.

RECOMMENDED READING

1. Edward Forrest, Activity-Based Management: A Comprehensive Implementation Guide.

2. Gary Cokins, Activity-based Cost Management: An Executive's Guide.

Advantages of small-scale operations

The advantages of working in small organizations are often of a psychosocial nature. They are difficult to measure and for this reason attract less interest than they should. Without small-scale advantages there would only be one company in every industry. Economies of scale would then be the decisive factor in the ability to compete. Advantages of small-scale operations include:

1. Motivation
2. Communication
3. Customization
4. Optimal processes
5. Economization of resources

6. Flexibility at work

7. Sickness absence – productivity

By 'motivation' we mean that people will devote more of their energies to work if they are motivated. This leads to a win-win situation in that employees feel better about their lives, while employers get more effectiveness from operations, and customers, hopefully, get greater value (quality in relation to price).

A small company enjoys better channels of communication than a large company. Studies carried out in the USA show that many managers in large companies spend 60 per cent of their available time in in-house meetings. This means that they are exposed to the same thoughts and meet the same people almost all of the time, not a good basis for effectiveness. In small companies, communication between management and employees takes place with much less expenditure of energy. It happens naturally in the cafeteria or wherever people congregate.

In small-scale environments a firm's co-workers are very sensitive to the requirements of their customers so that customization becomes practically a matter of course. The way to create customer satisfaction is usually obvious, as the distance to the customer is not as great as in environments dominated by large-scale production.

Processes can be seen from different perspectives; one example is Business Process Re-engineering. Work flow (see *Processes*) is the analytical element on which processes are based. The desired effect of a flow is first established, then activities and work tasks are integrated in order to produce this effect. In this way discontinuities and unnecessary work can be eliminated, leading to shorter transit times. Work-flows are much simpler in small-scale operations; the more complex the organization, the harder work-flows are to analyze.

Resources are usually in short supply in small-scale environments and it is important to get value for money. Money goes further, which tends to increase effectiveness. Flexibility of all personnel is a palpable advantage of small-scale operations. It is natural to help others beyond what is written in one's job specification and this too leads to operational effectiveness. For example, we once saw how a hard-pressed airline handled its ground support operations. Its crew efficiently carried out simple checks and other jobs, something that a large airline probably could not have done without calling in special personnel.

Sickness absence – productivity

Research has shown that sickness absence varies greatly depending on the size of an organization. In companies with fewer than five employees, sick absence is about 1.7 per cent, while in large organizations with more than 200 employees the figure is between five and six per cent. These figures reflect the presence of motivation and work satisfaction, as well as the fact that small working groups enjoy high productivity. This in turn shows that small companies can enjoy a competitive advantage and clearly speaks in favour of decentralized responsibility from both an employer and employee perspective.

In the section under *Decentralization* we give an account of a form of analysis which can be useful to organizations in their structural work and which balances small-scale advantages with economies of scale, and other aspects that should be taken into account.

RECOMMENDED READING

1. Bengt Karlöf, Strategic Tools and Processes.
2. Jamie S Walters, Big Vision, Small Business: Four Keys to Success Without Growing Big.
3. William Easterly, The Elusive Quest for Growth: Economists' Adventures and Misadventures in the Tropics.

Agenda analysis

Agenda analysis is a term used in strategy work, where an analysis of different factors is set in motion by a management group to reach a consensus on a strategic agenda. The group's strategic agenda indicates its priorities in the achievement of its goals.

An agenda analysis can actually be regarded as a tool for establishing priorities in any situation in which a group wishes to:

1. bring out and deal with possible differences of opinion; and
2. reach agreement on its priorities.

The procedure for carrying out an agenda analysis is as follows:

1. Identify candidates

Select the points the group wishes to prioritize and reach agreement on. These may be anything from a number of strategic actions to various areas for cutting costs, or the identification of possible market segments.

2. Individual ranking of candidates

Members of the group then rank each candidate. An effective way of doing this is by assigning points. Each group member has 100 points to distribute among the candidates as s/he sees fit. The distribution of points by members is checked and counted up according to the figures given below.

As can be seen by the distribution of points in the table below, candidates 1 and 4 are those which, on average, have been valued highest by members.

	Member 1	Member 2	Member 2	Member 3	Member 4	Total
Candidate 1	30	40	90	90	10	170
Candidate 2	10	0	0	0	40	50
Candidate 3	10	0	0	0	10	20
Candidate 4	40	50	10	10	0	100
Candidate 5	10	10	0	0	40	60
Total	100	100	100	100	100	(400)

If sensitive points are at issue, or the dynamics of the group so dictate it, voting may be carried out anonymously or via e-mail. However, the opportunity for a discussion on priorities and the relative merits of candidates will then have been forfeited.

3. Discussion of the result

An important part of agenda analysis is a discussion of the result. How is it that the priorities of member no. 4 differ so noticeably from those of the rest of the group? Why do members' no.1 and no.2 think that candidate 4 is so important?

By following this line of argument, the group become aware that it has different priorities. Its customary decision-making procedures can then come into play. However, it is more common for members of the group to find that they each see the candidates in a different light. When this is the case, the candidates should be clearly defined.

4. Iterations

Once the result of the exercise has been discussed and each candidate defined, participants should have the opportunity of repeating the exercise. This is allowed to continue until the group has reached agreement on an agenda, or realized that consensus cannot be achieved.

One of the strengths of this tool is that it reveals and deals with 'false consensus'. It is not unusual for all the members of a management group to put their names to a strategic plan because everyone has been able to get their key points on board. Once its priorities have been revealed, a group often sees the agreement it believed to be a reality, vanish into thin air.

If an agenda analysis is not carried out, there is a great risk that all the participants will come to act on a basis of their own priorities instead of those of their company. Another strength of agenda analysis is that it obliges participants to discuss candidates for prioritization, thus creating a unified viewpoint as to the merits of each candidate.

To focus on streamlining a company's in-house business can mean different things to different people. For one person it might be the development of efficient IT-based support systems, while for another it might be the study and improvement of in-house work processes. A third person might have in mind the creation of a culture that favours knowledge exchanges. A fourth may be thinking of making staff cuts.

This brief illustration of agenda analysis shows how important it can be to discuss the points on a list of priorities.

Balanced scorecard

Few can withstand the simple and obvious logic underlying balanced score-card, namely, that there are factors other than the financial which are important to control and follow up and that it can be a good idea to establish which factors these in fact are. We are not breaking fresh ground when we declare the importance of controlling an organization with parameters other than purely the financial. Customer satisfaction, co-worker satisfaction, process lead times and other non-financial values were given consideration long before balanced scorecard made its appearance. What was new about balanced scorecard was that it provided a simple, pedagogic structure for assessing such values. When Robert Kaplan and David Norton launched the concept of the balanced scorecard in the *Harvard Business Review* in 1994 and later in a book under the title of their concept, they postulated the idea of organizational control on a basis of four perspectives: finance, learning and growth, customers and internal processes.

Other thinkers on management have proposed different categories often based on the same basic themes: co-workers, customers, internal efficiency, finance and, sometimes, renewal business. For a more comprehensive appreciation of the different perspectives of organizational control, we can divide them into internal, external and profit perspectives. Minor perspectives commonly grouped under these three categories are shown in the tabulation below.

Balanced scorecard was not the first attempt to create a structure for control and follow-up of non-financial values. One of the earliest of these endeavours was the *tableau de bord*, which drew much attention in France in the 1960s. (See for example P Lauzel and A Cibert, *Des Ratios au Tableau de Bord*, second edition 1962.) Tableau de bord is very similar to balanced scorecard, but because what had been written on this model had never been translated from the French, it made no impression on the non-French speaking world. Curiously enough, the principles of tableau de bord had already been formulated in France at the end of the nineteenth century. Meanwhile Sweden has been represented by Karl-Erik Sveiby, who in 1989, together with the Konrad Group (the name has its origins in Konrad Day, a date in the Swedish calendar), published *The Invisible Balance Sheet* (*Den osynliga balansräkningen*) a practical guide for the measurement and review of an organization's intangible assets. The work which was popularized through concepts such as TQM (see *Quality*) also gave rise to a number of models clearly related to balanced scorecard.

The authors recommend that companies reflect on the areas of their organization that need control and review, instead of blindly turning to whatever standard models are up for grabs. An organization's suppliers might be one area that requires a special perspective, while for another organization this might be its products.

The balance in balanced scorecard is first and foremost the balance between financial and non-financial values. Unsurprisingly, it was relatively easy to sell the concept on this basis in the latter half of the 1990s when many companies wanted to lay emphasis on their intangible assets. In conferences on balanced scorecard in this period, the big gap between market value and book value was used as proof that company management were missing something important. Intellectual capital (see this term) was a term that was regularly used to describe the parts of a company's value that remained invisible for traditional accounting procedures.

INTERNAL PERSPECTIVE	EXTERNAL PERSPECTIVE	PERFORMANCE PERSPECTIVE
• Processes	• Customer	• Finance
• Efficiency	• Relations/stakeholders	• Economy
• Employee	• External business environment	• Owners
• Innovation/ renewal/learning	• Suppliers	• Profitability
• Organization	• Community	
• Products		
• Environment/quality		

However, the balance in balanced scorecard is of a more traditional character in that it pits leading metrics against lagging metrics. Leading metrics are measures that refer to earlier parts of a process and give early indications of the direction a company is taking, while lagging metrics measure the results. If we assume that happy employees make for more satisfied customers, and that this in the long-term will result in better profitability, then co-worker satisfaction is a leading metric while profitability is a lagging metric. Leading metrics are often found in the internal and, possibly, the external perspectives, while lagging metrics are to be found in the profitability perspective (see the table above).

Apart from juggling the financial against the non-financial, and leading metrics against lagging metrics, the balanced scorecard aims for a balance between internal and external focus.

A popular model for working with balanced scorecard is to describe, for each perspective:

1. the long-term goals of the organization.
2. what success factors have been established to achieve these goals.
3. what activities should be carried out to achieve goals.
4. what indicators should be measured to monitor development.

RECOMMENDED READING

1. Robert S Kaplan and David P Norton, The Balanced Scorecard: Translating Strategy into Action.
2. Paul R Niven, Balanced Scorecard Step-by-Step: Maximizing Performance and Maintaining Results.

Barriers

The word 'barrier' actually means, 'an elongated structure erected as an obstacle or shield'. By analogy, the word as used in the context of business strategy refers to the creation of obstacles either to prevent new competition from starting, or to prevent existing competitors from leaving the market.

The erection of a barrier is part of the struggle to gain a competitive edge.

The nature of the barrier may vary. Traditionally, it is a question of high capital intensity. In the airline business, the barriers consist of concessions and large sums of capital. In many kinds of consultancy business it is know-how that is the barrier. In the retail trade it is the location of the shop or some other competitive advantage that makes it hard for competitors to break in. Barriers of this kind are called entry barriers.

Examples:

- Economies of scale: high investment needed to achieve low production costs
- Differentiated product: customers loyal to one brand or supplier
- Capital requirement: high capital outlay for credit, image or whatever
- Changeover costs: cost to customer of changing suppliers
- Distribution channels: none available
- Components and raw materials: deliveries unobtainable
- Location: already occupied
- Lack of experience and know-how
- Expected retaliation: competitors will gang up on a newcomer
- Customer loyalty to strong brand
- International trade restrictions
- Price cutting
- Patents and licenses

In many industries, exit barriers have proved to be a serious obstacle to long-term profitability. The world shipbuilding industry is a classic example. Many nations have built huge shipyards and invested billions of dollars in them. When a situation of overcapacity arises, the investors fight tooth and nail to hold on to their investment, with the result that capacity is not knocked out fast enough to allow anybody to make a profit. The same thing has happened in the steel industry and to a certain extent in the aviation industry.

Examples of exit barriers:

- Write-off of heavy investments
- Prestige and image
- Management pride
- Government intervention
- High disengagement costs: restoration of site
- Trade union opposition
- Shared costs which will have to be borne by another product or market
- Suppliers, customers, distributors

The purpose of entry barriers is, of course, to deter new competition from trying to get established. The idea is to make the cost of admission to the marketplace so high as to risk a negative return on the capital that must be invested. Entry barriers can thus be designed either to raise the admission fee or to increase the risk to the newcomer.

Exit barriers, on the other hand, force business units to keep on operating in an industry where profitability is low or return on capital is negative. As we can see from the list above, exit barriers can be divided into three classes: socio-political, economic and emotional. The last-named group includes the situation where a successful conglomerate branches out into a new field and stubbornly keeps the venture going year after year despite heavy losses. Such situations are not uncommon, and they can often create serious problems for established companies in the industry concerned.

RECOMMENDED READING

1. Paul A Geroski, Market Dynamics and Entry.

2. Philip Kotler, Principles of Marketing.

3. W. Kip Viscusi, Economics of Regulation and Antitrust.

Basic business functions

There are four basic functions of business management that can help to understand any business. They are:

- Development

- Marketing – sales

- Production

- Administration

This classification is often highly instructive, for these basic functions apply to all types of company and all types of business unit.

Development comprises the development of products and markets, as well as of the organization and the people in it (see the entry under *Development*). Development implies adaptation to needs and is essential in all business activities.

Marketing (see *Market* and *Needs*) is the business of creating demand. Without demand, arising from the need structures of customers, business cannot exist. The term marketing also includes selling, that is, order acquisition.

Production is the total process of making the goods and performing the services that customers demand, and of bringing them to the customer. Distribution may belong to the production or marketing function depending on the type of industry and the importance of the distribution aspect to the business.

Administration covers all the actions required to control resources. In a business unit, the term administration comprises all the supporting functions necessary to doing business.

RECOMMENDED READING

1. Kim B Clark et al, Harvard Business Review on Managing the Value Chain.

2. Michael E Porter, Competitive Strategy: Creating and Sustaining Superior Performance.

Benchlearning®

It is an axiom that we should learn from the experiences of others without ourselves having to re-live those experiences. It is because of this axiom that humans have developed faster than animals. We have been able to store and impart knowledge and have thus created a bridge of learning, not only between different cultures and geographical areas but also in the temporal sense.

Benchlearning was developed in 1994 by Karlöf Consulting as a natural consequence of continually working with benchmarking. Benchmarking largely focuses on key ratios and processes. Benchlearning goes a couple of steps further: first, to causality, i.e. causal relationships, and then to organizational learning, or the insight developed within an organization of what makes for success in that organization.

All knowledge is based on experience. Learning is therefore really a question of systemizing experiences and devising problem-solving techniques to work on stored knowledge; naturally we also have to put our creativity to work. The advantage of benchlearning is that it provides us with a learning reflex, and thus a shortcut to knowledge, through systematically comparing ourselves with role models. We see ourselves reflected in others and consequently raise our awareness of our own organization at the same time as we get ideas to improve it.

In a world plagued by planned economy, i.e. one where suppliers have a monopoly and recipients of goods and services lack a free choice between different alternatives, it is important that competition – an extraordinarily effective force for development – should be encouraged. In addition to learning, benchlearning fosters the competitive instinct (which is an important aspect of acquiring information) and a more efficient organization, i.e. the creation of greater value and/or higher productivity.

The combination of development for both employer and employee creates a win-win situation in any organization. Employees become better motivated and the employer gets a more efficient organization which creates more value for customers and owners (or their equivalent). There is good reason, then, for claiming that benchlearning creates utility for the three primary stakeholder groups in all organizations: employees, customers (buyers) and owners (principals).

Legacy from benchmarking

Benchmarking was conceptualized in the Xerox group at the end of the 1970s, and the initiative spread throughout business and commerce as well as to other sectors of society. Benchmarking can be applied to calibrate processes wherever there is a similarity in the production of goods and services.

Benchmarking-related methods can be divided into types and variants:

1. Comparisons of de-standardized key ratios. This is done amazingly often.
2. Comparisons of standardized key ratios, i.e. 'apples with apples'.
3. Real benchmarking, which compares relevant key ratios, procedures and causes.
4. Benchlearning, which adds to the above organizational learning and motivation at work.

The first variant does not concern itself with comparable volumes, something that anyone involved in benchmarking soon discovers. Naturally, such comparisons will not be relevant.

Even where figures are standardized and irrelevant aspects have been eliminated, as in the second variant, the key ratios involved will elicit a reflex to make excuses because they are not tied in to causality; in other words, we will always be able to say that the comparison is irrelevant.

The third variant is generally initiated by management and can often prove a real springboard to improvement in an organization. This happens when people involved in the benchmarking process both understand that something is being done more efficiently, and *how* it is being done. Benchmarking should not be imitation, but a motivating source for our own creativity. Intelligent solutions from another environment must almost always be adapted to an organization's own, specific situation.

The fourth variant is benchlearning, which fosters knowledge of better working methods throughout the organization. Through benchlearning we can perceive the development of worker participation and the healthy process which leads to improvement through a better understanding of the whole organization and its relevant metrics. The difference to benchmarking is a question of degree rather than kind. Putting it simply, we can say that benchmarking stresses efficiency, while benchlearning puts more stress on learning in all aspects of the organization – which is not to say that it ignores efficiency for all that.

Both benchmarking and benchlearning are based on the simple theory that it is wise to learn from the experiences of others rather than to try to reinvent the wheel.

Experiences can be positive as well as negative; we can learn from mistakes as well as from the success stories. For example, by using benchmarking or its variant, the mistakes made by companies in establishing themselves in a foreign land can be avoided.

Benchlearning – building blocks

The four building blocks of benchlearning are:

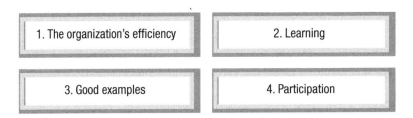

1. The organization's efficiency

2. Learning

3. Good examples

4. Participation

1. Effectiveness of the organization

Benchlearning was devized by Karlöf Consulting as a method that combines the creation of favourable conditions for learning with the ambition of improving organizational effectiveness. An organization's effectiveness, i.e. the ability to create value for customers, in relation to the cost of creating this value, forms the basis for development work through benchlearning. We can illustrate this by means of the effectiveness matrix.

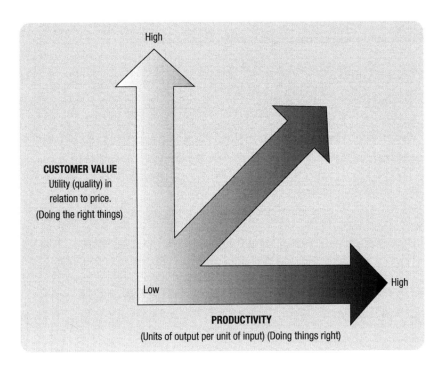

High

CUSTOMER VALUE
Utility (quality) in
relation to price.
(Doing the right things)

Low

High

PRODUCTIVITY
(Units of output per unit of input) (Doing things right)

It is important to find the right balance between customer value and productivity in the short and long-term if companies and organizations are to be successful. Business leaders are finding it increasingly more important to be able to answer the questions, "How do you know that your organization is efficient?" and, "How efficient can your organization be?"

2. Learning

Learning through benchlearning has two aims: to stimulate learning that is close to what is strategically or operatively essential in the company, and to develop the ability to learn new things. Both the desire to learn and the conditions for learning are thus involved.

3. Teambuilding

This word illustrates an important difference between benchmarking and benchlearning. Benchmarking often has a 'top down' perspective and is usually initiated by management to improve efficiency in the organization. In benchlearning the responsibility for change is spread over the organization. Employees are the ones affected by organizational change so it is they who should impel the work of change. For such work to have an effect it is logical that the people most affected by it should feel involved.

Broad participation also means that by involving an entire organization it is possible to utilize the power of the 'good example' to the utmost. An allusion to the 'burden of proof' clause from the law to support our case seems apposite here:

Persons instituting changes must commonly show evidence of why something should be changed. With a good example as evidence, the burden of proof shifts to the preservers of the status quo, who instead must show why something should not be changed.

4. Good examples

Good examples are used in benchlearning as a springboard to learning and improvement in an organization. The good example helps to raise ambition levels; it promotes improvement and new ideas; it helps to create an atmosphere of curiosity and open-mindedness in the learning organization.

The good example affects an organization's efficiency in two ways. In the first, the organization gets a yardstick of its position compared to other organizations in the outside world. It is then possible to make calibrations of efficiency and success and to set new goals for the organization in relation to these standards.

The second way in which the good example affects organizational efficiency has more to do with *how* it does this: how has the good example worked to reach its level of efficiency? Sometimes it could be instructive to look at a bad example to avoid those mistakes.

The method

A system has been developed for working methodically with benchlearning. The steps in the process given below can be replaced by other steps, depending on context.

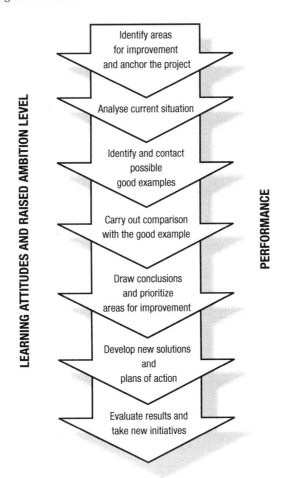

Applications

Learning from the experience of others has a variety of applications. Here are some of them:

1. Improvement in previously identified problem areas
2. Calibration of efficiency
3. Creation of a learning organization
4. Searching for areas to improve in
5. Learning in decentralized systems
6. Making use of synergies
7. Bridging differences in company cultures after mergers
8. Evaluation of strategic alternatives
9. Benchlearning as a sequel to benchmarking
10. Benchlearning as a working method in networks
11. Benchlearning for type situations in management and strategy

Let us repeat what we said earlier: the difference between benchmarking and benchlearning is a question of degree rather than kind. Benchmarking has come to be used for the comparison of more or less standardized key ratios; in benchlearning, the stress is on co-worker participation (teambuilding), learning throughout the organization and the opportunities that are offered to create a self-improvement system of people and working groups.

RECOMMENDED READING

Bengt Karlöf, Kurt Lundgren and Marie Edenfeldt Froment, Benchlearning: Good Examples as a Lever for Development.

Benchmarking

Benchmarking has dramatically grown in popularity and use ever since the Xerox Group introduced the term into management at the end of the 1970s. It was then something of a shock to find that the Japanese were selling small and medium-sized copiers at prices lower than Xerox' production costs. Management put this down to the Japanese predilection for price dumping. On closer inspection it was found that the Japanese had made a breakthrough in both design and production and that the Xerox productivity goals fell well short of what was needed. It was at this point that benchmarking was introduced as a means of stepping up development. Since then, benchmarking has spread like wildfire from Anglo-Saxon countries to the rest of the world.

A benchmark is a term used in surveying and means a fixed point, i.e. a point – often red – marked out in the bedrock or some other immovable mass. It is used as a reference for establishing altitudes and locations for buildings, and other construction work. Because it comes up with reference points where none previously existed, benchmarking has become deservedly popular.

The greater part of the world's organized business is done under the conditions of a planned economy in the sense that a manager bears the responsibility for part of a company, organization or administration in the public sector where there is an absence of real competition and the money comes not from the users or customers, but from higher up. In other words, businesses are financed by principals.

A line manager in a large airline does not have the option of hiring planes from Air Kazakstan to cut costs in interest and depreciation. Neither can s/he use pilots from Malev, the national Hungarian air carrier, or Lot, the Polish equivalent, where a pilot trained on Airbus or Boeing costs a fraction of the cost to train their own pilots. In the same way, it would be unthinkable to make use of cabin staff from Malaysian Airlines who, in addition to being cheaper, are highly reputed. For these needs, our line manager is referred to his or her technical and flight operation departments. These act as a monopoly and the line manager will not have a free choice between suppliers. A planned economy is thus in control, lacking any reference points for efficiency.

The lack of reference points in parts of systems where competition does not exist, is an important reason for the existence of benchmarking. (It is interesting that in English we use the same word for aspects of a game or sport as we would for the more serious business of business opposition: *competition*.) The element of competition in an activity plays a developing role by raising our ambition level and creating an interest in learning, which in turn promotes efficiency and competitiveness. In all the areas where competition does not exist, the marking of reference points through benchmarking constitutes a valuable exercise.

The theory can be seen in the diagram below.

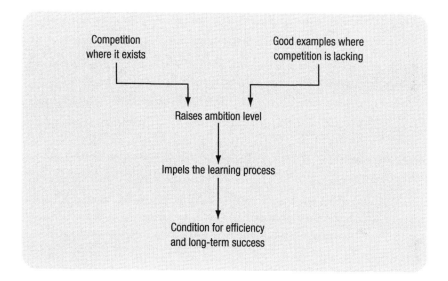

To the extent that it has spread, benchmarking has been trivialized, so that the word itself is now semantically vague. Benchmarking has gradually come to be interpreted as simply a comparison of key ratios, without reference to causality, learning or progress. The danger here is that benchmarking will degenerate into an organizational rain dance – an academic study not without interest but an exercise that does not have any noticeable effects.

The use and misuse of benchmarking may be illustrated at four different levels:

1. **De-standardized key ratios** result in the comparison of metrics that do not reflect the same work content, so that what we get is

not a comparison between apples and apples but rather between apples and whole baskets of fruit. Comparisons of this kind are far too common, particularly in the public sector.

We have encountered situations in which comparisons were made of the cost of an operation for patients with a particular complaint, or the maintenance costs of a road of a particular type. In each case the work involved, on closer inspection, was found to differ considerably. Costs for such things as cleaning and maintenance may be involved, or even more important things like indirect costs, depreciation periods, and so on.

It is an easy matter for analytically minded people to collect key ratios together, neglect to check that the work involved in one case is consistent with another, reproduce the results in a correlation chart in an Excel file and then think that some sort of progress has been made.

2. **Standardized key ratios**. Obviously, it is much better to have carried out a standardization process, i.e. to end up with compa-rable figures. This variation of benchmarking is extremely useful for diagnostics – identifying which areas should be chosen for careful examination. The standardization procedure is largely a kind of art, often calling for careful analysis and special measurement. Exact correspondences can seldom, if ever, be achieved. On the other hand, we should take standardization as far as it is possible without falling prey to the excuse that differences are so great that the whole exercise is meaningless and ought to be abandoned.

3. **Genuine benchmarking** is just as much about standardized key ratios as documented procedures with comparable work content or causality. By this we mean not only that somebody performs better, but also *why* and *how*. If we can say that a telecoms oper-ator has much lower costs for fault localization, the result will not be anything in particular even if we accept that we can carry out a comparative study of their figures. Insight and the beginning of the learning process first occurs with an understanding of why an operator is so much better. Their technical support may be superior, or their help desk may be manned by technicians.

4. **Benchlearning** is a methodology developed by Karlöf Consulting that can help organizations further on their way towards progress through participation and the learning process. By creating an environment in which everyone in an organization can understand why and how they can do better, a system of continual self-improvement is developed. See also the previous section on *Benchlearning*.

Benchmarking can be used in almost any situation. The need to quantify may vary. The less precise a matter is, the more difficult it will be to create quantitative metrics. Benchmarking can thus encompass many things: from compilations of key ratios to the documentation of procedures and the inspirational lessons of role models.

In a benchmarking sketch of a bank's productivity, which we offer here, costs per office have been divided into five types: overheads, premises, cash, back office and foreign exchange. The bar chart illustrates several important study points. The first thing is that an analysis should include 100 per cent of the bank's costs. If we only looked at a part of these, some costs could easily be attributed to another part of the business, which would complicate the standardization process. Secondly, distribution of costs, i.e. the type of cost and the place it is incurred, is important. We have chosen a relatively simple cost distribution for convenience. Thirdly, the way costs are demarcated is important. In this case we have defined the work involved per cost category. Fourthly, our comparison illustrates a common phenomenon, i.e. that the best office is by no means the best in everything. Office A, with the highest costs per credit account, has the lowest level of costs for cash function. Fifthly, the choice of metrics is significant. Here we have fixed on costs per credit account.

This benchmarking exercise is thus about productivity; we are not considering the quality of an account in this analysis.

We could also benchmark customer quality per account, but we would have to begin with a set of conditions focused more on quality.

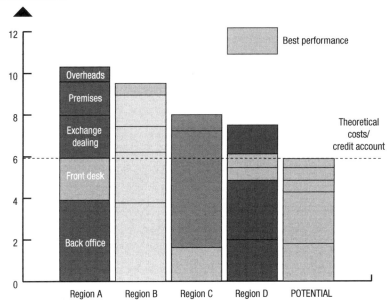

Costs/credit account

Best performance

Theoretical
costs/
credit account

Overheads

Premises

Exchange
dealing

Front desk

Back office

Region A   Region B   Region C   Region D   POTENTIAL

The column on the far left represents best practice. If all the offices were best in each cost category, productivity would theoretically be given by the column on the right and the sum potential for improvement could be calculated, even if this had to be at different times. For example, it would be time wasting to reduce the costs for premises if we were in the middle of a rental agreement.

Finally, we would like to emphasise the great importance of causality, i.e. the reason for a better performance by a particular office. Office A, with the worst productivity excepting in cash function, has studied the flow of customers during the different hours of the day and days of the week, and has decided to opt for one permanent member of staff. The other staff are part-time and fit in with customer needs. This in turn provides a lesson that should lead to a change of behaviour in other offices.

Benchmarking appeals to the competitive instinct in people. The representation below illustrates how the creativity of one organization can inspire another to a performance better than its own.

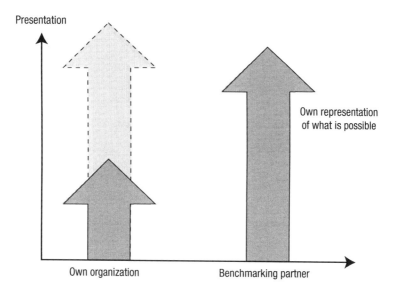

Presentation

Own representation
of what is possible

Own organization

Benchmarking partner

A colleague once told us of how she had thought of contracting a builder to renovate her bathroom. When she heard that her neighbour, a fireman, had done the same job himself, she and her husband decided to do the work themselves and save money. Their own idea of what was possible had changed and the bathroom renovation became a notable success.

In its most developed form, benchmarking is not merely about making comparisons with role models. It is also about learning from mistakes. Many organizations fail to learn from their experiences; we have found companies in telecommunications, the airlines and the energy sector which have not learned from their own history. This may have been partly due to staff turnover and a natural tendency to forget mistakes.

A postal service in one country has regularly carried out unsuccessful 'business development projects' which do not seem to have affected their experience curve in the slightest. If an organization is to carry out comprehensive cultural changes, experiences from other organizations can be very useful, as can be success factors and mistakes from the past. This is the way to avoid pitfalls. The origins of benchmarking can be found in the thesis that it is better to learn from the mistakes of others, rather than commit them yourself.

We have noticed that in large organizations it is usually the performance-oriented people who are keen to use benchmarking. There are individuals who, from a behavioural point of view, are relationship or power oriented and who will do anything to avoid criticism of their own performance. Then again there are the performance-oriented people who are conscious of the need to improve and do not see this as a fault, but rather as an opportunity to get better at their job and thus gain greater work satisfaction.

Let us note some of the uses of benchmarking:

1. Calibration of one's efficiency against others
2. Source of inspiration to improve procedures
3. Source of expertise in any given situation, e.g. strategy development
4. Diagnostic search tool to improve areas of the whole organization

The fundamental idea in benchmarking is to find common reference points in a variety of situations, while what motivates it should be efficiency, i.e. the relation between value and productivity. There is a whole section devoted to efficiency in this book; it should be the *sine qua non* for all organizations.

An obvious advantage with benchmarking is that it can be applied to almost any organizational situation. A disadvantage is the risk of trivializing the benchmarking process through the use of de-standardized key ratios.

Some criticisms of benchmarking

On several occasions we have encountered criticisms of benchmarking generally expressed as follows:

1. Benchmarking leads to imitation and is not conducive to the learning process.
2. You can only become as good as your best competitor, which won't give you a competitive edge.

Strangely enough, such criticism comes mainly from academic circles. In our opinion, it is based on a fundamental misconception of benchmarking. The following quote above gives an unequivocal reply to such criticism.

> *"Benchmarking is not imitation and almost never consists of a comparison with competitors."*

In the large number of projects that we have participated in, competitors have never played a part – unless it was a question of a European airline carrying out benchmarking in respect of say, Quantas, with its base in Australia, when the common competitive terrain was so small as to be negligible. Benchmarking involves open comparison and it would obviously be difficult to find a partner among the competition. Typical in benchmarking is that a substantial process, such as the maintenance of light aircraft or invoicing, is selected and a partner found – the industry is irrelevant – with the qualifications to be a role model. A typical example was the occasion when Xerox wanted to streamline its small general goods business.

In this example, the mail-order company L.L. Bean, whose core business was the logistics of small goods, was consulted.

The other criticism of benchmarking concerns imitation. Benchmarking should be about inspiration, not imitation. People should never have their creative intelligence denied them. The imitation criticism has unfortunately been given some credence. A collaborative partner should serve as a mirror encouraging one's own organization to press on with improvements. On the other hand, fanatical belief in a system or method is always dangerous, so it is important to be aware of criticism.

RECOMMENDED READING

1. Bengt Karlöf, Kurt Lundgven and Marie Edenfeldt Froment, Benchlearning: Good Examples as a Lever for Development.

2. Christopher E. Bogarn and Michael J English, Benchmarking for Best Practices: Winning Through Innovative Adaption.

Board work

The role of the board of directors in a company's development is complicated, and it is changing. There is a movement afoot for increasing the responsibility of boards both in their entirety and where individual members are concerned. This development has meant that board members must familiarize themselves more thoroughly than ever with the organization for which they are responsible. Each member must be able to make businesslike evaluations both together with management, and independently of management and the managing director.

It is not an exaggeration to say that board work has been the centre of attention in recent years and come in for some criticism. Without going into details, there is a general understanding that too little is spoken of strategy and business development in boards and too much of history, financial reviews and general information. A number of studies also point to a lack of time and resources available to boards to deal with strategy work.

It is surely possible to improve the work of directors by placing greater emphasis on knowledge and by a more intelligent use of their time in favour of strategic questions. One problem in this context is that a board is not necessarily chosen on the basis of its business ability. In many cases, board members are appointed by big capital owners to run the financial management. This type of member does not always create the best conditions for a company's business development. Naturally these observations will not be valid in every case, especially where new and small companies are concerned. Serious discussions of strategy may take place in many of their boardrooms, in particular where members have been chosen on the basis of their business competence and knowledge of the industry.

Topics currently discussed in relation to board work are:

- Distribution of roles: owners – board – management
- Lack of competence in questions concerning foreign countries
- A board's ability to stand up to strong management
- Remuneration. The board's role in arranging 'soft landings' for the management of large companies

- 'Professional' board members. Can one person really belong to the boards of over 30 companies at the same time and take his or her responsibilities seriously? Some of the leading personalities in industry and commerce seem to have so many board duties to perform.
- Diversity in relation to age, sex, background, etc.
- Rendering an account of options

The role and work of boards has come to the fore during the last ten to twenty years mostly because of two factors. First, there has been a sharp reaction in the USA against under-performing companies characterized by strong management and decorative boards. A pioneer in this connection was CalPers, the Californian pension fund for public employees, which began a movement that soon spread to the big asset management companies. CalPers was at the fore in seeking a change from management power to owner power, which came to be called corporate governance.

The second circumstance that has led to a focus on board work is the abuse of management power which has occurred in a number of companies. A symbol of this has been Enron Corporation, the giant conglomerate but there are other numerous examples such as WorldCom and Global Crossing. In periods of extremely fast expansion, deregulation and a blind faith in IT and telecommunications, managements have snatched back the initiative and, through boards overcome by the heady atmosphere of success, given themselves unreasonably high salaries that have also resulted in short-term increases in the values of the companies concerned. Managements were enticed through generous option conditions to discount long-term contracts and take them up as income while carrying forward expenses which in fact should have been entered as costs. In other words, the books were cooked so that the business should appear to be more successful than in fact it was.

So the balance of power between the boardroom and management has gone one way and now another. Boards are currently clear winners in the struggle. More or less anonymous owners of capital have appreciated the role the boardroom plays in the creation of value, while politicians feel obliged to intervene in concerns of ethics and equal distribution of the sexes. Board work is thus subject to a number of influences which are sure to keep this important area in a state of flux.

A board of directors can be said to have a dual role inasmuch as it must satisfy owner ambitions and requirements, and at the same time exercise a management function in relation to company management. This is shown in the illustration.

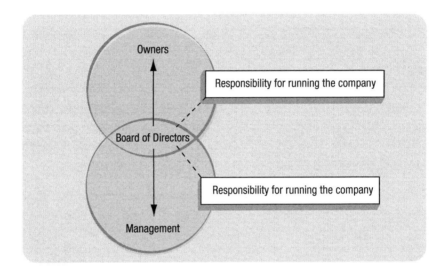

A board is the link between company management and owners, a function requiring multi-directional communication.

A board has to represent all the owners of a company and possess a breadth of competence in order to take care of the company's capacity for renewal, deal with risks, etc.

The term 'corporate governance' reflects an owner perspective rather than management's operative and strategic perspective. It is an expression of owner revolt against management's traditional upper hand. The growth of owner control is giving boards a more prominent role but at the same time there is a need for the distribution of responsibility between boards and management to be clarified. A current trend is for a more even gender distribution in boards.

How is an active board created?

There is a tendency to see board membership as some form of reward or as the means of representing a particular customer group, employees, etc. Some constructive advice in the creation of active boards:

- Require owners to establish clear goals for company operations.

- Choose board members on the basis of the competences required to develop the company in the next three to five years towards established goals.

- Take great care with the selection of a chairman of the board. This is a fundamental requirement for good board work.

A board's duel role:

- Choose a board chairman with personal integrity - a conductor rather than a soloist.

- Do not take too many similar competences on board. A good combination might be two wielders of power, two with business backgrounds and a monitor.

- Sitting on boards is not an honorary function. Appoint members for three to five years at a time or let them go when their competence is no longer relevant.

- Begin by inviting candidates to a number of board meetings in order to see how comfortable they will be with the normal work of the board.

- If you are stuck with a passive board of directors, work to gradually weed out the `honorary' members to obtain the competence you require.

Research recently carried out in the USA shows that the traditional rules for the comportment of boards of directors do little to explain a company's success. A comparison of ruined companies (Enron, Global Crossing) with successful companies like General Electric and Disney Corporation found that there were no great differences in attendance of members, knowledge of companies, company shareholdings, number of board duties, etc. The authors stated in their report that traditional parameters alone could not account for a successful board of directors. Special emphasis was given to the importance of an open atmosphere where members felt they could speak freely, rather than one characterized by 'group think' or deferential attitudes. Also stressed was the importance of creative discussions of company strategy as opposed to routine reporting or the formalization of decisions already made in practice. Questions of strategy are in short supply in boardrooms.

Remember:

- Hold board meetings at least five or six times a year.
- One of the board meetings of the year should be devoted to strategy and last a whole day, preferably an overnight stay from lunch on one day to lunch on the next.

This becomes more important as the size of a board increases.

- Boards should be kept informed on a regular basis. A letter once a month from the managing director dealing with three problems, three items of a more optimistic nature and the more important coming events, should be sufficient.
- Ensure that information about the company and the industry from external sources (and not only from the managing director) is made available to board members.
- Let the board chairman and managing director prepare meetings and establish agendas together.
- Ensure that the 'right' questions are taken up at board meetings.
- Set up agendas so that the most important questions are dealt with first when the attention is less inclined to wander. Routine reports should be left to the end, if included at all.

We believe that boards, while retaining positions of relatively great power, will become more accountable, i.e. greater attention will be paid to how they perform and the results they achieve.

Role of a board of directors in strategy work

A board of directors can have several roles in strategy work depending on how it is elected, the size of the company in question and where the company is in its development. The principal duty of the directors in relation to strategy is normally to see to it that the company has actually determined its strategy work. It is then up to management to carry out this work. Of course there are important exceptions to this general rule where the distribution of work is concerned. The directors of many companies which start and grow quickly often have special skills that are of great value in strategy work, so that we would naturally expect these people to be included in the work.

The role of a board of directors in strategy work can be seen in the illustration below.

Their job essentially is to:

1. initiate strategy work and see to it that it is pursued.
2. set ambition levels for finance, growth, etc.
3. make initial decisions on the strategic agenda.
4. continually follow up the strategic agenda.

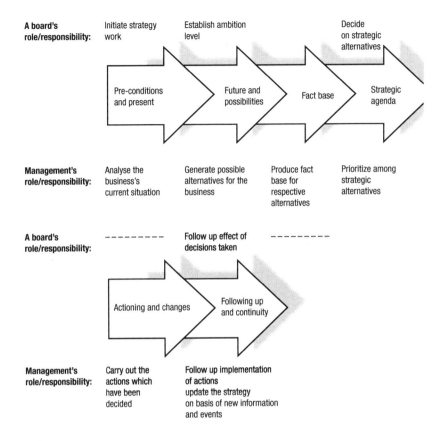

A board's role/responsibility:	Initiate strategy work	Establish ambition level		Decide on strategic alternatives
	Pre-conditions and present	Future and possibilities	Fact base	Strategic agenda
Management's role/responsibility:	Analyse the business's current situation	Generate possible alternatives for the business	Produce fact base for respective alternatives	Prioritize among strategic alternatives

A board's role/responsibility:	- - - - - - - -	Follow up effect of decisions taken	- - - - - - - -
	Actioning and changes	Following up and continuity	
Management's role/responsibility:	Carry out the actions which have been decided	Follow up implementation of actions update the strategy on basis of new information and events	

Naturally it is an over-simplification to describe the reality of strategic work in six simple steps, as we have. While a company is breaking down strategies into plans of action, changes may occur in the external environment which necessitate a return to the strategic agenda to check that its basic assumptions are still valid. The steps in the sequence should not be regarded as concrete milestones, therefore, but rather as guides in strategy work.

RECOMMENDED READING

1. Ralph D Ward, 21st Century Coporate Board.

2. Walter J Salmon, Harvard Business Review on Corporate Governance.

3. Jay A Conger et al, Corporate Boards: New Strategies for Adding Value at the Top.

Boston matrix (BCG matrix)

At the end of the 1960s, Bruce Henderson, founder of the Boston Consulting Group, BCG, developed his portfolio matrix. The effect on the business world was dramatic.

Henderson first came up with the concept of an *experience curve*, which differs widely from the *learning curve*, a concept formulated many years before and which states that staff productivity increases according to the number of times a particular work task is carried out.

The experience curve does not have the inherent threshold effects of the learning curve. The experience curve states that when a particular task is duplicated, the cost of carrying it out the second time will fall by about 20 per cent. Thus, by doubling our sales force, customer sales costs will fall by about 20 per cent. The same thing applies to invoicing, production, etc. For more on this, see the entry *Experience curve*.

The other important principle in the BCG concept was relative market share, which was calculated in relation to the biggest competitor.

The experience curve was combined with relative market share and the life cycle curve in the well-known BCG matrix shown in the figure below. The matrix was popularized by the use of symbols mainly representing animals. Such terms as 'dogs', 'wildcats', 'star' and 'cash cow' subsequently came into business use, whereupon the Boston matrix was referred to as the 'BCG zoo'.

If we look at the four squares of the BCG zoo and try to predict cash flow for the next 3.5 years, we begin to make out certain patterns. The dog or the star should have a minimal positive or negative cash flow. The cash cow delivers very positive cash flow, while the wildcat has negative cash flow.

When portfolio strategy was in its infancy, balancing the cash flow was one of group management's most important functions. The theory was that cash flow should be created in the cash cow and invested in the wildcat in order to increase market share and reach a strong competitive position. This would then bring the unit into the star square. When the market gradually stopped growing, the star business would tumble into the cash cow.

The underlying idea of the BCG matrix is that the best strategy is to dominate market share when the market is mature. The thinking goes like this:

1. Profitability is greatest when the market matures.

2. A dominating market share gives the highest accumulated production volume.

3. According to the experience curve, high volume leads to lower production costs.

4. Low production costs can either be used to lower prices and take market share, or to increase profit margins.

The BCG matrix proved a great success and most of the big American companies used it to review their business units.

BCG's competitors naturally wanted to get on the band wagon and both McKinsey and Arthur D Little developed a method involving matrices of nine cells instead of the BCG four-cell model (see for example *Industry attraction and strategic position*).

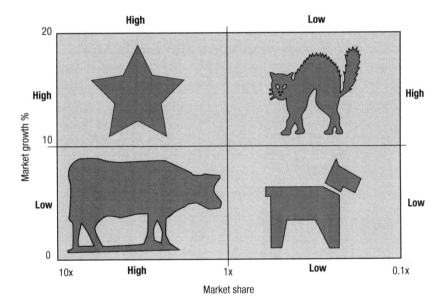

The Boston matrix has come in for harsh criticism. Here are two examples of the risks involved in connection with its use.

James Ferguson, Managing Director of a foodstuffs group, tells the story of the company's coffee business, known for, among other things, the Maxwell House brand. According to the prevailing portfolio pundits, this unit was classed as a cash cow. It was therefore supposed to create positive cash flow and not to develop and grow. The management of the unit consequently relaxed and were on the way to missing the wave of brewed and freeze-dried coffees, which were of course making a great breakthrough in the early market.

The other example concerns General Electric, a great pioneer of portfolio strategy. General Electric began to apply strategic management to its portfolio as early as the 1960s. Since then they have realized the limitations and dangers of BCG. Railway engines powered by electricity, lighting and white goods were some of the businesses that were financially starved for many years before the need for investment was discovered and applied to these business units.

Richard Hamermesh, who has made a study of the disadvantages of the BCG matrix, considered that portfolio planning on the basis of early methods was very useful when decisions had to be made concerning which business units were to be sold off, but was much less useful in connection with growth and business development. Richard Hammermesh gives good advice in this respect:

1. Do not confuse resource allocation with strategy. Planning is not a substitute for visionary leadership.

2. Pay careful attention to the strategy of each business unit and not only the strategy for the whole portfolio, which is of course the aim of portfolio planning.

3. Involve line managers in the planning process. Line managers and not personnel managers should plan strategy.

4. Do not confuse strategic planning with strategic thinking. The discipline involved in strategic planning helps in the development of strategic thinking, but they are in no way identical.

The fourth point has been called into question by many business commentators. It seems that the discipline of rigorous planning is deleterious to strategic thinking. Creativity in the sense of the ability to integrate empirical elements in new ways is a requirement in strategic planning. The rigorous discipline called for in a planning process will curb the ability of its participants to think creatively, and the result will be a second-rate strategy.

RECOMMENDED READING

Carl W Stern and George Stalk Jr (ed), Perspectives on Strategy from The Boston Consulting Group.

BPR (Business Process Re-engineering)

Business Process Re-engineering was one of the most highly touted management concepts in the early 1990s. The underlying idea was to redefine and invigorate out-of-date processes that were frustrating large organizations and leading to inefficiency.

Michael Hammer is generally considered to be the father of re-engineering. In 1990 he introduced the concept in an article in the Harvard Business Review and, in 1993, together with James Champy, he published *Re-engineering the Corporation*, regarded as one of the standard works on the subject. Hammer challenged management thinking of the time, advocating drastic change rather than incremental improvements. BPR is founded on the idea that an organization starts with an empty sheet of paper before defining its processes, in an attempt to put its history and old routines to one side. BPR can be regarded as diametrically opposed to Kaizen (see this entry), which is based on the idea of slow and gradual improvement. Expressions meaning to obliterate were sedulously used by Hammer.

As suddenly as BPR appeared on the management scene, just as sudden was its departure. There are several reasons for this. The main reason was probably a blind faith in BPR as the key to an organization's efficiency: all that had to be done was to implement it. The importance of company culture and the need to implement change through the company's co-workers, was forgotten. Critics have rather unkindly suggested that it is typical that BPR should have been developed by a former professor of computer science at MIT. Employees were expected to quickly familiarize themselves with the new charts that someone (often a consultant) had drawn up. This rather technocratic approach to business development has caused its critics to see in BPR a rediscovery of taylorism. Someone even went so far as to compare the BPR mentality of 'knocking down to build up' with Mao's cultural revolution.

Another problem was that the concept came to be seen simply as hunting down costs and making staff cuts. A study made in 1994 of 624 companies which had worked with the concept showed that in the USA, an average of 336 jobs per BPR project disappeared. The corresponding figure for Europe was 760. BPR made its appearance during a period of recession and heavy competition, one in which IT moreover came to play a major role in companies. Many organizations had to make cutbacks and dispose of activities that did not create direct value, and BPR was a useful tool for this purpose. It is easier to tell your workforce that you are downsizing or introducing BPR, than to tell them that you are making cutbacks.

It may be a rare thing nowadays to hear a company say that it is working with BPR, but the fact is that many organizations today have well defined and documented processes that are regularly reviewed and developed. The concept of BPR has contributed to an understanding of company processes and has provided many useful tools for analyzing them. It has also offered food for thought in the debate on what companies ought to concentrate on and what could be better done by others (see the entry on *Outsourcing*).

RECOMMENDED READING

1. Joe Peppard, Essence of Business Process Re-Engineering.
2. Michael Hammer and James A Champy, Re-Engingeering the Corporation.

Branding

A *brand* is a distinguishing mark of a company or product and the sum of the external world's associations with this mark. Brands are usually registered or trademarked with a regulatory authority. In current English we normally use the word trademark to refer to brand in the legal sense of the word. Because a trademark can be distinguished, it cannot be confused with an already existing *trademark*. A trademark is protected for a period of 20 years that is renewable indefinitely. Trademark legislation places two fundamental demands on a trademark:

1. It must be capable of being reproduced graphically.
2. It must be able to distinguish one product from another.

A legal trademark is usually identified by the symbols ™ or ®, the latter symbol indicating that it has been registered with The United States Patent and Trademark Office.

More recently, the commercial, strategic aspects of a trademark (brand) have won general acceptance. In this sense, a brand is defined as something experienced; it is the external world's association with a company or product name. The most common definition of brand is a variation on the following:

'A brand is a word, mark, symbol or design that identifies a product or differentiates a company and its product from others.'

There are two important aspects of a brand: its *spread* and its *power*. 'Spread' refers to how well-known a brand is, while 'power' refers to what it is known for. A brand's spread and power form the basis for its value. A study carried out in 2002 by J P Morgan Chase attributes to the world's ten strongest brands the following values (in billions of dollars):

1. Coca-Cola (69.6).
2. Microsoft (64.1).
3. IBM (51.2).
4. GE (41.3).
5. Intel (30.9).
6. Nokia (30.0).

7. Disney (29.3).

8. McDonald's (26.4).

9. Marlboro (21.2).

10. Mercedes (21.0).

How is it that Coca-Cola can be valued at close to 70 billion dollars? 'The Pepsi Challenge' may give an explanation. Pepsi issued a challenge to Coca-Cola to allow a large test group to carry out a 'blind' test of the two beverages. The result was that 51 per cent preferred Pepsi, while 44 per cent preferred Coke. The remaining 5 per cent did not have any special preference. When the same test was carried out with participants knowing what they were drinking, the result was 63 per cent to 23 per cent in Coca-Cola's favour!

There is considerable evidence to show that we as customers are loyal to brands and are prepared to pay much more for a product with a strong brand. Brands even affect the way we act in that we use them to boost our own image. How much would people be willing to pay for a Rolex watch if it was impossible to identify as a Rolex? Who buys a Rolex watch because it tells the time better than a cheaper watch?

Work with branding usually aims to answer the following questions:

1. What does the brand stand for today and who is aware of it? What position does the brand have in the market?

2. What do we want a brand to represent and who do we want to recognize it? What position do we want a brand to have in the market?

3. How can we close the gap between points 1 and 2, above?

4. How do we know that we are moving in the right direction?

Profile studies are normally carried out in order to answer question 1, above. By 'profile' we mean the characteristics for which a company or part of a company is known by an important target group. A company profile is the image a company or product has in the target group, where image is the way the public interprets reality. A company's profile is its active offering of competitive advantages, while image is the recipient's passive understanding of the sender, i.e. company or product.

The figure opposite shows how some management consultancy firms are interpreted by the market. This was a real study and was part of a survey carried out by Testologen AB, the Swedish market research company.

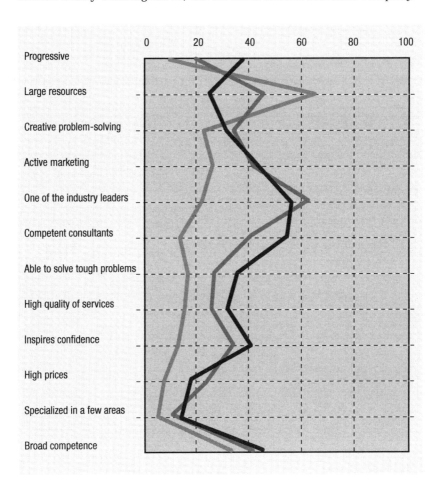

Dr Frans Melin, a researcher of brands at Lund University, has identified brand-building as a process comprising six steps:

1. Product attributes

First, a product must have a quality and functional value that are demanded by the market. Then it is important to consider how the product can be developed by other attributes such as packaging design.

2. Brand identity

Brand identity relates to how a company wants its brand to be perceived. Image, which is closely related to identity, describes how the public perceives a brand.

3. Core value

The core value of a brand derives from those factors, emotional or functional, which are believed to produce a long-term, differentiating advantage. A brand's core value should therefore be unique and hard to imitate.

4. Positioning

The purpose of external positioning is to establish a certain perceived position in the consumer's mind. However, first there should be internal positioning, i.e. a place should be established for the brand in the collective mind of the organization. Careful analysis of a brand's core value will create the conditions for effective positioning.

5. Marketing communication

Market communication (advertising, etc.) should be carried out from a long-term perspective, where persistence is the watchword. Effective positioning is achieved by communicating a brand's core value to desired target groups. A unique communicative identity should be uniformly conveyed through all marketing channels.

6. Internal brand loyalty

Internal loyalty to the brand is an important component in the management of accumulative brand capital. It can be maintained through in-house communication and the publication of guidelines, for instance in the form of a brand manual.

Ries and Ries have described 22 rules for effective brand building. Below is a summary of their main points.

Conclusion 1
A brand loses in strength when it includes too much information

Focus is vital for a brand. Identify the core value and build the brand around it. Expanding a brand may give short-term returns but will eventually contribute to undermining it. This thesis is far from being accepted by other researchers and practicing managers.

Conclusion 2
First publicity, then advertising

A success factor for a new brand is to generate positive *publicity* (as opposed to advertising) in the media.

The best way to do this is to be the first brand in a new category. When the novelty value has subsided, there has to be investment to maintain the brand's position. This should be treated as an investment, not a cost. Brand leadership is the most effective message to communicate ('biggest' rather than 'best', regardless of what people say, as 'biggest' is an indication of 'best').

Conclusion 3
The importance of being the owner of a word in the customer's mind

History is the proof of this. Volvo owns the word 'security' in the car market, which is not to say that their cars are always the safest ones.

In brand building, a distinguishing attribute has to be identified and then adhered to and imprinted in the minds of customers. In the interests of clarity, there should be a focus on the message going out while other attributes should be toned down.

Conclusion 4
An impression of quality is more important than actual quality

Quality is of course important for a brand. Studies show that brands connected to quality in the customer's mind are more successful in respect of both market share and profitability. However, studies also show that in principle there is no connection between a product's success in the market and success in quality tests. The important thing then is to create an impression of quality in a market. In this connection, it is important to be perceived as a specialist, to have a good brand name, and to charge high prices.

Conclusion 5
Leading brands should develop their category

A leading brand should market the category (which it has often created) and welcome competing brands. Pepsi-Cola's entry into the cola drinks category was the best thing that could have happened to Coca-Cola. Buyers like to have a selection to choose from. If a category is short on brands, buyers may become suspicious and buy from another category.

Conclusion 6
Keep concept separate

It is important to differentiate between a company and its brand. Ries and Ries believe that a brand should be given precedence over the company which has developed it. The authors also criticize the widespread use of sub-brands as they tend to dilute the power of the core brand. Mega-branding, master-branding, sub-branding and so on are fine but they are not customer-driven concepts. The customer has to understand the distinction and draw lines between them.

Singularity is a concept that Ries and Ries often return to.

Conclusion 7
Persistence is decisive

Brands must be built from a long-term perspective. Success is measured over decades, not years. Volvo has communicated 'security' for almost 40 years, BMW has been getting 'fun to drive' across for almost 30. Where brands are concerned, it is important to keep a tight hold on creativity and not overdo the message. Then there are situations where it can be necessary to change or get rid of a brand, but this is a long, expensive process.

RECOMMENDED READING

1. Al Ries and Laura Ries, The 22 Immutable Laws of Branding.
2. David E Aaker, Building Strong Brands.
3. Erich Joachimsthaler et al, Harvard Business Review on Brand Management.

Business concept (Corporate mission)

An enterprise's business concept describes its fundamental aim. In non-commercial businesses, the business concept is often called the operational concept, or simply the business objective. The terms corporate or business mission are often used by both commercial and non-commercial organizations.

An important distinction should be made between the term 'business concept' as applied to a group and as applied to its business units, although it is unnecessary to get into pointless discussions about the idea of a business concept for groups if one does not actually exist. (A group consists of different business units each with its own business concept.) It may however, be meaningful to talk about a *portfolio* concept, which describes how a concern can best coordinate its business units and create synergies between them.

A business concept should always start with the needs of customers or buyers. In this connection it is important to distinguish between needs and demand. A need to satisfy one's hunger can result in a demand for porridge, a fillet steak, or fish. A need for cold can lead to a demand for ice, a fridge, or for a trip to more northerly latitudes (more southerly ones for those in the southern hemisphere). The latter case was vividly exemplified by the two companies which at the beginning of the 1900s were engaged in the business of sawing and delivering ice. The business concept of one of them was to sell ice, while that of the other was to sell cold. After the introduction of the refrigerator, one of the companies remained. You don't need to be a genius to guess which one.

This example also says something about defining core competence. The delivery of ice was an undertaking that embraced what for the time was advanced logistics. Surely this competence could have been used in some other connection after the advent of the fridge?

More about the distinction between needs and demand can be found under *Needs*.

Philip Kotler compares a business concept with the 'invisible hand' which leads it along the right tracks. Kotler believes that a good business concept is:

- Market-oriented. A business concept should be based on customer utility and the needs that the business satisfies in the market.

- Possible. It should be attainable but still be challenging; it should be all-embracing but not vague.

- Motivating. Co-workers should know what the business concept is and believe in it.

- Specific. A business concept should be relatively easy to define and simple to communicate (avoid mumbo jumbo).

Furthermore, a business concept should be able to answer the question: 'Why should we be the ones who customers buy their services or goods from?'

So far we have looked at some important aspects underlying a business concept. These can now be summarized under the following five points:

1. Needs/demand
2. Customers/distributors
3. Offering of goods and services
4. Core competence
5. Competitive edge

A useful exercise for testing a business concept and improving it is to go through the five defining elements, above. Here are some questions that might help in this work:

- What needs underlie customer demand? Are there any problems in connection with the use of a particular product or service? Should we carry out a study to find ways to improve needs satisfaction?

- Who are the customers whose needs we are to satisfy? Who makes the decision to buy? Are there gaps between the distributor and the end-user?

- Can we think of more effective combinations of goods and services to provide needs satisfaction? Can we add anything to make what we have to offer more attractive, or take away components that cost money but do not give value?

- Do we need to have more skills and expertise than we have now? Are we living on out-dated skills which are no longer meaningful?

- What separates us from the competition? How do people react to our brand? What is the advantage for our customers?

- How do we formulate our business concept on the basis of customer needs? Is our business concept credible? What code words can we use to help to formulate it?

- How can we exploit our business concept in respect of co-workers, customers and owners? Should we try it out to get feedback?

Another idea we can put to work is what Abell calls the three dimensions of the business concept. These are:

1. **What?** What needs (functions) of the customer are met by our business concept?

2. **Who?** What customer segments will we direct our business concept to?

3. **How?** What technology and products are used to meet needs in selected customer segments?

RECOMMENDED READING

1. Philip Kotler, Marketing Management.

2. Richard O'Hallaron and David O'Hallaron, The Mission Primer: Four Steps to an Effective Mission Statement.

Business development

There is a choice between two main approaches in any strategic process. Either a strategy for a business is pursued in roughly its present form, that is, without any spectacular plans for expansion, or a development process is pursued which aims at a much higher ambition level in respect of market share, expansion of the served market, or new goods and services.

The term 'business development' has a great attraction when it means a sudden, reckless expansion. We define business development as a special case of the development of a business strategy, oriented to growth and characterized by commercial risk-taking and pertaining to the revenue entry of the profit and loss statement. Strategy questions can essentially focus on either of two functions.

1. Making important decisions on the future development of current operations.
2. Creating and making use of new business opportunities.

Both types of strategy development are essential. The former is important at all times, while the latter – making use of new business opportunities – is not necessarily a decisive factor in the successful development of a business. On the other hand, there are a number of points which can form the basis for the search for new business opportunities:

1. The company is capital rich and is looking for investment opportunities.
2. An external threat in the shape of new technology, deregulation, or intense competition.
3. Favourable conditions
4. Entrepreneurs in the company wish to impel business development.

Easy access to capital as a result of the success of previous operations will probably drive a company to acquisitions or organic business development. The tax system existing in Europe and many other parts of the world creates lock-in effects that make it very expensive to distribute capital to shareholders and puts pressure on management to act. Dangers may present themselves in different forms. Digital satellite technology may threaten terrestrial radio and TV, for instance. In preserving an organization's size and avoiding recidivism, management suffering similar threats is put under pressure. The same thing applies to deregulation where monopolies are given free rein and competition is allowed. A third point may be that business opportunities present themselves. Existing customers may clearly be looking for greater supply capacity, that is, more products or services. Other possibilities might suddenly present themselves: launching the company into what had been a protected market, or benefiting from spin-offs through technological synergy.

The fourth point, one which may seem irrelevant but which in fact can play a major role, is that in management there may exist people with entrepreneurial flair who are looking for greater responsibilities and seeking to drive on various types of development processes. We define an entrepreneur as someone who is creative, has high performance expectations and is not averse to taking risks. These attributes can be found in certain people. For a successful outcome, meanwhile, generous portions of judgment and tenacity, not necessarily present in such people, are required. The difference between an active entrepreneur and an injudicious enthusiast can be a fine one.

There are many examples of business development where an enterprising person took charge of a part of a company and developed it into an independent business. Catering in SAS was developed into Service Partner and sold. Car handling equipment in Volvo was developed into Olofström. Their systems are now sold to motor works all over the world.

There are different ways of identifying business opportunities. The sources given below can be useful:

1. An inventory of business opportunities in the company
2. Customer needs remaining satisfied.
3. New geographical markets
4. New customer groups
5. New technology
6. New distribution channels

The use of one of these sources does not rule out using one or more of the others at the same time. In fact, highly satisfactory results can be achieved by the use of various combinations.

Another aim of business development is to revitalize the existing main business and to increase the radiation of outwardly directed energy at the expense of internal energy consumption.

We resort to these somewhat grandiose expressions after having observed a number of organizations which, as they grew, began to expend more and more energy on maintaining and preserving the basic organization itself. Internal conferences, reshuffling production apparatus and personnel, a constant growth of internal communications, and so on, make it all too easy to forget about customers and to use up more and more energy on in-house matters. This is one of the main reasons why companies lose their ability to compete. The increasing consumption of energy internally is usually accompanied by decreasing alertness to the changing pattern of customer needs.

Business development can also be defined as increasing delivery capacity. This means that customers are encouraged to decide to buy goods and services that were not previously part of the product range. Unfortunately, this kind of expansion is often undertaken without prior analysis of 'ideal' delivery capacity, i.e. of how many buying decisions customers are prepared to make at the same time.

Traditional strategy strives for efficient utilization of resources in the form of capital and costs. The experience curves and optimization models developed in the 1950s and 1960s all had that aim. The rationale for striving in that direction was that goods were in short supply in most areas and demand could therefore be taken for granted. After the cataclysmic events of the mid-1970s, corporate development came to focus on customer value. This was how the concept of business development came to embrace a holistic view in the sense that all the dimensions of business management had to be included in the work of strategy. We refer the reader to the section on *Efficiency* for an illustration of this holistic view.

It is an essential part of businessmanship to balance the components of efficient resource utilization and customer-perceived value against each other.

The traditional view of business in Europe differs from that which prevails in the USA. Ever since the *experience* curve was first described in America in 1926, the emphasis of commercial operations there has been heavily on cost advantages in manufacturing. The large, homogeneous market of the United States, free from regional barriers, has stimulated cost-based – and thus price-based – competition. In Europe, on the other hand, we have had a jumble of small regional and national markets which has prompted greater interest in quality as a means of competition.

Value is the quotient of quality and price, so concentrating on *either* costs or business development is not a satisfactory solution. It is thus the task of leadership to balance the parameters according to the situation. We have worked with a number of similar situations in strategic planning, and one of these categories was business development. Below we briefly describe some of these situations, which may perhaps trigger inspiration in your business development.

Expanded delivery capacity. To primarily offer new products to existing customers. Companies can increase sales to existing customers through expanded delivery capacity. By simplifying customer purchasing, customer-perceived quality can be enhanced. Decisions can thus be based on a value analysis of the customer purchase situation.

New customer groups. Identifying buyers in parallel with the traditional market. New customer groups can both contribute to expansion (greater revenue) and productivity (better use of resources) in that they often complement existing customer groups. Take, for example, tourist class customers as a complement to business travellers on airlines, or DIY customers as a complement to professionals in the power tools market. Tourist class passengers fly on weekends, and DIY customers buy power tools on the weekends too.

New geographical markets. Establishing ourselves in geographical markets in which we have not previously been active. A growing company may wish to branch out into the European market. It is important to take into account the conditions and culture of each country or region.

Globalization. Expanding potential/served markets to include the whole world. Globalization may lead to economies of scale in a larger served market. This may be vital when competing with global competitors. A country known for its competence in a particular area would obviously benefit from globalization.

Synergy. The use of skull and scale advantages. Synergy is about achieving lower Costs, or the better use of a company's skills through advantages of skull and scale (greater knowledge mass) while creating higher customer value. Unfortunately, the term synergy is both vague and often used incorrectly. Synergy is often given as a reason for mergers. The benefits of synergy are often exaggerated in order to promote various kinds of structural change.

Strategy as investment. Financial sacrifice in the present for future profit. Many strategic decisions damage the profit and loss statement and cannot be activated in the balance sheet. It is often easier for companies to make decisions about investments that can be activated in accounts than about investments which will only be entered as a cost. It is therefore important that management communicate effectively, both internally and externally, in respect of the possible outcome of an investment.

Organic or structural growth. Expanding through one's own businessmanship or through acquisitions. As regards whether to strive for organic or structural growth, the question can often be resolved by striking a balance between the need for security and the advantage of shared values on the one hand, and fast growth, on the other, in order to become a real player in the market. Examples of both kinds of growth can be found in IT and finance. It is important for management to remember that growth based on financial strength is very risky if the business is not managed profitably and earns market share.

Market conditions – timing. The ability to introduce new products at the right time for market acceptance. The experts, too, can sometimes misjudge the right time to enter the market, and this can lead to costly investments. In this connection, we could look at Ericsson Information Systems, EIS, in the 1980s, when an attempt was made to integrate data communications and telephony. With hindsight, we can see that this was a mistake but it was not obvious then.

The pressure of technology. Developments in technology drive demand. Rapidly expanding industries often have to wait for the manifestation of demand, as their customers may as yet be unaware of their products. 'Supply creates its own demand'. Communication between Stockholm and Gothenburg may lead to the demand for a train ticket, a flight, or a video conference! If customers do not realize that the video conference alternative exists, there will be no demand for it.

RECOMMENDED READING

1. David A Aaker, Developing Business Strategies, 6th Edition

2. Jim Collins, Good to Great: Why Some Companies Make the Leap... and Others Don't

3. Gary Hamel, Leading the Revolution: How to Thrive in Turbulent Times by Making Innovation a Way of Life

The business life cycle

Growth and capital needs can be traced to the life cycle curve represented in the first figure, below.

The graduation of the time axis varies depending on the business; there are countless variations on this theme. In business, one of the main functions of leadership is to stretch out the business life cycle over time, by changing the offering of goods/services or by entering new markets.

In the same diagram we could insert the profits for all the companies in a particular industry on the time axis. Then we would see that a business' total profit is maximized before the market reaches its peak. If such life cycle curves were accurate, we would do best to go into a business at point 1 and getting out of it at point 2 (see the second figure). During this interval there is rapid growth in both profit and volume. We can develop the business life cycle concept by dividing it into phases, and this is done in the third figure.

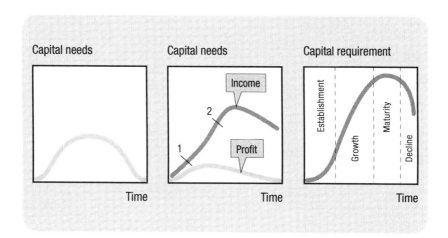

A diversified portfolio will probably have businesses in every one of the four phases of launch, growth, maturity and decline. Thus, at a given point in time, certain business units will have just started, others will be coming into rapid growth, some will have reached their peak, while others will be in decline.

If we know a business unit's position in the life cycle curve and must allocate capital, then in theory we should be able to find certain guidelines. It is important to note that as the number of competitors increases, structuring becomes tighter ahead of market maturity and possible decline.

Traditional portfolio analysis began with the business life cycle and described the market in each of the four phases. On this basis, conclusions could be drawn about competitors, performance levels and strategy. A number of guidelines emerged based on a business' position on the life cycle curve. Terminology has changed somewhat, so that the four phases are now usually called:

1. Market launch
2. Market penetration
3. Defence of position
4. Market exit, that is, winding-up of the business unit.

A series of recommendations have been developed for each phase in order to put these theoretical ideas into concrete form and make them useful for heads of department.

During the *launch phase*, previous users have to be persuaded to buy the product or service. During this time, much of management's capacity goes towards solving questions of finance and looking after production.

During *growth*, the important thing is to penetrate the market and persuade customers to buy our brand and not any others. At the same time, energy must be used to extend the products offered, thereby maximizing sales and market share. Production should be trimmed so that economies of scale can be attained and we can go down the *experience curve* (see this term).

During the *maturity phase* it is important to defend the brand and maybe structure the business in the acquisition of competitors. This is not the time to add new products. Instead, existing ones should be trimmed back. During this phase we should also work on capital rationalization and produce to satisfy orders, increasing volume if necessary.

During the *decline phase*, attention should be given to reducing costs. Preparation should be made for exiting the market by milking the brand for all it's worth.

RECOMMENDED READING

1. Lawrence M Miller, Barbarians to Bureaucrats: Corporate Life Cycle Strategies.
2. Don Nyman, Maintenance Planning, Scheduling and Coordination.

Business model (business logic)

It is often useful to divide a business into different groups with common characteristics. A common such division is shown in the figure below.

Extraction and cultivation	The production of goods and services	Distribution	Speculation (Trade)	Production of services	Knowledge

From earliest times there has been a shift in business operations, from cultivation through to production and on to distribution and knowledge. Speculation, whether in tulips in the Holland of the 17th century, spices, property or shares, has always existed.

A short explanation of the above business typology is given below.

Extraction is the age-old utilization of natural resources. *Cultivation* is characterized by a similar use of nature. The predominant notion for a long time was that access to natural resources was the basis for wealth, something that has been refuted and not least by Japan. However, natural resources are still the main source of livelihood for many nations, especially those involved with oil extraction.

Production largely depends on the attainment of technological advantage, which in turn allows the creation of economies of scale and the cutting of costs. The fundamental strategy is that raw products, which have been extracted or bought, are processed into finished or semi-finished goods. These are then processed further, or sold to an end-user in the consumer chain.

Distribution seeks to optimize the transfer of goods and services on the basis of a deep insight into the needs structures of buyer and seller. The distribution function has gone through great changes as a result of the appearance of information technology in combination with shorter and shorter product life cycles. In many cases, the distributor's role in the value chain has diminished drastically or disappeared completely.

Speculation, similarly to distribution, involves *trade,* but here the driving force is the possibility of profit through a superior ability to assess price and price development. Trade in this context may be with raw products, property, shares, options, currencies, and many other things.

Service production is a term used for the more or less systematized services which our society today demands and supplies. This may vary from qualified medical services to the provision of financial services. A knotty problem in the production of services is how to build healthy *structure capital* in the form of systems, processes, procedures and a strong brand.

Knowledge companies have gained in importance as the knowledge component of products and services has grown. This is the case in both traditional industries and businesses such as consultancies and educational institutions, which have the development and provision of knowledge as their business concept. More on knowledge companies can be found under *Knowledge Management.*

A more detailed description of the different types of business was given by the Swedish business consultant Eric Giertz in 1999. He sets out six main types of business, including a number of sub-categories. These are given below.

1. Raw product acquisition

The extraction and sorting of raw products. Examples of businesses are agriculture, stock-raising, forestry, fishing, mining and oil-drilling. Important points are commonly the efficient sorting of material at source, rational information and transport systems, and a high utility of fixed assets.

2. Production

a. *Contract work*

    Flexible, module-based production for customer orders in small series. Examples of businesses are processing plants, machine shops and binding departments. Important points are changeover and transit times, degree of coverage for personnel and machines, delivery punctuality and service level.

b. *Labour-intensive process production*

Production with relatively few raw products processed in a process-oriented production flow.

Examples of businesses are dairies, sawmills, textile factories and pharmaceutical production.

Important points are commonly the mechanization of handling information, short changeover times and low costs for labour and raw products.

c. *Capital intensive process production*

Production with little personnel requirements but costly production plants, where a few products are processed in a relatively slow production line. Examples of businesses are pulp factories, printing plants and chemicals production. Important points are commonly short changeover times and high utility of fixed assets.

d. *Assembly*

Production through the assembly of sub-components. Examples of businesses are engine, electronics and instrument assembly. Important points are commonly stock control, transit times and delivery service.

3. Goods distribution

a. *Freight transportation*

The transportation of physical goods. Examples of businesses are haulage contractors, shipping, delivery firms, air and rail transport. Important points are commonly delivery punctuality, high cover and loss minimizing (mishandling).

b. *Reshipment*

The discharging, re-stowing, storing and loading of physical goods onto transport carriers. Examples of businesses are ports, airports, sorting centres and regional warehouses.

Important points are commonly good information systems, systematization and orderliness and long waiting periods for transport carriers.

c. *Retail*

The sale of physical goods within a delimited geographical area. Examples of businesses are department stores, kiosks and petrol stations. Important points are commonly high service levels, clear profiling and a lean trading stock.

4. Basic public services

a. *Exercise of authority*

Takes care of public interests. Examples of businesses are public administration, trade associations and political organizations. The most important point is often contact with the grass roots.

b. *Institutional production of services*

Supplies services which cannot or should not be controlled by the requirements, or readiness to pay, of the market. Examples of businesses are grant-controlled services, the police, defence, prison welfare and basic research. Important points are commonly short turnaround times, continuous operational development and correct procedure (observance of regulations and guidelines).

c. *Subscriber-related administration*

Distribution to a fixed group of subscribers within a geographical area. Examples of businesses are electricity boards, gas boards and radio and TV transmitters. Important points are usually ease of accessibility and preventive maintenance.

5. Service production

a. *Local manual service production*

Service production based on the ability of co-workers to apply their skills in a local market. Examples of businesses are car repairers, property management, hairdressers and dentists. Important points are commonly high and regular staff cover, emulation of 'the good example', customer service and delivery punctuality.

b. *Knowledge-intensive commissioned business*

Production based on the ability of co-workers within delimited areas to apply their expert knowledge to solve customer needs. Examples of businesses are consultancies, development departments, financial consultation and architect services.

Important points are often specialist knowledge, flexibility, high service level, development and streamlining of working methods and co-worker cover.

c. *Local consumer service*

Delivers service to physical persons in a delimited geographical area. Examples of businesses are hotels, gyms, public transport, cinemas and swimming baths.

Important points are in general quality assured working methods and a high service level.

d. *Hiring out*

Offers the occasional use of resources against payment. Examples of businesses are the hiring out of machines, vehicles, flats, premises and clothes. Important points are commonly high service levels and maintenance of the fixed assets.

e. *Teaching*

Local and teacher-led transfer of knowledge. Examples of businesses are schools and educational associations. Important points are usually a clear profile and the creation of commitment and interest on the part of participants.

f.   *Distance support*

Service or interviews involving people over great distances geographically. Examples of businesses are telephone services, help desks, call centres, telephone banking and taxi switchboards.

Important points are commonly service-oriented staff with good language skills and short handling times.

g. *Artistry*

Through artistry, people are provided with stimulation, entertainment and suspense.

Examples of businesses are those run by musicians, artists, actors and practitioners of sport.

The most important point is commonly to become known and 'get a name' for oneself.

6. Web services

a. *Publishing*

The engagement and coordination of work input from experts, employees and suppliers in specific organizations. Examples of businesses are project management, book publishing, building development, exhibition management and tour operating.

Important points most often involve professional procurement, and keeping within timeframes and under cost ceilings.

b. *Chain organizing*

Central quality assurance and product range coordination for actors in different geographical markets. Examples of businesses are franchisers and customers' cooperatives.

Important points are commonly brand building together with the standardization and quality assurance of products.

c. *Brokerage*

Trades in capital, goods and services by matching offers with demand. Examples of businesses are sales representatives, financial brokerages, auction houses and producers of gaming machines.

Important points are commonly relatively high levels of invoicing and market segmentation.

RECOMMENDED READING

1. Derek F Abell, Defining The Business: The Starting Point of Strategic Planning.

2. Michael Treacy and Fred Wiersman, The Discipline of Market Leaders: Choose Your Customers, Narrow Your Focus, Dominate Your Market.

3. Eric Giertz, Measuring Success: Identifying Performance Indicators

Business plan

The term 'business plan' is used to indicate everything from budget-type documents to assist financial evaluation, to strategy plans with the aim of ensuring long-term success. The most efficient way of working in strategy work has been shown to be with a rolling strategic agenda, that is, with a number of main areas marked out for change and alternative options. In strategy work nowadays, less is spoken about the 'plan' and more about strategic thinking and the implementation of the strategic agenda.

A business plan should be very comprehensive and cover all the principal areas of an organization. The following checklist of eleven headings may help with the writing of a business plan. Each section may be more or less important, depending on its relevance to the business. The eleven elements of the business plan can also be used in other structures, such as the *Balanced Scorecard*.

- Business concept/corporate mission
- Strategy – vision/ambition and agenda
- Product development plan
- Production
- Marketing plan, market size and customer groups
- Sales plan
- Administration and IT plan
- Personnel and competence development
- Organization plan
- Investments
- Finances

Business concept is also called *corporate mission* in many businesses. The elements listed above are however, much the same in any organization and comprise needs/demand, customers/distributors, offering of goods and services, essential core skills and competitive edge, i.e. why customers will turn to one company or organization for their goods and services, and not another. Time spent working on corporate mission is time well spent, as we are forced to review factors on which the success of our organization may very well depend.

Strategy is defined here as a pattern of decisions and actions in the present to ensure future success and make the most of opportunities. The idea of a vision can sometimes be very important in strategy work; in other contexts it might be more helpful to think of ambition level. By strategic agenda we mean a list of points that feature in an organization's future success.

Developing new products in the form of goods and services in order to expand or supplement existing delivery capacity is always an important question, one that should be based on satisfying the needs of customers or buyers. For more on this see the section under Value.

Production is an issue in many aspects of business, for the more capital and costs that are bound up in the production apparatus, the more important it is to maintain high and consistent capacity utilization.

Market plan is perhaps the most important component in a business plan, at any rate in an organization under competitive pressure. Market dimension has two polarities: innovation and new products on the one hand, and the satisfaction of customer needs on the other.

Sales function is often neglected in business. Few areas give faster profits and greater value in an organization than investment in its sales. We therefore recommend that the sales plan not be developed together with the market plan but that it should be the object of special attention.

Administration comprises ordinary production, wages and invoicing, as well as more important support activities like systems development, and so on.

Personnel, with its learning and skills, is becoming more and more important for all kinds of organization. Together with customers and owners, personnel constitutes the most important stakeholder group as it is this category that will provide needs satisfaction and shareholder value.

Organization is a topic much beloved by people who like to tinker with things and complicate them. Organization is basically about work in all its forms, including distribution and specialization. A flexible organization with long-term stability often provides a counter-balance to inclination for structural change.

Investment is an important part of an organization's resources. By investment we mean a financial sacrifice made in the present for future returns. More and more resources of an investment nature can be found booked as a cost in the profit and loss statement. Events of recent years have revealed the number of investments that failed to give the expected profits.

Finances provide the yardstick with which most organizations are measured, with the exception of certain non-profit organizations. Important questions concerning liquidity, financing, accounting, etc, are also grouped under this point.

RECOMMENDED READING

1. Rhonda Abrams och Eugene Kleiner, The Successful Business Plan: Secrets and Strategies.
2. Art Dethomas et al., Writing a Convincing Business Plan.

Business unit

A business unit is an organizational entity which in all essential respects acts as an independent enterprise for business purposes. A business strategy should be formulated for business units if they are to compete and be successful in the market. In order to be called a business unit, an organizational entity must:

1. satisfy customer needs in an external market.
2. work to compete with external companies.
3. have its own business strategy and business concept.
4. be performance driven and take responsibility for profits and losses.
5. be decentralized from the parent organization (even if certain resources and business interests are shared).

It has become popular in large organizations to create business drive and entrepreneurship through the organization of activities into strategic business units, known as SBUs. By the establishment of business units, responsibility can be decentralized and given over to a number of leaders who will then be able to focus on competing and meeting goals within a limited area. A business unit is structured so that the parent company has the role of portfolio administrator and owner. Business units normally have their own boards on which both representatives from the parent company and external board members are represented.

The father of business unit thinking may well have been Alfred P. Sloan, who during his time in the different positions of Manager, Managing Director and Group Chief Executive of General Motors (GM), looked for ways to enlarge the company while at the same time making it flexible. When Sloan took over, GM was a complex structure where different makes of car competed with each other in much the same way as with their biggest competitor, Ford. Sloan's solution was to organize the company into five car divisions and three component divisions. Each division had a managing director with commercial and strategic responsibility. This led to innovative business development where, for example, the component divisions began to sell components to external players. This structure was introduced in the 1920s and by 1925 GM had surpassed Ford to become number one in the automobile business. Sloan's organizational model, which he called 'federal decentralization', was firmly based on business unit thinking and came to be a model for many other businesses. Nowadays, it is mostly the rule, rather than the exception, that large companies are constructed around business units. Sloan's ideas came to be honoured and promoted by such management gurus as Peter Drucker and Alfred Chandler.

Gradually however, GM came up against problems that led to big reverses during the 1960s. By then, their organizational structure had generated a morass of bureaucracy where central units wanted to be all-powerful, controlling the divisions. As a result, separation of the company into divisions ended up contributing to the organizational sluggishness that it had been supposed to counteract.

Both academics and workers in the field today agree that group management should not get involved, if at all possible, in the day-to-day activities of business units; they should avoid bothering them with unnecessary bureaucracy and simply keep out of the way.

RECOMMENDED READING

1. Alfred P Sloan Jr, My Years With General Motors.
2. Michael E Porter, Competitive Strategy: Techniques For Analyzing Industries And Competitors.

Businessmanship

The old concept of the businessman has once again come into favour. According to a dictionary definition, a businessman is a person whose work involves financial transactions on a professional basis. In the modern world of finance, the term 'businessman' can be defined as follows:

"A businessman is a person who is able to understand the structure of needs of his customers, combining this with knowledge about the rational use of capital and costs, so that economic value can be created. The businessman can creatively combine needs and production resources, and will have the capital, costs and energy to allow a business to get started. The businessman can function in a market economy, that is, one in which the customer has a choice between different alternatives."

The problem with businessmanship is that it is not a discipline in the usual academic sense. Meanwhile, certain disciplines associated with business-manship have progressed; these include accounting, financing, marketing, distribution, and so on.

During the 1900s, businessmanship was influenced by different sciences. Mathematics has been necessary for accounting and cost-benefit analy-sis. Biology has been very influential through cybernetics, as has psychology and, from time to time, even religion and philosophy.

Little research has been dedicated to businessmanship as a whole because of its very complexity.

Our intention is to show the reader that businessmanship involves the ability to have a comprehensive understanding of creating value for customers while making a rational use of resources.

A rather different kind of businessmanship is characterized by the ability to see structural solutions. A certain type of financier has the ability to purchase companies, dispose of assets or separate business units in a company, and divide it up so that its different businesses end up with a more efficient structure. This has less to do with customer-experienced value and more to do with an ability to perceive optimal business structures.

Businessmanship is in short supply in big companies and technocratic environments. The demand for businessmen is sharply increasing at the moment, and this is sure to put a premium on expertise.

It is not uncommon for the terms 'business transaction' and 'business relationship' to be confused. People lacking in solid business experience sometimes have a tendency to attribute an element of trickery to businessmanship that in the short term could maximise their own advantage to the detriment of another party. In a business transaction, such as selling a bike or a car to someone, where we are unlikely to do business again, it is possible to maximise short term self-interest.

However, it is more common to build up a business relationship in the belief that it will last and prove of value to the parties involved.

There has been a considerable movement against deregulation and exposure to competition from the latter half of the 1980s into the new millennium and, at the same time, an increasing demand for businessmanship and businesslike behaviour. Individuals who have toiled within a planned economy as 'bureaucrats' sometimes betray a misapprehension concerning the significance of the term businessmanship. Those sectors of society which have previously escaped the rigours of value creation and competition from others must now be brought to understand and master the building blocks of management and indeed, of businessmanship.

Returning to our definition, we could replace the word 'businessman' by the phrase 'person responsible for a business' and apply it to senior employees in the public sector, or to the entire organizational world for that matter. Perhaps the last sentence in our definition could be modified to read: "The businessman functions in a market economy where customers have a choice between different alternatives".

If we look at other sectors of society, we see that this element of choice is not primarily one between comparable alternatives. Here people can choose between, say, membership of a society and something completely different. In situations involving the pure exercise of authority, our concept must be modified further if it is to be applicable, mainly because of the complexity of the needs structure and the fact that we are then operating in a monopoly-type situation.

Study points in this section are:

1. The definition of businessmanship
2. The complexity of competences and the lack of academic treatment
3. The difference between business relationships and business transactions
4. Changing societal conditions which place similar demands in other environments, such as the public sector and non-profit organizations

---

RECOMMENDED READING

Robert T Kiyosaki and Sharon L Lechter, Rich Dad, Poor Dad: What the Rich Teach Their Kids About Money That the Poor and Middle Class Do Not!

Capital rationalization

In capital-intensive industries, profitability metrics are focused on the return on investment (ROI) formula:

$$ROI = \frac{Revenues - costs}{Capital}$$

The rationalization of the use of capital is a key concept for all industries in which capital intensity is an essential factor. Capital in company operations is usually divided into three main categories:

1. Fixed assets
2. Inventory
3. Cash management

If the difference between revenue and costs is constant, halving employed capital will lead to the ROI being doubled. Within the PIMS framework (Profit Impact of Market Strategy), capital intensity is said to be one of the single most important factors for profitability in a large number (over 3,000) of business units. This relationship can be looked at in different ways. The connection between tied-up capital and value-added productivity is shown in the figure.

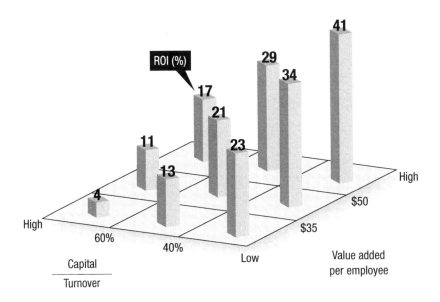

There is therefore every reason to work constructively and creatively with the use of capital. Many factors can affect the level of working capital. There are three factors that tend to increase tied-up capital in a business and which at the same time fall within the scope of management control:

1. The marketing organization's ambition to increase sales through short delivery times and improved service.

2. A distribution system that has been developed with many inventory points.

3. The efficiency of the production process in handling both inventory and fixed assets.

Two important tools for working with capital are the Wilson formula and the Du Pont formula.

The Wilson formula

By means of the Wilson formula we can calculate an order quantity in terms of money once we know the following: warehousing cost, administrative reordering cost, interest, volume (demand per period) and manufacturing cost.

The simplest formula can be given as:

$$q = \sqrt{\frac{2Kd}{h}}$$

Where:

q = Order quantity in number of units

K = Administrative reordering cost

d = Demand in number of units per period

h = Warehousing cost per unit and period ((material + processing) x internal rate of return).

However, a number of conditions must be fulfilled if the Wilson formula is to be relevant:

1. Constant and continuous demand
2. Constant lead time for receiving ordered goods
3. Constant administrative re-ordering costs and warehousing costs
4. No shortages
5. Entire order quantity delivered to the warehouse on one and the same occasion
6. Price/cost independent of time requirements and ordered quantity

A number of attempts have been made to escape from the unrealistic demands of the formula; supplements to it have entailed the need for more data and have affected the precision of the Wilson formula only marginally.

The Du Pont formula

This formula was first used around 1910 by the Du Pont Powder Company in Wilmington, Delaware. It is now more widely used than ever and was of great importance in Swedish industry from the middle of the 1970s for investment in capital rationalization.

In the Du Pont formula, ROI on capital employed (Rc) is determined as the product of two factors, profit margin and the rate of turnover of this capital. This can be seen in the following formula:

$$Rc = \frac{Surplus}{Turnover} \times \frac{Turnover}{Capital\ employed}$$

By using the Du Pont model we can see that low profitability by no means only depends on profit margin but also to a very high degree on capital turnover. The formula can be looked at in different ways but the diagram below represents the most common of these.

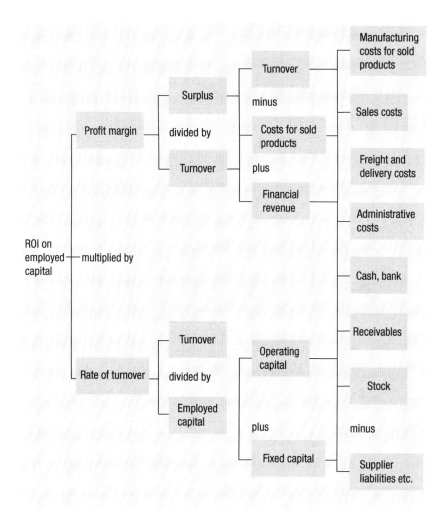

The model illustrated above has great value as a pedagogic tool for clarifying the relationship between revenues, costs, capital, margin and profit.

RECOMMENDED READING

1. Monte Swain and Jan Bell, The Theory of Constraints and Throughput Accounting.

2. Shannon P Pratt, Cost of Capital: Methods and Applications.

Change management

All organizations are in need of effectively organized change. This area, which is often called Change Management, deals with initiating, monitoring and following up actions to bring about change in an organization. Changes may be revolutionary or step-by-step changes towards long-term goals, or anything between these two extremes.

The perception of change naturally varies from one organization to another, both on the individual and organizational level. In some organizations, change is a daily affair, while others are characterized by what could be termed organizational sloth. On the individual plane people sometimes speak of the 20-60-20 rule, which gives a rough division of employee attitudes to major changes: 20 per cent are opposed to change, 60 per cent sit on the fence and 20 per cent are wholeheartedly in favour of change. A pitfall in the work of change is to devote too much energy to trying to change the attitudes of the very critical employees. This rarely gives results; instead it will send signals to the organization that their attitude merits management attention. A better approach is to give the enthusiastic employees a high profile and turn them into ambassadors for the work of change. The 20-60-20 rule is of course a pedagogical support and has no scientific basis.

According to Lars H Bruzelius and Per-Hugo Skärvad, the organization experts, opposition to change is especially strong when:

- changes are drastic and radical.
- changes are sudden and unexpected.
- changes have potentially negative consequences for people involved.
- there is strong support for whatever it is that is marked down for change.
- aims are so vague as to cause uncertainty.
- previous changes have not turned out well.

There may be many more reasons for opposition to change. One of these may well be the habits that have become established at the workplace. We human beings are creatures of habit, as the saying goes. A striking example of this is use of the qwerty keyboard, so called because QWERTY are the first six letters in the upper left-hand corner of the keyboard. This layout was devized in 1873 to slow down typing speeds so that typewriter keys would not jam. The new idea was introduced because it was inherently inefficient! In spite of the fact that the original reason for the keyboard no longer exists, qwerty has survived and followed us into the computer age. All efforts to change the layout of the qwerty keyboard, even by its inventor, have met with failure. It would be interesting to know what loss in productivity has been occasioned by this particular custom.

Opposition to change commonly arises when employees do not have confidence in management and the people who have been put in charge of carrying out the process of change. Similarly, it is important that management should show confidence in their employees by listening to them and inviting them to take part in the process.

Research and other recorded evidence has revealed a number of characteristics of successful processes of change. The most important principle and one shared by all the studies was the importance of developing the understanding and commitment of co-workers to the work of change. This has been confirmed by Rosabeth Moss Kanter, a Harvard professor and author of the bestseller *The Change Masters,* and her studies of empowerment in change processes.

If co-workers are to be motivated to work for change, it is important that they should understand what is going to be changed and why the changes are going to be introduced. Some ways of doing this are:

- Produce a simple plan showing goals, sub-goals, activities and expected results.
- Supplement this plan with a communication plan.
- Involve co-workers or their representatives in these plans and make sure that their skills are taken on board.
- Be clear about the need for change. Create a crisis if you have to!
- Identify key figures in the organization and ensure that they unequivocally and publicly back the changes.
- Work with a clear and positive vision of what life in the workplace will be like after changes have been implemented (fear of the unknown is one of the principal obstacles to change).

The creation of a *fair process* (see this term) that deals with the above points is essential to the success of the process of change.

An effective way of producing change is to make use of the power inherent in the 'good example'. Here we could take a leaf from the book of the legal profession in alluding to the burden of proof:

Persons instituting changes must normally show evidence of why something should be changed. With a good example, the burden of proof shifts to the preservers of the status quo who instead should show why something should not be changed.

Dealing with 'preservers of the status quo' is one of the challenges of working with change. Such extremely cautious people do not usually harbour ill will when confronted with talk of change, they simply fear whatever this might bring; or they may think that change is not possible. Anxiety about change can be overcome by speaking of the possible results of change through a good example. If this works even the sceptics will be convinced that change is possible, as "it worked for so-and-so". For more on working with good examples, see *Benchlearning*.

Change management is a big subject. The abundance of literature dealing with the subject testifies to this as do the many theories that have been devoted to it in the field of organizational development. In a book of this size it can only be given a fraction of the attention it deserves.

RECOMMENDED READING

1. John P Kotter, Leading Change.
2. Rosabeth Moss Kanter, The Change Masters: Innovation and Entrepreneurship in the American Corporation.
3. William Bridges, Managing Transitions: Making the Most of Change.

Communication

The word 'communication' comes from the Latin *communis*, which means 'together' and *communicare*, which can mean variously 'to share, 'to impart', 'to unite', 'to participate in'. Communication implies an exchange of information between sender and receiver. Sometimes the communication flow is unidirectional, as is often the case with advertising through the mass media. However, bi-directional flow by means of mass communication has become increasingly more common with the advent of the Internet.

Communication can be verbal (expressed by speech or writing) or non-verbal (body language, tone of voice, what is left unspoken, etc). According to Dr. Elayne Savage, a communication coach, two-thirds of the communication between a salesman and his or her potential customer is non-verbal. Studies carried out by, among others, Wiio (1973) and Patty (1982) show that the distribution of information received by the brain is as follows:

1. Sight (83 per cent).
2. Hearing (11 per cent)
3. Smell (3.5 per cent).
4. Taste (1.5 per cent)
5. Touch (1 per cent)

Verbal communication imparts a *denotative* meaning (the meaning is in the word itself) and a *connotative* meaning (the feelings and associations suggested by the word). Communication flow is often described using Harold Lasswell's five Ws: *Who* (sender) said *what* (message) to *whom* (receiver) in *which* medium (channel) and with *what* effect (effect)?

An overview of a communication process is shown in the model below.

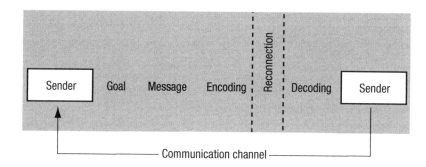

85

The process starts when a goal for communication is established. For example, much energy is spent at this stage in marketing communication, while the formulation of the goal in personal communication of course occurs implicitly. Regardless of the different forms communication might take, there is always a conscious or unconscious goal (even in small talk, where the goal is to pass the time). When a goal has been established, the sender forms a message that satisfies this goal. What is the core of the communication to be? The message is then coded in a certain sequence of words, for example, or a text or communicative picture. The coded message passes through a communication channel such as a letter, telephone conversation, direct communication, e-mail, mass media, through a messenger, etc. The receiver gets the coded message and decodes it, which might happen in the case of a letter by reading and interpreting it. A connection is then re-established with the sender. The sender can take an active role in reconnection by, for example, carrying out a survey in order to find out how a particular marketing announcement has been received. Otherwise reconnection occurs indirectly through the receiver's response, which might be a telephone conversation or the determination to buy more or less of the sender's products.

A number of obstacles or problems are commonly associated with the different stages of the communication process:

1. **Sender problems**. Example: the sender has a good idea which s/he is timid about communicating at a meeting with superiors.

2. **Coding problems**. Example: due to confusion while speaking or poor writing ability, a person does not succeed in getting his/her message across.

3. **Communication channel problems**. Example: the receiver is overwhelmed by e-mails and deletes the message by mistake or a help desk telephone with long waiting times is used.

4. **Decoding problems**. Example: the receiver does not understand the models on which the sender bases his/her message.

5. **Receiver problems**. Example: the receiver is momentarily completely taken up with something outside the realm of the sender's message.

6. **Reconnection problems**. Example: the receiver feels that reconnection is undesirable or will not have any effect.

Apart from the above process-related communication obstacles, there are many other obstacles of a different nature to consider: physical ones (distance, time zones, etc), semantic ones (interpretation of language, which is especially important for communication between different disciplines, e.g. medicine and the law) and psychological obstacles (perhaps different social classes or values are involved). Psycho-social factors, and especially culture and religion, are extremely important in international trade. A tragic example of poor communication apparently led to the atomic bomb being dropped on Hiroshima. Japan's answer to the American ultimatum to give up is said to have been 'mokusatsu' which was wrongly translated to mean 'disregard' instead of the correct, 'await comment until a decision has been made'.

Internal and external communication are key areas for many companies and organizations. The importance of internal communication is increasing now that many companies have to adjust to the imperatives of good knowledge management. Organization structures are also becoming more complicated and need to be well coordinated. External communication is becoming increasingly more important to distinguish companies from their competitors and in respect of brand management (see *trademark*). The classifications of conscious and unconscious can be applied to both external and internal communication. Examples of different kinds of organizational communication are given in the following matrix.

From an organizational perspective, it is important to repeatedly check who the organization's important communication partners are. This can be done by means of a stakeholder analysis (see the section under this term). Meanwhile, research has shown that the following seven categories are the most important for large companies in respect of their communication needs:

1. Advertising (announcements, mail-shots, etc)
2. Co-worker communication
3. Media relations
4. Shareholder relations
5. Consumer communication

6. Local community relations

7. Relations with public administrative bodies

The same research reveals that there is a trend towards centralization of the communication functions in organizations. It is more and more common in business to find a top manager, possibly a member of the Group or company management team, with responsibility for a centralized communication department. The driving forces underlying this trend are the importance of coordinated communication and the care that organizations must take with their brands.

We conclude this section with Johari Window the well-known model developed by Joseph Luft and Harry Ingham. This model, the name of which is a composite of its authors' first names, is used to understand what is going on in the communication between, for example, a manager and his or her subordinate. It is based on the simple idea that there are things that the manager knows but which the subordinate does not, and things which the subordinate knows but not the manager (see the following figure).

	UNCONSCIOUS/INFORMAL	CONSCIOUS/FORMAL
INTERNAL	• Non-formal communication (gossip) • Non-verbal communication (body language, etc.)	• Meetings • Manager-employee conversations • Intranets • Staff magazines
EXTERNAL	• Co-workers as ambassadors • Gossip from for example previously employed co-workers • Spread of information from pleased and displeased customers	• Plans • Marketing • The company's web site • Annual report and other financial results • Annual meetings, etc.

According to the model, the manager and employee have two choices: to work together and extend the open areas, or to try to hide information and manipulate one another. The model can be used to understand the game which goes on to a greater or lesser degree when people interact with each other.

RECOMMENDED READING

1. Courtland L Bovée, John V Thill and Barbara E Schatzman, Business Communication Today.

2. Ralph G Nichols et al, Harvard Business Review on Effective Communication.

3. Robert B Cialdini, Influence: Science and Practice.

4. W Timothy Coombs, Ongoing Crisis Communication: Planning, Managing, and Responding.

Companization

A wave of companization has rolled over Western Europe, mainly, in the last couple of decades. There are a number of reasons for this:

1. Deregulation, privatization and competition in public sector institutions have led to the need for legal units with defined business concepts.

2. In groups of companies that are diversified portfolios, a reasonable evaluatio often puts the whole at a lower value than the sum of the parts. Companization has thus been encouraged to clarify the value of business units.

3. Reward systems and a desire to be the absolute master over some area has in many cases led to the companization of product or market areas.

It is of course very difficult to sell or buy a business unless it is operated as a company or at any rate has its own profit and loss statement and preferably its own balance sheet.

Traditional state-run businesses have often been companized for all of the above three reasons. There are many examples too of companies quoted on the stock-market that have been undervalued because shareholders have not been aware of their true value. This is usually called investment company discount. This discount expresses a negative value and is often considered to be a direct measure of confidence in the management to create value in the group.

Looking back a few decades, it is possible to say that in boom times there was a desire in managers to create their own empires with all the perquisites of title, pay, prestige and status. In the same way that acquisitions, mergers and disposals are often impelled for irrational reasons, the ambition for power for instance, companization can sometimes be staged for mysterious motives. It is therefore essential to be clear about the structure of motives behind a proposal to set up a company. Some of the motives we have found are:

1. A functional unit has a large proportion (over 50 per cent) of external deliveries.

2. Preparation for sale of part of the business.

3. A function that was once strategically important to the business has become trivial and inefficient.

4. The core business is subject to restrictions that can be evaded by setting up a separate company.

5. The legal structure in a given environment requires the existence of a company with a board of directors, etc.

6. A tactical move in bargaining with unions.

7. Somebody wants to put 'Managing Director' on their business card.

8. A desire for a higher degree of independence from principals.

It is therefore advisable to define the motives for companization to avoid making it a solution in search of a problem.

In connection with deregulation, we have often observed a nostalgic desire to become an independent company. Somehow it is seen as a kind of organizational nirvana that will create opportunities and lead to more or less realistic visions on the part of the advocates.

As with most things in management, companization can be abused or taken too far and have negative effects. The basic idea is to create companies around business units that compete as efficiently as possible by creating value for customers, staff and owners. However, where deregulation during the last two decades is concerned, companization has been taken into the realms of the absurd and has done nothing for stakeholders. A traditional railway monopoly which has grown organically may suffer if the business is divided. Factors in the company's growth may be inherent its monopolistic situation and thus need to be changed, or they may have their origins in natural synergies that may not always be apparent.

If, in the case of the rail giant, maintenance and repairs are hived off into a separate company, then an organization with a reputation for regularity, punctuality and operational safety may be broken up. The same thing is true of property, the importance of which is due to a process, i.e. its value depends entirely on the business operated there. A railway station that is to continue to function as such has no real property value over and above its function as a station. It may not then be a good idea to companize this type of property. If the freight business is impelled to integrate with passenger traffic and considerable resources have been allocated, there may be good reason to consider the options carefully before the businesses are companized.

We should always ask ourselves whether the motives underlying companization cannot be dealt with in some simpler way, perhaps by studying the profit and loss statement and balance sheet or through a consideration of possible degrees of independence, management award systems, and so on. The motives for companization should be subjected to very careful examination.

RECOMMENDED READING

1. Alfred Schipke, Why Do Governments Divest: The Macroeconomics of Privatization.

2. Richard Pipes, Ownership and Freedom: The Fundamentals of Democracy.

Competence

A common definition of competence is:

Competence = Knowledge + experience + ability

Knowledge comprises a co-worker's training and qualifications. Experience is framed by time and work content. *Ability* refers to the capacity to utilize knowledge and experience to solve problems. *Will* is sometimes emphasized in definitions of competence.

Competence is related to the framework of an organization's aims and an individual's place in that framework. A professor of astrophysics will not automatically make a competent engine driver or administrative director. The manager of a sales department is not necessarily competent enough for his job, although s/he might have enjoyed many years of success as a successful salesperson.

	Known by the manager	Unknown by the manager
Known by the subordinate	Open areas	Hidden areas
Unknown by the subordinate	Hidden areas	Unknown

Competence is commonly divided into categories that are relevant for companies. The following classification is fairly common:

1. *Organization specific* competence, which is directly related to industry or company structure. Examples of competences that fall into this category are knowledge of a company's products.

2. *Business-related* competence is, as its name suggests, competence that is directly connected to business enterprises. Examples of this sort of competence are sales ability, negotiation technique and project leadership. Businessmanship is an important part of business-related competence.

3. *Personal* competence comprises abilities that are not directly connected to work but which nevertheless stand the employee in good stead there. Examples of this are social competence and the ability to work in groups.

When competence is analyzed from a company perspective it is often done by means of a gap analysis where the competence of today is set against the competence needed to carry out strategies and realize a vision. This is often done using a radar diagram as in the illustration that follows.

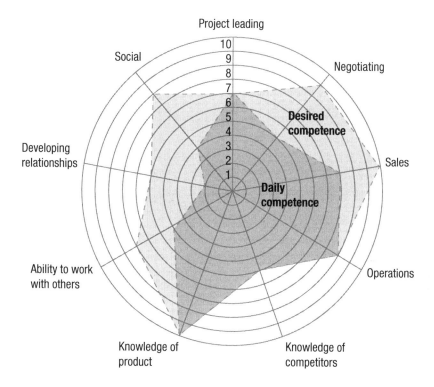

Core competence is a popular term. This is the competence on which a company's corporate mission is based and in which it must seek to be best in its industry. Knowledge of one's core competence and knowing 'what we can be the best in the world at' was shown to be a distinguishing characteristic of top companies in a comprehensive study carried out by James Collins. Visionary companies constantly seek new business opportunities and areas where they can apply their core competence. At the other end of the competence scale, as it were, is *hygiene competence*, which is the minimum level of general competence normally necessary to be a player in a particular market.

Another common term is *Competence* management, which is about attracting, developing and keeping competence in organizations. An important aspect of competence management is the ability to close the gap as in the gap analysis mentioned above and thereby ensure that the organization is properly equipped to meet future requirements. Competence management must therefore go hand in hand with a company's strategy development and business environmental analysis.

RECOMMENDED READING

1. Bengt Karlöf, Kurt Lundgren and Marie Edenfeldt Froment, Benchlearning: Good Examples as a Lever for Development.

2. Bradford D Smart, Topgrading: How Leading Companies Win by Hiring, Coaching and Keeping the Best People.

3. Patricia Pulliam Phillips, The Bottom Line on ROI: Basics, Benefits, & Barriers to Measuring Training & Performance Improvement.

Competition

Competition is defined as 'rivalry or contest, often between more or less well-matched contenders'. From the term 'competition' we can derive many different concepts and models, all of them based on an ability to compete, that is, the ability of a product to be perceived as a better alternative than the one offered by competing companies. Some of these concepts are described below:

Comparative advantage is a theory which holds that production of goods is subject to relative advantages or disadvantages that vary from one country to another, and that countries therefore benefit from specializing in the production of some goods, while importing others. This implies that even if a country is more efficient in absolute terms in producing two kinds of goods, it should opt to produce one and import the other.

An analogous situation is that of an experienced business strategist who also happens to be the world's fastest typist. Just as the strategist can earn more money by developing business and paying someone else to do his typing, so a country can benefit from concentrating its resources on areas where its comparative advantage is greatest.

Competitive profile is a graph that compares the cost structures of a business unit with those of another. It highlights the areas in which the unit enjoys advantages of scale of one kind or another.

Competitive edge is what all (competitive) business strategies aim for. Many factors can give a competitive edge; they include more efficient production, ownership of patents, good advertising, good management and good customer relations. (See also this term.)

Forces of competition are the factors that determine the state of competition in an industry. The five factors defined by Michael E Porter are:

1. Competition between existing companies

2. The bargaining power of buyers

3. The bargaining power of suppliers

4. The threat from new entrants

5. The threat of substitute products or services

See also *Porter's five competitive forces.*

Competitive position is the position that a company occupies in its industry with reference to current results and its strengths and weaknesses relative to its competitors. A business unit with a strong competitive position usually has a competitive edge protected by high entry barriers. Business units like that generally have a return on investment above average for their industry. Market share or relative market share (a company's share compared to its two or three strongest competitors) is often an essential component of competitive position. See also *Industry attraction and strategic position.*

Competitive strategy is a synonym for business strategy. It refers to the sum of the ways in which a business unit should behave in order to be competitive in its industry. (See also *Strategy.*)

RECOMMENDED READING

1. Jack Trout, Differentiate Or Die: Survival in Our Era of Killer Competition.

2. Michael E Porter, Michael E Porter on Competition.

Competitive edge

The whole object of business strategy is to gain a strategic advantage (or competitive edge). This strategic advantage should be of a kind that can be utilized as soon as possible and last as long as possible. Its function is to generate profits above the industry average and to gain market share.

Michael E Porter has defined three basic strategies that companies can adopt in order to reach a competitive advantage: differentiation, total cost superiority and focusing. These are shown in the model below.

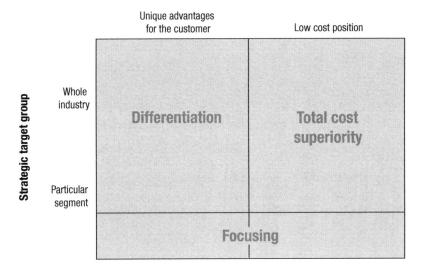

Differentiation means to distinguish products or services from those of the competitors. Differentiation can be through design, trademark, technology, distribution networks and many other factors. *Total cost superiority* is a method of utilizing the experience curve (see this term) to reach superior cost structures in an industry. Cost superiority represents a competitive advantage as it gives higher margins and prepares a company for price wars and price squeezes by customers. *Focusing* is to seek competitive advantage by focusing on a particular customer, target group, geographic market, etc. A company can have differentiation and/or cost advantages in respect of the market segment focused on.

Nowadays companies are talking more and more about finding their USP (Unique Selling Point). A USP is usually why customers will come to one company rather than to its competitors. It must be the most important of all competitive advantages.

Competitive advantage is increasingly found outside the four marketing Ps of product, price, place and promotion, due to tougher competition, shorter product cycles and imitation. The popularity of trademarks and the intensity with which they are marketed are becoming increasingly more important to distinguish between companies (see *Trademark*). It is important to point out that it is the customers' and stakeholders' experience of the product or trademark as unique or worth its price, which will determine whether there is in fact a competitive advantage – and not the 'objective truth'. A key to success in the hunt for competitive edge is therefore to get to know one's customers and their needs structures.

A comprehensive study has revealed that one of the differences between successful and unsuccessful companies is that the successful ones compete against themselves rather than their competitors (see the section on *Collins' and Porras' strategic success factors*). Instead of making war against your competitors, why not have a love affair with your customers?

RECOMMENDED READING

1. Gary Hamel with C K Prahalad, Competing for the Future.

2. Michael E Porter, Competitive Strategy: Creating and Sustaining Superior Performance.

3. Michael Treacy and Fred Wiersman, The Discipline of Market Leaders: Choose Your Customers, Narrow Your Focus, Dominate Your Market.

Conjoint analysis (simulated trade-off situations)

The idea of effectiveness is founded on the principle that all organized activity is for the purpose of creating a value that is higher than the cost of producing this value.

The two main components of any analysis of a company's effectiveness must then be its production costs and the readiness of its customers to pay for what it produces (i.e. customer utility). Production costs are based on calculable quantities while customer value is subjective and thus exists in the eye of the beholder. The shortage of goods during much of the last century focused the minds of business management on questions of productivity. To own a refrigerator – any one – was better than no refrigerator at all. The basic supply of goods was a priority in the whole world during the first half of the last century and mainly in the planned economies of former communist states during the second half, when customer value was not nearly as important as production costs.

As competition, i.e. the choice between several alternatives, has increased, customer value has grown more and more important to a company's success and survival. As a result, there have been a number of initiatives for the evaluation of customer value. Indicators like 'satisfied customer index' have become very popular, but often lead to disappointment when results fail to suggest a concrete course of action. If a satisfied customer index goes in six months from 82 per cent to 74 per cent for satisfied or very satisfied customers, we are still none the wiser as to how we can improve the situation.

There is an anecdote about an American telecoms operator that is instructive and furthermore, true. In study after study they got more and more satisfied customers, all the while losing market share to their competitors. A closer analysis showed that their customers thought that they were more expensive than the competition; obviously price played an important part in the choice of supplier.

There is a growing demand in business for tools that can give an indication of appropriate therapy and not simply make sweeping diagnostic statements. Conjoint (trade-off) analysis is one of the best known of these tools. This method displays customer preference and willingness to pay for different utility functions and provides complete or part profiles for management decision-making. As in the case of *yield management*, management is presented with clear choices in relation to price optimization, volumes, and so on. The tool has proved very useful to the Ford Group, which has, in recent years, become known for its progressive work in pricing, customer demand and product design.

Conjoint analysis is a powerful analytical tool for measuring customer behaviour (decisions) – as distinguished from attitudes – in simulated trade-off situations. The method uses customer evaluations of a product's different attributes and indicates which of these are most important to the consumer in financial terms, i.e. willingness to pay or price elasticity.

Conjoint analysis comes up with quantitative values to indicate the importance of one utility function in relation to another. The method can be used to facilitate:

1. determining the attributes a new or repositioned product or service should have.

2. pricing, on the basis of the customer's willingness to pay.

3. calculations of sales volumes at different price levels.

4. studies of the prospects for a new product or service.

Suppose for example, that you have to take a plane to New York for a meeting. Which of these two flight options would you choose?

- Company A that will be leaving two hours before or after the time you want to travel and which often arrives late in New York. The plane will be making two stop-overs and will probably be half empty. The air hostesses are friendly and considerate and you have a choice of two films to pass the time.

- Company B which will be leaving for New York four hours before or after the time you wanted to leave and which almost never arrives late. The flight is non-stop and the plane will probably be 90 per cent full. Air hostesses are reserved and only magazines are provided for your in-flight entertainment.

Companies naturally want to know what the consumer really wants from a product or service. Our example above shows how complicated the problem can be. In the first place, the alternatives which the customer has to choose between are multi-dimensional, i.e. they have several 'utilities'. Second, the customer has to make a comprehensive decision about the relative value of the total utility of all the alternatives, that is, s/he must order them in respect of some criterion. Conjoint analysis can sort out the relative importance of a product's different characteristics or product concepts.

There are other ways of determining the relative importance of a utility function. The simplest of these is to ask people which function of a product they think is the most important. The problem is that people will usually say that all the functions are important. In market research on choice of passenger car, for instance, many of the respondents say they would like a car that uses little petrol, looks sporty, is spacious, is low-priced, and so on. This line of enquiry tends to tell us more about respondents' attitudes, which is not particularly useful when we come to decide what choices these people would actually make in a buying situation.

Conjoint analysis on the other hand forces the respondent to make choices. Is the desire for one utility function great enough to warrant the sacrifice of another? If a function has to be sacrificed, which one should it be? This information is obtained by giving respondents the product concepts, which represent different combinations of utility functions and their levels (the different values they represent). Conjoint analysis, then, can produce realistic and useful information.

Three areas in which conjoint analysis can be used are of particular interest. First, we can gain insight into how consumers make choices in an existing market and get information on how they perceive the competing alternatives; this can be valuable when designing market communication programmes. Second, this type of analysis can suggest new configurations of products or services which consumers may find more attractive than the competing alternatives. Finally, utility functions can be used to carry out strategic market simulations used to evaluate the implications (volume, results) of changes in marketing strategy.

To illustrate how a conjoint analysis can be used, let us assume that a company is interested in putting a cleaning agent on the market. The management has identified five utility functions which it assumes will influence customer behaviour more than others:

1. Packaging
2. Branding
3. Price
4. Whether their cleaning agent will be 'best in test'
5. If it carries a money-back guarantee

The company has produced three different types of packaging (A, B and C). It has also come up with three different name brands: K2R, Glory and Bisell. The cleaning agent is to be priced at 29, 39 or 59. In addition, the analysis is to reveal what value customers place on the agent's being 'best in test', and whether a money-back guarantee is to be offered. There is a total of 3 x 3 x 3 x 2 x 2 = 108 possible combinations for the five factors we listed.

Conjoint analysis utilizes a special experimental design concept that includes the principle of orthogonality, which selects combinations so that independent alternative combinations are excluded from the total. In this case the 108 combinations are reduced to 18! These 18 combinations of cleaning agent with different presentation and price are shown to potential customers who are then asked to rank them in the order in which they would probably buy them.

Various computer programs have been devized to calculate utility functions which determine how meaningful each of the five factors is for a customer's choice. This technique gives us a utility function for each level of every factor and thus allows the levels of best customer-perceived utility to be combined. See the figures below.

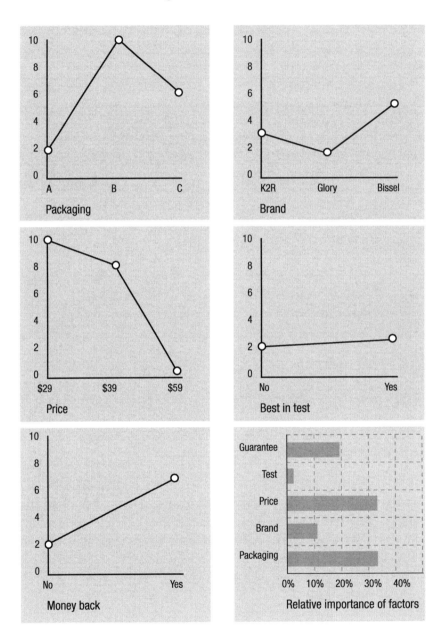

We have not given an account here of the multivariable statistical analysis that underlies conjoint analysis, but recommend the interested reader to contact a good consultancy firm with experience in projects involving the method. There are a number of pitfalls associated with conjoint analysis but experience can help to avoid them.

RECOMMENDED READING

1. Anders Gustafsson, Andreas Herrmann and Frank Huber (editors), Conjoint Measurement: Methods and Applications.

2. Jordan J Louviere, Analyzing Decision Making: Metric Conjoint Analysis.

Control systems

The heading of this entry really ought to be 'profit control systems', because the shorter term 'control systems' refers to the process of obtaining organized information about the extent to which operations are achieving their set goals. Surprisingly often, we find that control systems are not congruent with the goal image. In many cases this is because the goal image has not been precisely defined in terms of money, or of quantities like orders received or market share, or of customer-perceived quality. If we have established the principal factors of quality as the customer perceives it, we can also measure and record those factors without having to go out and ask customers so often that it causes undue expense to us or undue annoyance to them.

One of the commonest pitfalls is an excess of ambition in the construction of control systems. This may be because the designers of the system have set their sights too high, or because the criteria have been sloppily defined, with the result that the designers try to satisfy too many demands without establishing what the users of the system actually need. Such system failures often lead to prolonged and serious effects that are very difficult to remedy. A large Swedish company, three years after launching its control system, still had no follow-up reports in its organization, or at any rate none that the recipients bothered to read. Reporting discipline had declined to an abysmal level because the organization did not perceive reporting as meaningful as long as nothing came out of it. In that particular case, the failure could be ascribed to undue ambition; they had tried to construct a system capable of solving all the information problems in a huge organization.

RECOMMENDED READING

1. Bob Frost, Measuring Performance: Using the New Metrics to Deploy Strategy and Improve Performance.

2. Richard L Lynch and Kelvin F Cross, Measure Up! How to Measure Corporate Performance.

CRM

Customer Relationship Management, CRM, concerns the technique of getting, developing and hanging on to good customer relations by finding out as much as possible about customer needs and wishes. The concept of CRM has come to be synonymous with systems developed by the SAP company (Systems, Applications, Products), Siebel and others to facilitate the work of CRM. Many people have these systems in mind when CRM is used today.

CRM techniques are largely based on integrating all the systems in an organization: customer service, sales support, pricing and so on. CRM had a number of precursors such as SFA (Sales Force Automation), which provided support for sales and marketing activities and CSS (Customer Service and Support) which offers support for after-sales activities like customer service, complaints, call centres, etc.

Implementing a CRM system can be dangerous, as many companies have found to their cost, as the technology involved tends to dictate the course of planning. The most intelligent way to manage customer relations is for customer orientation personnel to first set up a goal and then establish how this goal can best be achieved. A goal might be to change the company culture or modify customer service procedures. Once these priorities have been established it might be interesting to see if there is a system that can support the customer strategies and working methods already in place.

CRM has come to be a very vague term. Going through the abundance of different definitions the term has given rise to, it seems that organizations can call any activity that has the slightest connection to marketing or customer relations, CRM. In other words, the term has come to mean all things to all men. The principle of acquiring more insight into customer needs and wishes in order to build stronger customer relations is of course extremely important, and a question of survival for many organizations. Evert Gummesson, a professor at the Stockholm University School of Business, splits the concept into hCRM (human CRM) and eCRM (electronic CRM). hCRM focuses on inter-personal relationships, eCRM on system-based relationship management.

RECOMMENDED READING

1. Evert Gummesson, Total Relationship Marketing.
2. Jill Dyché, The CRM Handbook: A Business Guide to Customer Relationship Management.
3. Patricia B Ramaswamy et al, Harvard Business Review on Customer Relationship Management.

Culture

When we think of *culture* we usually think in terms of nations, ethnic groups and religions, but the word has entered popular use to describe the distinguishing characteristics of businesses and organizations. Henceforth we will be using the term *company* culture, but it is just as relevant for all kinds of organization.

The term *company culture* has been established in management since the middle of the 1980s. An organization's culture is formed by the values and standards, explicit or otherwise, which have emerged from past events and strong personalities or through the work of development.

Someone once said that the company culture was an employee's inner compass. It is a company's culture that determines the length and frequency of meetings, the mode of dress, the conditions for dialogue in the company, the length of reports, and so on.

A company culture helps co-workers to feel that they belong. The person who has perhaps done most to call attention to company culture is Edgar H Schein, a professor at MIT, with his book *Organizational Culture and Leadership*, which appeared in 1985. Schein affirmed how difficult it was to change a company's culture and he cites the CEOs who have been outstandingly successful in this area. An example is Jack Welch, who famously revolutionized General Electric's company culture with his vision of a hybrid enterprise ("the body of a large company, the soul of a small company").

Success in changing the culture of an organization, according to Schein, lies in getting consensus in the following five areas:

1. The organization's corporate mission or primary task
2. Goals in the work of change
3. Methods for achieving these goals
4. How progress is measured
5. Strategies for support or repair actions

Are there cultural patterns which have been more successful than others? A study carried out by Jim Collins and his team of researchers in which they analyzed and compared 28 companies over a period of five years showed that top companies were able to combine two somewhat contradictory criteria: discipline and entrepreneurship. When organizations grow and become more complex, discipline takes on a greater cultural role in driving them forward. Discipline can also smother the energy and risk-taking initiatives of the entrepreneurial spirit and lead to an organization's bureaucratization. According to Collins, a combination of discipline and entrepreneurship is the recipe for success.

The Swedish company IKEA is a good example of this combination. IKEA, with Ingvar Kamprad, its founder, at the fore, has worked on its company culture for a long time. Kamprad minted a number of catchphrases in his pamphlet, *The testament of a furniture dealer*, which is given to new employees:

- "Expensive solutions are often underwritten by mediocrities"
- "Making mistakes is the privilege of people who act."
- "Don't waste your strength in convincing me; carry out your project instead."
- "Constant planning is a company's most common cause of death."

The above quotations show the importance of discipline, mainly in connection with an awareness of costs, and give evidence of a marked entrepreneurial company culture. IKEA spreads its culture through the use of symbols (myths and images), standard bearers, cultural ambassadors and by the example of its managers.

McDonald's, with its slogan of QSCV (Quality, Service, Cleanliness and Value), is another example of a well-established company culture. These values are the mortar that holds together McDonald's innumerable restaurants around the world, and they are drummed into managers at McDonald's Hamburger University in Chicago. McDonald's has a heavy manual describing how their message is put into practice. All their new employees undergo a baptism of fire in QSCV. Films on QSCV are always running during breaks. Ray Kroc, founder of the McDonald's chain but now deceased, has become a symbol for QSCV.

Many other examples could be given, including the story of how Apple and Microsoft, through discipline and entrepreneurship, graduated from an operation in a garage to become what they are today.

A comprehensive study of cultural differences in different countries has been carried out by Geert Hofstede, Emeritus Professor of Organizational Anthropology and International Management at Maastricht University, and can be found in his book, *Culture's Consequences*. The framework used by Hofstede for his research can also be applied to throw light on cultural patterns in organizations. Hofstede worked with four variables:

1. Individualism/collectivism
2. Power distance

3. Uncertainty avoidance

4. Masculine/feminine

Some of the pitfalls of strong company cultures are:

1. Strong cultures can lead to sectarianism where thinking outside what is acceptable is easily dismissed; thus good ideas can end up in the waste bin.

2. There is also a risk that conformism allied to a strong culture impedes the work of change when this becomes necessary. If a company suddenly has to change its approach because of market conditions, changes may be slow to come. We can cite the example of Ericsson, which has had to meet the challenge of changing from a technology-driven culture, successful at an early stage of the market's development, to a customer-oriented culture in order to remain competitive.

3. Cultural differences between countries are often forgotten when companies expand on a global basis. A business that has thrived in England may not be successful at all in China or Finland.

4. Finally, there is the risk that work on company culture may be aiming more at the general well-being of its co-workers than at improving levels of businessmanship. 'Happy employees equals happy customers' is a dangerous over-simplification in business. In the long run, happy employees want their company to survive and be successful.

With the right approach, a company's culture is an effective means of managing and holding the organization together. See the section under Values, which is closely connected to the idea of company culture.

RECOMMENDED READING

1. Edgar H Schein, Organizational Culture and Leadership.

2. Fons Trompenaars and Charles Hampden Turner, Riding the Waves of Culture: Understanding Cultural Diversity in Business.

3. Geert Hofstede, Cultures and Organizations: Software of the Mind.

Customer relations

Studies have shown that the cost of replacing a lost customer is from five to seven times greater than the cost of raising the value delivered to an existing customer. Taking care of customer relations is of vital importance for the health of most businesses, and the signs are that this is going to be even more important in the future.

Sales organizations play an important role in building long-term customer relations. It is common for a special salesperson to be appointed to be in charge of customer relations. Titles such as Key Account Manager (KAM) and Relationship Manager are becoming more and more common.

A success factor in building good customer relations is to continually measure and evaluate customer satisfaction in different areas and, if need be, to take appropriate action. A rule of thumb is that every customer account should be reviewed at least once a year. This can be appreciated by customers, especially as it is one customer meeting that will not focus on selling. See *Sales force* for more information on customer metrics.

The trouble with customer surveys is that they only give us an index and do not tell us what action to take to develop customer relations. They can even be dangerous if a customer sees that no action has been taken on something that s/he complained about in a survey. In order to avoid this, it is important for questions in surveys to be precise and for the results to be quickly communicated to the operative parts of the organization which can then deal with what may be an unsatisfactory state of affairs.

A Problem Detection Study (PDS) is a method that can be used to identify areas for improvement. Instead of asking how satisfied they are, customers are asked to formulate the problems they experience and to rank them in order of importance. This method reveals the areas in which company action will have the greatest positive effect on customer satisfaction. More about PDS can be found in the section of that name.

Good customer relations often become what can only be called a partnership between the supplier and the customer, so much so sometimes that it can be difficult to draw a boundary between the two businesses. Systems and processes become so integrated that the companies collaborate in all areas, with the exception of direct sales.

RECOMMENDED READING

1. Evert Gummesson, Total Relationship Marketing.

2. Jill Griffin, Customer Loyalty: How to Earn It, How to Keep It.

3. Kenneth Blanchard and Sheldon Bowles, Raving Fans: A Revolutionary Approach to Customer Service.

4. Sallie Sherman, Joseph Sperry and Samuel Reese, The Seven Keys to Managing Strategic Accounts.

Customers

By customers we mean regular buyers of goods or services. Potential customers are usually included in the abstract concept of market. The concept of a customer is appearing more and more in non-commercial activities where the term used to be 'user' or 'buyer'. In this respect, a customer is the person who receives and evaluates a producing unit's goods or services.

Greater local and global competition, shorter product cycles, more and more imitation and consolidated purchasing, have all given the customer increasingly greater power in many industries. The building of long-term customer relations characterized by satisfaction and loyalty has thus become more of a priority than ever. For more on this see *Sales force*.

The customer was not nearly so important during the years from the end of World War II to the mid-1970s as s/he is today. When demand exceeded supply, much less attention was paid to the customer's wishes than has been the case since the mid-1970s. Customers were formerly regarded as an abstract mass who were charged handling fees and subjected to a rationalization process designed to make them buy as much as possible every time they placed an order. Producers put their own production apparatus first and tried to adapt customer behaviour to it.

Since the mid-1970s, producers have had to focus their attention on the customer and his need structures in order to influence customer demand for their products. Large corporations still have a tendency to treat the customer as an abstraction. Comet-like careers in big organizations tend to make high-ranking executives uninterested in who their customers actually are, or what their underlying need structures might be. In this case, the term customer refers to executives and individuals who make or influence buying decisions.

It is sometimes difficult to identify the customer in the sense of discovering the need structures to be satisfied, especially where there are dealer structures, which are becoming increasingly common. In the pharmaceutical industry there are at least three categories of person who could aspire to being customers: the patients/end-users, the doctors/pharmacists, pharmaceutical committees and other organs that influence decision-making. It is important then to sort out what we mean and not simply babble about 'the customer'. The same is true for schools. Is it the pupils, their parents or society as represented by the government of the day, who are to be seen as the customers?

The most generally businesslike definition of customer is: the physical person who makes decisions on purchasing or utility outside of the traditional buying situation.

RECOMMENDED READING

1. Bradley T Gale, Managing Customer Value: Creating Quality & Service That Customers Can See.
2. Gerald Zaltman, How Customers Think: Essential Insights into the Mind of the Market.

Decentralization

A process of decentralization is under way almost all over the world, in business as well as in public administration and non-profit organizations. The aim of this process is often to make operations more efficient by utilizing people's intelligence so as to increase an organization's pool of wisdom. Another important aim is to put the responsibility for decisions close to customers and the market in the hands of people who know them best.

Decentralization is impelled by three principal motives:

1. Organizations become more market-oriented and thus more efficient in respect of the people they serve.

2. People feel more involved, which encourages motivation, entrepreneurship and job satisfaction.

3. People want to be their own masters instead of being bossed around.

Decentralization is desirable by both management and employees in times of prosperity. It is easy to accept delegated responsibility when success is assured. But decentralization is not such a cut-and-dried affair in times of adversity. It is hard for people to have to reduce volumes, cut capacity and fire colleagues. And it is not pleasant to have the responsibility to decentralize when there are hard decisions to be made in respect of the productivity axis (see the section on *Efficiency*). In the good times, decisions are primarily about expansion and customer value. In a slump, belts are tightened and the hair shirts are brought out.

The early 20th century witnessed dramatic developments in people's working lives. When Fredric W Taylor developed his theories on scientific management (see *Taylorism*) it was an extremely small section of the working population that had any kind of management responsibility. The majority of wage-earners carried out more or less repetitive work without the need for problem solving skills or decision-making.

Nowadays there are a great many more work arenas and the situation could not be more different. A vast number of jobs now carry some responsibility, people have to think about the work they do and management skills are required of many people, whatever their position in the organization. Routine production work is now mostly assigned to machines, leading increasingly to the intellectualization of most of our work. From a management perspective, organizations have simply become more customer-oriented and efficient, while the working environment is giving employees more job satisfaction and an opportunity to exercise their creativity.

One of the principal causes of decentralization is competitive pressure, i.e. customers can choose between several good alternatives. When there is little pressure from competitors the need for market and customer orientation is less obvious. Corporate thinking can be left to top management with the rest of the organization following orders. This is an extremely inefficient way to lead a company however when competitive pressure is high. Substantive decision-making is too far removed from customers who then turn to more agile organizations that respond more quickly to their needs. Decentralization then becomes a question of self-preservation and competitive ability. Studies have shown that decentralization is highly desirable to increase efficiency where customer utility is concerned but is considerably less effective in relation to the cost dimension. This can be seen in organizations that have felt it necessary to lower their cost levels. Decentralization then tends to go overboard, with top management taking over control. Of course the world is not so constituted that only one course – centralization or decentralization – has to be the right one. The intelligent approach is to strike a balance between these two opposites and look at a number of factors:

Centralized/decentralized

1. What essential functions ought to be kept together from the standpoint of overall strategy?

2. Which functions call for local initiatives, customer-perceived value and variation?

3. What economies of scale, i.e. advantages of 'scale and skull', are there?

4. What is necessary to manage the organization?

5. How do small-scale advantages affect the efficiency of the organization?

In many systems largely shielded from competition, a kind of anarchistic decentralization can be made to work. By this we mean a division of responsibility without the need for a cohesive executive.

A slight, inadvertent shift to decentralization can sometimes be discerned, particularly in the transition period when regulated public systems begin to face competition and the balance between centralization and decentralization has not been sufficiently pondered. The following points can be made:

1. It may be strategically necessary to keep brand, R&D and marketing together.

2. Functions that require local initiatives are often connected to sales, service and after-sales.

3. An analysis of how the advantages of scale and skull (or the total competence of an organization) relate to efficiency, is often lacking. An important function at a bank can appear to be cost-motivated, while one of its branch offices is busy creating customer value which, however significant, may well escape analysis.

4. Sometimes, in decentralized systems, there is not sufficient analysis of cause and effect and this can make the work of management difficult. Certain expenses may be activated in the balance sheet in one place while they appear as a cost in the profit and loss account in another. Customer contracts stretching over several years may be taken up as income in one region but split into periods in another.

5. Small-scale advantages need to be commented on separately as they are often behavioural in character and ignored by technocrats. Small-scale advantages are difficult to measure and therefore get less attention than they deserve. Without small-scale advantages there would only be one company in every industry, as the ability to compete would be determined by size.

The following small-scale advantages have been identified:

1. Motivation and energy

2. Communication

3. Customization

4. Optimal processes

5. Economization of resources

6. Flexibility in the use of personnel

7. Sick absence – productivity

Small-scale advantages may sometimes be impossible to measure but an awareness of the factors present in a given situation can affect the outcome. Analyzes have revealed that the advantages of a decentralized structure are mainly due to sales, service and after-sales. Consideration should thus be given to what is best done by centralization and, on the other hand, what issues are best served by decentralization. Some of the hazards of organization rationality are:

1. Coordination mania

2. Compromise

3. Lack of flexibility

The dilemma of organization that always calls for 'manual control' is the dichotomy between rational, large-scale, coordinated solutions on the one hand and the efficiency-boosting effects of small-scale entrepreneurship on the other. It is a sound general rule that decentralized entrepreneurship is a good thing in good times, whereas many questions require centralized action in bad times. See *Small-scale advantages*.

RECOMMENDED READING

1. Henry Mintzberg, Structures in Fives: Designing Effective Organizations.

2. Kenneth H Blanchard, Empowerment Takes More Than a Minute.

3. Robert Heller and Tim Hindle, How to Delegate.

Decision methodology

Most people are probably not acquainted with decision theory, in spite of the fact that our daily lives are full of decisions that must be made involving work, relationships, the acquisition of wealth, etc.

We often have to make decisions which may have serious consequences, in a climate of uncertainty, and great sums of money may be involved. This is especially true of decisions taken in business, political situations, in war and peace or in human relationships important to us. If we are familiar with decision theory we can learn to make decisions more effectively while dealing with the consequences of those decisions.

PrOACT

In their book *Smart Choices,* John S Hammond, Ralph L Keeney and Howard Raiffa describe a methodology called PrOACT an acronym that derives from the first five elements of the decision-making process. These elements are given below.

1. Problem
2. Objectives
3. Alternative
4. Consequences
5. Trade-offs
6. Uncertainty
7. Risk tolerance
8. Linked decisions

We describe PrOACT in detail as a working method because we have found it to be more useful and comprehensive than other methods in the field of decision theory. PrOACT seeks to analyze and clarify situations in which we make complex decisions. For very complex decisions, it may be necessary to go through all eight steps of the process carefully. However, it often suffices to select a number of elements that are especially relevant to a situation and go on working with these.

Has the problem been correctly formulated? The problem has to be correctly formulated for best results and complex problems must be formulated clearly and concisely. The answer depends on the question, as it is said. Are the goals we want to reach clear? It is important to have a clear picture of what we want to achieve in order to make the right decision.

Have the different alternatives been identified? It is important to clarify the alternatives available to us. Have the consequences of applying alternatives been thought out? It is not easy to assess the consequences of our decisions, but we must try.

What trade-offs need to be made? It is not unusual to find that our goals conflict in some way with the decisions we have to take to achieve those goals. Sometimes it may be necessary to go ahead anyway and try to establish a balance between conflicting issues; sometimes it may be necessary to relinquish a goal in favour of another goal.

Are there any doubts? Before making a decision, it is essential to try to identify and clear up any doubts that we may have. Are we really at ease with changes in the external business environment?

What risk tolerance is there? The person responsible for making a decision should look carefully at the risks involved; if a decision carries an unacceptable level of risk, it should not be considered.

How are decisions linked together? A decision made today will affect future decisions; our goals for tomorrow will affect our decisions today.

Decision-making traps

There are a number of pitfalls connected to decision-making. Many of the 'traps' we describe can also be used consciously in attempting to influence the decisions of others, for example in negotiating. The very best defence against these hazards is to be aware of them.

The anchoring trap

We tend to 'anchor' our thinking and give disproportionate importance to the first piece of information that crosses our path. If the magnitude of something is hinted at in a discussion, it will tend to dominate what follows. This can be exploited in negotiations, for example.

The status quo trap

This refers to our tendency to want to keep things as they are. In business, to deviate from the status quo involves taking responsibility upon oneself and thus risk criticism. This hazard is one to watch out for in repressive environments.

The sunk cost trap

The sunk cost trap is related to our desire to be consistent and follow decisions we have previously made. This can often be observed in business. Products are pushed for far too long in the hope that their prospects will improve. It goes against the grain to have to admit that a product has been a bad investment and abandon it.

The confirming evidence trap

We tend to seek proof that supports our viewpoint or the decision that we have taken intuitively. This can certainly be observed in politics, when two political opponents with the same information find arguments to support their own orientation.

The framing trap

The framing trap is a hazard that we may meet through the way a problem is framed or presented. The way a problem is presented considerably influences the alternatives we choose. It has been shown that problems that are presented as a gain lead to lower risk-taking than problems presented as a loss.

The estimation and prediction trap

People are strongly inclined to overestimate both their own performance and their ability to foresee the future and as a result, wrong decisions are often made. The University of Michigan carried out a study where top executives in a number of companies were asked their opinions on certain matters. The following statistics emerged from the study:

- 50 per cent thought that, in respect of performance and quality, their own company was among the top 10 per cent in their industry.

- 75 per cent of managers thought that their company was in the top 25 per cent in respect of performance and quality.

- 90 per cent of managers thought that they were in the upper half of their industry.

The caution trap

Certain people find that it is always easier to be cautious and careful in their actions instead of taking risks.

The impression trap

As human beings we tend to be unduly influenced by unusual events in our immediate environment. Under these circumstances, objectivity and a sense of proportion are often abandoned. Examples of such events are aircraft accidents, illnesses around us and traffic accidents.

The only real defence against all of these traps is to be aware of them. We therefore advise readers to give a little extra thought to those 'go – no go' project decisions, evaluations of their company's performance vis-à-vis the competition, and so on. It can often be a good idea to invite someone from outside the company to question its decisions and assumptions, i.e. to play the devil's advocate.

RECOMMENDED READING

1. John S Hammond, Ralph L Keeney and Howard Raiffa, Smart Choices: A Practical Guide to Making Better Decisions.

2. Robert B Cialdini, Influence: Science and Practice.

3. Scott Plous, The Psychology of Judgment and Decision Making.

Deregulation

Deregulation refers to industries or areas where competition was either non-existent, or strictly limited by regulation or legislation and where the limitations are eased or abolished. The classic case with which most people associate the word is the deregulation of air passenger traffic in the USA, initiated in 1978 by the Carter administration. Deregulation of telecommunications in the United States and of banking and currency trading in Western Europe have since come to highlight a new kind of strategic situation that scarcely existed before 1978. Today in many industries, countries and, not least, in the EU, we are witnessing both fear and joy in connection with the general deregulation which is proceeding at a variable pace – most recently from 2003 in agriculture within the EU.

To understand deregulation and the business opportunities it offers, we should first try to understand the factors that led to deregulation being imposed in the first place, and how things have changed since that happened. In the case of airline traffic, it was considerations of safety that made governments all over the world feel, after World War II, that regulation was necessary. The underlying idea was that unrestricted competition would tempt airlines to cut corners on safety.

What has happened since then is that safety in aviation has steadily improved and has now reached a level that would once have been almost inconceivable. Since the beginning of the 1960s, with the exception of 1985, the number of scheduled airline passengers killed in accidents has fallen steadily when measured per passenger-kilometre.

Many of the regulated monopolies were originally set up because the technologies and investments involved made competition impossible. Telecommunications were long regarded as a 'natural' monopoly, but modern radio technology, optic fibre cables strung along railway lines, satellites and, not least, the Internet, have made the business an attractive proposition for new operators. This creates problems for the former monopolists, one being how to generate a sense of success in their organizations. Being forced to yield market share can cause psychological and organizational upsets of an often unforeseen kind.

The disadvantages of regulation had grown more and more apparent in the light of the impressive improvement in efficiency that has taken place in private enterprise throughout the world, partly as a result of the energy crisis of the mid-1970s. It has become increasingly obvious that efficiency is decidedly poorer in regulated industries. This is of course due to the deadwood that organizations accumulate when they do not have to worry about competition.

As national economies have got deeper into trouble, the efficiency of regulated industries has become more and more of an embarrassment. This is probably one of the chief explanations for the wave of deregulation now mainly sweeping the Western world.

Clearly there is a risk that businesses which used to be regulated will lack the ability and will to compete in the new environment in which they find themselves. This lack of competitiveness will naturally not only apply to production, i.e. in cost per unit produced, but just as much on the other axis of efficiency, i.e. value as a function of utility and price. The 'soft' customer utility functions on the service side are often underdeveloped. This is natural and understandable in an environment shielded from competition. Spectacular improvements in productivity can be observed in deregulated industries, clear evidence that regulation causes inefficiency due to a lack of competition.

According to all the theories, a company in a monopoly position ought to generate abnormally high profits. But such is hardly ever the case in practice, because companies that are shielded from competition let their cost levels drift upward through a surfeit of capital and costs to the point where their profits are not much better.

There are different aspects to deregulation: the deregulated business that must transform itself in a competitive culture, and the part of the industry formerly existing under different conditions now presented with new business opportunities. Yet a third aspect in this connection is that companies might fall for fashionable solutions which can lead them into a maze, with negative consequences.

Poorly planned divisions of rail or airline companies and slipshod separations between a company's infrastructure and operations have, in many cases, led to teething problems that have proved expensive to correct. The company that has been regulated must face up to a cultural revolution. The monopolistic or, through state control, partly monopolistic airline must compete with new low-priced operators which have identified passenger demand for low prices as the decisive component in customer value. Such situations call for a complete change in an organization's attitude to performance.

The deregulated unit generally has far too low operational productivity, i.e. too many staff. Further, the business has generally underestimated price as a means of competition. By this we mean the great importance that customers attach to price when there is a free choice between different alternatives.

A third factor is the investment structure a company has got into. As soon as it is confronted with competition it will by definition lose market share, and when this happens its boots will be too big, not only in terms of staff, but also in terms of premises, machinery and other parts of its infrastructure. To give an example, a traditionally monopolistic European telecommunications operator was found to provide 26 sq. metres of office space per office employee, while the corresponding figure for Bell Canada was 14 sq. metres. For other competitors the figure was still lower. The deregulated party therefore has to go through a baptism of fire by streamlining its operations, i.e. it must generate greater productivity and customer value.

Infra-structural sources of revenue such as the operation of rail tracks or telecom networks, or access to airport departure times, are often lost. In cases where businesses succeed in keeping control over their infrastructure, they often, in a defensive strategy, milk this cash cow through high prices. This can lead to disputes with new competitors and loss of the cash cow, which is transferred directly to the state in question.

The challenge of turning a national behemoth into a lean operator in a competitive market is a monumental one. It is all too easy to sneer at organizations which take up the challenge and struggle in the process. However, in our opinion they are due the greatest respect in their efforts to effect a cultural transformation that can secure a future for the company and its stakeholders.

While for some players deregulation may represent an uncertain future, for others it is often just the opposite. Suddenly, opportunities are there to create new TV channels, new airlines, new telecom operators or new energy companies.

Meanwhile, inherent in this apparently cosy scenario great dangers await the new players. One is to underestimate the formerly regulated company's influence on society. Appearances are always against monopolists. They have very little goodwill because people hate not to have alternative suppliers. It is therefore common to find entrepreneurs rushing into new business opportunities, underestimating both the costs of getting into the market and the strong position of the former monopolist – not least with the authorities. It is not unusual to see large numbers of new market entrants coming to grief in deregulated markets. This can be observed in the airline business in the USA, in telecoms, energy, and so on.

New companies underestimate the time it takes to gain acceptance for new brands and new products, also known as the modernity trap. The costs of running a business in a previously regulated area are often underestimated. The operational side of things may well seem uncomplicated and easy to manage at much lower costs, and lead to dramatic price reductions. But unsuspected and unforeseen details may intrude upon start-up, raising costs and leading to losses and market exit. It can thus be a difficult situation for the deregulated company as well as its new competitors. The newly deregulated business undoubtedly finds the situation most difficult, however. It often has to deal with a comprehensive lack of efficiency in both production and customer value, while customers' sympathies often shift to what is perceived to be the underdog.

As the situation calls for special management competence, the benchmarking of other deregulation exercises is strongly recommended.

We bring this section to a close by pointing out that there are naturally cases where regulation may be necessary for, among other things, social or ethical reasons.

RECOMMENDED READING

1. Daniel Yergin med Joseph Stanislaw, The Commanding Heights: The Battle Between Government and the Marketplace that is Remaking the Modern World.

2. William Emmons III, The Evolving Bargain: Strategic Implications of Deregulation and Privatization.

Development

Development can be described as change from a more primitive to a more sophisticated state. In a glossary of business terms, development definitely rates a place today. The term is used in two principal senses:

1. To denote one of the four basic functions of a company (the other three being marketing, production and administration).

2. To denote a method of tackling issues that gets things moving in the right direction.

The development function in a company usually devotes its effort to product development, or to concept development in the case of knowledge industries.

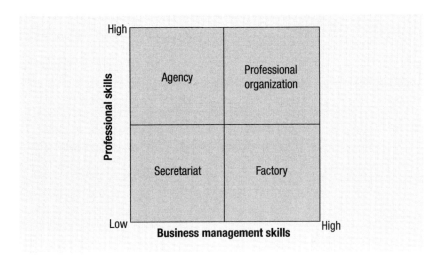

124

This is what we naturally associate with the word development. In recent times a couple of other terms have come into use which compete with the traditional use of the word development in industry. One is *market development*, which refers to expansion of existing clientele (served market), and the other is *organization development*, which refers to the development of individuals, groups, areas of responsibility, control systems, incentives and so on.

Nevertheless, by far the most important meaning of the word development is still the development of goods and services in the company to satisfy customers' underlying need structures, and thereby increase demand for one's own product. In a modern business development process, we cannot take it for granted that development resources should be used to improve product performance. In many cases they should be devoted to other functions instead, ones where the greatest possible increase of customer satisfaction can be achieved, which will in turn create competitive advantages. In short, business development is a matter of allocating resources to where they will produce the greatest possible competitive edge in the shortest possible time.

The second sense of the term development can be most simply explained by contrasting it to dealing with problems of administration. Matters that are dealt with are matters that call attention to themselves. They arise in every kind of activity. Prices must be adjusted, employees must be recruited, budgets must be drawn up, progress reports must be analyzed, etc. Dealing with issues is the main function of administrative management, or what Joseph Schumpeter, the well-known economist, calls static efficiency.

The characteristic feature of development issues, on the other hand, is that we have to go out and look for them. That is why they must be pursued with extra energy. Strategy work is a good example of this kind of development question.

The ability to handle development issues is what largely characterizes modern management. Maximum efficiency in administering the status quo has given way to efficiency in developing one's area of responsibility. The business development concept has come to be a characteristic of offensive strategies designed to make the business grow rather than to conserve its resources. Both ingredients are of course necessary to successful business management. The newly discovered development aspect of business management sometimes tempts managers into flamboyancy and reckless use of resources, which of course is not a good thing.

RECOMMENDED READING

1. Jim Collins, Good to Great: Why Some Companies Make the Leap… and Others Don't.

2. Michael Fullan, Leading in a Culture of Change.

Displayed thinking (graphic visualizing)

Effective communication is one of the hygiene factors (see Needs) for motivating co-workers. Someone responsible for strategy development in a large company told us recently that they had passed the stage of treating their strategy plan as a confidential document accessible to only the chosen few and now put it on the company's Intranet. The reason for this move was the absurdity of a strategic plan hidden from the very people it was made for. The company naturally ran a security risk by making their plan available to a larger circle but the alternative was not to use the plan at all. It would become an intellectual exercise and end up on a bookshelf (or as in this case, a safe). If communication within an organization is to be effective then it is important for the entire management experience to be documented so that it can be easily visualized and communicated.

Mike Vance, the former Managing Director of Walt Disney developed a technique which he called 'displayed thinking', where wall charts, and so on, are used to display the elements of a strategy. Information and various parameters will have been communicated to management, so managers can get involved quickly and contribute to the discussion. In this way, well-grounded decisions with a broad and solid factual base can be made.

Visualizing the process stimulates participants to learn from each other and build on what they already know. This is especially important, as different people will probably be taking part over a long period of time. Displayed thinking can be carried out in workshops using flipcharts or wall charts to document ideas that pop up along the way. It is very important to record the different interconnecting ideas, so that when the whole process has been documented it can be intelligible to everyone.

Displayed thinking in a frank and open atmosphere may seem to be a simple enough thing to arrange, but in fact managements often fail to grasp the opportunity to do so. Our experience is that companies can greatly benefit from this kind of visualization process as it has been described above, both where their processes are concerned and psychologically, when progress in the work becomes more evident.

Strategic Visioning is a method developed by Grove Consultants in San Francisco to work with displayed thinking in connection with strategy development. Some features of the concept are that it:

- stimulates holistic thinking.
- facilitates working in large groups.
- stimulates the creativity of both the individual and the group.
- promotes consensus, where everyone can contribute and be given a hearing.
- combines text, image and colour in large (1.5 x 3m) graphics to make use of the analytical and creative skills of all the participants.

The method is based on a number of factors; the ability to lead a seminar with a big visual component is one of them. Imagery and metaphor are used to reflect patterns of thought which are organized to achieve the desired result of the group taking part in the exercise. Simple though the graphics may be, they can set the scene for a unique opportunity to stimulate the thoughts and feelings of people in an entire organization. The kind of graphic that might be used at a strategic visioning session is shown below. The figure shows representations of an organization's strengths, weaknesses, threats and opportunities, its long-term vision and how to get there (strategic agenda), as well as important values in the work of development.

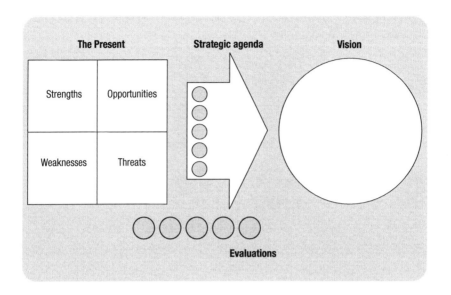

The Present   Strategic agenda   Vision

Strengths   Opportunities

Weaknesses   Threats

Evaluations

RECOMMENDED READING

David Sibbet, Principles of Facilitation: The Purpose and Potential of Leading Group Process.

Distribution

The dictionary gives two definitions for distribution:

1. Agreed or regular allocation and delivery of goods.

2. The totality of operations undertaken to make goods or services available to customers.

The term 'distribution' had wide currency at the end of the 1950s and during the 1960s when shortages of goods in most western countries gave way to surpluses. The production component of the price of goods fell and the concept of marketing emerged. At that time, the term distribution was often used as a synonym for marketing, and terminological confusion prevailed.

In modern usage, the term distribution has tended to revert to its original meaning of physical movement of goods. In this sense, the term distribution comprises two aspects:

1. The creation of a high level of customer service

2. Management of resources in respect of tied-up capital and transportation costs.

The essential thing is to make it clear which sense of the word is being used.

RECOMMENDED READING

1. Jeremy F Shapiro, Modelling the Supply Chain.

2. Sunil Chopra and Peter Meindl, Supply Chain Management: Strategy, Planning, and Operation.

Diversification

The idea of diversification has a varied history. It was in high fashion in connection with corporate development in the late 1960s and early 1970s, but fell on hard times when concentration on principal business gained the upper hand over diversification.

Diversification strategies tend to be popular when market prospects are good and companies generate capital with little prospect of expansion through their principal business. Globalization has to some extent restrained the tendency to diversify by offering the possibility of expansion through new markets.

A number of companies use a strong brand to lever themselves into diversification. Virgin is perhaps the best-known example of this. With 'low-budget' as their lowest common denominator, they have started companies in a number of different industries. Examples of these are the Virgin Flying Club, Virgin Cars, Virgin Travelstore, Virgin Trains, Virgin Mobile and Virgin Drinks.

One or more of the following factors are usually behind a diversification strategy:

1. Spreading risks, i.e. equalization of the financial position over a period of time.

2. Financial reasons, i.e. to reach higher margins and greater profitability.

3. Synergic reasons, i.e. the value of the business portfolio generated by diversification is greater than the value of the sum of its parts.

4. Entrepreneurial reasons, i.e. the risks and opportunities offered by diversification are an exciting challenge.

Some of the potential hazards inherent in diversification are:

1. A blind faith in *synergies* (see this section).

2. The brand is bled dry and loses its meaning for customers (see the section on Brand).

3. New areas are not properly understood, leading to unsuccessful investment.

4. Global competition has made it increasingly important to be the best in one's business area, but of course this gets harder as the number of areas increase.

RECOMMENDED READING

1. B. Joseph Pine II and James H Gilmore, The Experience Economy: Work Is Theatre & Every Business a Stage.

2. David Gewirtz, The Flexible Enterprise: How to Reinvent Your Company, Unlock Your Strengths, and Prosper in a Changing World.

3. Robert E Hoskisson et al. Downscoping: How to Tame the Diversified Firm.

Effectiveness

Companies today have to be effective to a degree that was scarcely imagined only a decade ago. Tighter budgets and various kinds of cutbacks have even affected non-profit organizations and trade unions, and there is an ever greater demand for the profit and loss statement to reflect the use of resources. Members of organizations wonder what they are getting for their subscriptions, the tax payer ponders the use of his or her contributions, and so on.

Whether as individuals or organizations, we strive for effectiveness in everything we do. By this we mean that utility is created for someone in relation to the work and resources necessary to create this utility. At the very least, we create utility for ourselves, but through organizations we generally strive to create utility for someone else: customers, shareholders, employees, members or fellow citizens.

The term 'effectiveness' is often, but incorrectly, used as a synonym for productivity, i.e. the ability to produce something without regard for its market value. Productivity simply requires that what is produced will also command a value in a market.

It is important to get the semantics right. The two words 'effectiveness' and 'efficiency' are similar. *Efficiency* is the quality of being efficient and has nothing to do with the relationship between quality and cost or between value and productivity as dealt with in this book. Let us quote a passage from the book *The Management Challenge*:

"Balancing Effectiveness and Efficiency

Distinguishing between effectiveness and efficiency is much more than an exercise in semantics. The relationship between these two terms is important, and it presents managers with a never-ending dilemma. Effectiveness entails achieving a stated objective. Swinging a sledgehammer against the wall, for example, would be an effective way to kill a bothersome fly. But given the reality of limited resources, effectiveness alone is not enough. Efficiency enters the picture when the resources required to achieve an objective are weighed against what was actually accomplished. The more favourable the ratio of benefits to costs, the greater the efficiency. Although a sledgehammer is an effective tool for killing flies, it is highly inefficient when the wasted effort and smashed walls are taken into consideration. A fly swatter is both an effective and an efficient tool for killing a single housefly."

Effectiveness is defined in the above passage as the attainment of a fixed organizational, qualitative goal. *Efficiency,* on the other hand, connects the consumption of resources to what actually has been attained, and this corresponds to the definition of productivity in use today. The question of the value of what has been achieved is another link in the chain of thought, that is, whether this value is meaningful.

Definition of effectiveness

We would like to define the term effectiveness and, in doing so, distinguish it from other closely related terms for clarity. We may start as follows:

All organized activity is based on creating a value that is higher than the cost of producing and delivering this value – this thesis is central to our idea of effectiveness.

Profitability is an expression of effectiveness in relation to an organizational whole. However, most management responsibility generally concerns not whole organizations, with a balance sheet and profit and loss statement to give proof of effectiveness, but for example:

1. company processes and functions.
2. the public sector.
3. different types of organization.

Without making claims to scientific exactness, we would say that at least 90 per cent of all management responsibility is to be found in units that lack the means of measuring their profitability and which to some extent, therefore, function in a planned economy. This applies to all parts of a company that deliver to the organization internally.

It is primarily the relationship between value and productivity – not either just one or the other but the balance between the two – that is fundamental in a company's operations. Effectiveness is an inherent factor in all organizations that is fundamental to their success and very existence. Profitability, as an expression of effectiveness, reflects the relationship between customer value and productivity but otherwise, and specifically for the in-house functions of a company that deliver to the whole organization, there is no profit and loss statement that will give this information. A graphic representation of effectiveness is given below.

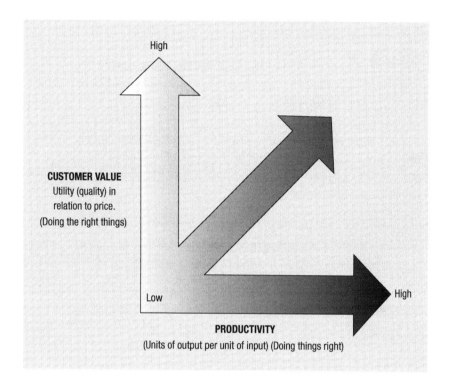

Value is the relationship between utility (quality) and price, while productivity is the cost of producing and delivering something.

The basic parameters of effectiveness, value and productivity, are illustrated in the figure. The internal departments of an organization have to be prepared for maximum productivity. But for external customers, value should be optimized so that price and quality (utility) are optimally balanced. Of course the consumers of goods and services, whether they be called customers or buyers, have no short-term interest in a company's productivity. But it is this productivity that in the long-term will determine the price of goods and services. If this price is too low for too long, the organization will not be able to exist without a continuous injection of capital.

Productivity is thus in the long run the important component of price. It is the denominator in the value fraction. For a better understanding of the two–dimensional aspect of effectiveness, we can begin by saying that there are two ways, and combinations of these ways, in which we can be efficient.

Productivity

Car manufacture provides us with a good example of the different aspects of productivity, not least because most people know something of the business having at sometime owned a car. Some of the world's large car manufacturers have problems with their productivity. Their customers would like to pay for cars that have been produced and delivered, but a car's production costs, including marketing and distribution, are higher than the price of the car, whether it be a Vauxhall or a Saab.

A car producer can see his problem as one of productivity, which in the industry is measured on an aggregate level, the yardstick being the number of assembly hours per unit produced. A car producer can thus identify a want of effectiveness as a problem with productivity.

Value

The other side to effectiveness can be illustrated by a supplier who may have acceptable productivity, but the value of what is supplied is too low or not measured on the open market. In the tax-financed public sector, or in non-profit organizations, assessments of effectiveness tend to be vague, if they are carried out at all. Different people become involved at different times, or the period covered is not long enough to be useful.

This sort of situation where customers lack a free choice between alternatives, is given the epithet of 'planned economy' in this book. Such conditions are not the preserve of the public sector, however.

Planned economy situations exist wherever departments, functions, business units and so on, are in-house suppliers in an organization. A whole company may be subjected to heavy competition but its departments enjoy a monopoly situation as internal suppliers.

The psychological balance

There is much psychology in the concept of effectiveness. The idea of value, for instance, is often connected in people's minds with positive decisions, ones that make customers, employees and owners happy. Productivity, on the other hand, is often associated with negative decisions, perhaps in the form of capacity reduction or personnel cutbacks.

Conditions, psychologically speaking, are therefore rather different on the two axes of customer value and productivity, and this can cause problems for management. Risk-taking managers with a desire to create value often emerge in prosperous times, but they are unlikely to want to face up to productivity questions later on. They are replaced in slumps by tough technocrats capable of grasping the nettle, but it is doubtful whether these are the same people that should be in charge of the company's business development when the business climate improves.

Four questions on effectiveness

We have discussed two important aspects of effectiveness. Given that there are two main ways in which an organization can become efficient, it is possible to identify some relevant questions:

1. **How should we define what we produce and deliver?** This may be passenger cars, environmental inspections, or the results of a study on some matter calling for a decision.

2. **How can we calculate cost per delivered unit?** This can be estimated in euros per piece, units per man-hour, inspections per hour or assembly hours per vehicle. The productivity quotient is a fundamental parameter of effectiveness.

3. **Which individuals assess what we produce and deliver?** In a free market, it is we the consumers who make the decision to buy or not to buy. In complex systems with planned economies, assessments

based on different criteria are made by different people at different times, which makes this question considerably hard to answer.

4. **What criteria do these individuals use for their assessments?** Depending on the business environment, criteria may vary; be vague; be impossible to grasp; be unknown, or show great variation.

The reader should now have some idea of effectiveness and productivity and of how they differ. The value of something may be great even if the company's productivity is abominable. This often applies to the really big projects, where costing may have been optimistic but the value delivered in the end phenomenal. Examples are the Panama Canal, the Sydney opera house or the Eurotunnel.

A number of concepts have emerged in the train of efficiency work, concepts such as BPR (Business Process Re-engineering), TQM (Total Quality Management), the measurement of transit times, and so on. All of them are well founded and useful in most cases but should not draw our attention from the central fact that effectiveness is achieved by increasing customer value and/or raising productivity.

The realization that effectiveness is fundamental to all organized activity is spreading swiftly and making the traditional merits of productivity harder and harder to live with. Managers are realizing that they have to find, in their part of the organization, the criteria for effectiveness that will ensure continued existence of their departments.

RECOMMENDED READING

1. Robert D Buzzell, PIMS Principles

2. Bradley T Gale, Managing Customer Value: Creating Quality and Service That Customers Can See.

3. Douglas K Smith, Make Success Measurable: A Mindbook-Workbook for Setting Goals and Taking Action.

Entrepreneurship

The word 'entrepreneur' comes from the French *entreprendre* and roughly means to set about, undertake. Opinions vary as to what makes an entrepreneur, but we can mention some of the things that entrepreneurs do. They:

1. build and create organizations.
2. combine things in new ways.
3. actively study possibilities.
4. deal with uncertainty.
5. get elements in production to work together.
6. identify and take action in respect of shortcomings or gaps in the market.

It seems that the concept of entrepreneurship can mean different things to different people. Even researchers have failed to agree on a definition of the word. Joseph Schumpeter was an Austrian economist prominent in research into entrepreneurship. Schumpeter reasoned that entrepreneurship involved the creative identification and development of:

1. new products.
2. new production methods.
3. new markets.
4. new forms of organization.

The word entrepreneurship has now entered the vocabulary of management circles, normally carrying the meaning of new ideas and creative development in the framework of large organizations.

Peter Drucker, the well-known consultant, has come up with a contemporary definition. Drucker says that entrepreneurship is really about seizing the possibilities that come with change, rather than bringing about change itself. Drucker defines an entrepreneur as a person who "…always searches for change, responds to it and exploits it as an opportunity." Change may be found everywhere, in technology, consumer behaviour and social norms.

Entrepreneurship is often interpreted as another form of capitalism. The capitalist and entrepreneur may well be found in one and the same person but a closer look reveals two completely different values. The confusion of roles may come from the fact that entrepreneurs often earn a lot of money and appear to be capitalists in the sense that they have been successful enough to finance their own companies.

Manfred Kets de Vries in an article in the *Harvard Business Review* entitled 'The Dark Side of Entrepreneurship' (1985) reflects on the darker side of entrepreneurship. He believes that the personal qualities, which make for a successful entrepreneur are the same ones that contribute to his or her demise. Entrepreneurs are often control freaks with an eye for detail, two important attributes for building an organization. But these qualities can be a drag on an organization's growth if the entrepreneur is not able to survey everything that happens and becomes frustrated as a result.

To understand how familiarity with entrepreneurship can best be used, we have to go back to what motivates people. David McClelland has identified three different motivational needs:

1. Power
2. Affiliation
3. Achievement

Someone motivated by power wants to be in authority and have influence over others, and wants to see his or her ideas prevail. Good performance is secondary; the important thing is to have made an impact. The authority-motivated driver produces a need to dominate over his or her environment.

The affiliation-motivated person wants to have friendly relationships and be held in popular regard, and sees interaction with other people as his or her motivational force. To be affiliation-motivated does not necessarily imply a lack of power or disregard for good performance, but the over-riding preoccupation is to interact with others rather than to attain power or out-perform his associates.

The achievement-oriented person too may have good relationships with others, as well as being both powerful and influential, but what drives them is the desire to do a good job. It is worth noting that the importance of good performance is growing in the world, not only in business but also in public-sector and non-profit organizations where performance is now a measure of the very ability to exist. The reason for this is something called *metacompetition,* a development where resources are limited and customers' time and money are objects of competition.

Some motivation inhibitors are:

- Stagnation
- Bureaucracy and ceremony
- Planning and negotiations with unions
- Reasoning, tactics and diplomacy

RECOMMENDED READING

1. Amar Bhldt et al, Harvard Business Review on Entrepreneurship.
2. David C McClelland, Human Motivation.
3. Peter F Drucker, Innovation and Entrepreneurship.

EVA – Economic Value Added

EVA is a financial management system which shows an enterprise's net operating profit after taxes minus the cost of invested capital.

The world's leading authority on EVA is Bennett Stewart, a senior partner at Stern Stewart and Co. To explain EVA he uses the analogy of the earnings which the owner of a little family business puts into a shoebox at the end of the week. EVA has played a significant role in the movement towards shareholder value which, according to one school of thought, has become a leading indicator of a company's success. According to this school, shareholders, who provide a company with its capital, only invest in order to get a return on their investment. This unbalanced view of shareholder activity has come in for increasing criticism, for example by business writers who believe that it has led to disastrous errors and enticed managements into dubious or even criminal accounting methods that have misled shareholders in relation to actual profits.

EVA is a well-established concept, but it is only in the last ten years that it has become an important yardstick for financial departments, which have increasingly used the measure for planning and performance management.

This school of thought maintains that EVA is a better measure of a company's value than its returns. For example, the Chairman of AT&T has declared that an almost perfect correlation has been found between the company's stock market value and its EVA. The efficient use of invested capital is the key to the creation of value: this is the message also going out to the people in charge of an organization's business processes. The main difference between EVA on the one hand and earnings per share, return on assets and discounted cash flow (the most common measures of performance) on the other are as follows:

- Earnings per share say nothing about the cost of creating these earnings. If for example capital costs in the form of loans, bonds and assets come to 12 per cent of investment, returns of 10 per cent will in fact represent a financial loss and not a gain. Profits also affect taxes, which diminish cash flow. EVA represents actual cash flow after taxes, interest and other financial obligations.

- Return on capital is a good measure of financial performance but does not take into account capital costs. In its years of greatest profitability, IBM for example recorded over more than an 11 per cent return on assets but its capital costs came to almost 13 per cent. A large company can borrow capital cheaply through favourable rates of interest and high share prices and this capital can be invested in companies fo returns which seem reasonable. The company is now encouraged to expand and does not think about the actual returns in the form of EVA.

- Discounted cash flow is not far from EVA conceptually if the discounted interest can be equated to capital costs.

We have to make two calculations to establish a company's capital costs; one is simple, the other one more complicated. The simple one applies to the cost of liabilities, which is the interest rate applied to loans and bonds after tax. The more complicated calculation involves an estimation of the replacement value of current assets and a calculation of shareholders' expected returns based on the prices they paid for shares (or whether they have decided to keep those shares). Investors can choose between investing in gilt-edged companies or buying shares that carry more risk. They know that the higher the return, the greater the risk they run. In order to attract investors, weak companies have to offer an advantage in the form of share prices that are lower than those of stronger companies.

Proponents of EVA claim that the management of capital is a company's principal business process. This truth is obscured by accounting systems which charge to expenses wages, software development, rents, training and other costs necessary for operations; these are systems which also enter redundancies, cutbacks, and so on, as extraordinary items in the profit and loss account. It is in fact easy to see whether by capitalizing processes or entering costs as liabilities a contribution is made to the amount of economic value added: EVA.

An article in *Fortune* magazine, 'The real key to creating wealth', summarized the essentials of EVA. Here is an extract from the article:

"How much capital is tied up in your operation? Even if you don't know the answer, you know what it consists of – what you paid for real estate, machines, vehicles and the like, plus working capital. But proponents of EVA say there is more. What about the money your company spends on R&D? On employee training? These are investments meant to pay off for years; but accounting rules say you can't treat them that way; you have to call them expenses, like the amount you spend on electricity. EVA proponents say forget the accounting rules. For internal purposes, call these things what they are: capital investments. No one can say what their useful life is, so make your best guess – say five years. It's truer than calling them expenses."

The purely financial perspective of business has been severely criticized. In their rush to be seen as financially sound, many managements have been enticed into fraudulent accounting practices in balancing costs, entering long customer contracts as yield, unreasonably extending depreciation on goodwill, and so on. CVA – Cash Value Added, and MVA – Market Value Added, are extrapolations of EVA.

RECOMMENDED READING

1. James L Grant, Foundations of Economic Value Added.

2. John D Martin and J William Petty, Value Based Management: The Corporate Response to the Shareholder Revolution.

3. S David Young and Stephen F O'Byrne, EVA and Value-Based Management: A Practical Guide to Implementation.

Experience curve

Experience Curve, a term used to express the effects of large-scale production on the learning process, was introduced in the 1920s. It has had enormous importance and has served as a basis for a number of strategy models, such as the Boston Matrix (see this term). It is usually applied to the manufacturing industry but is useful in many other areas as well.

The theory underlying the experience curve implies that a large market share is valuable because it offers opportunities to increase production capacity and thus move down the experience curve in the direction of lower production costs (see the figure).

Newspaper computer systems (UK)

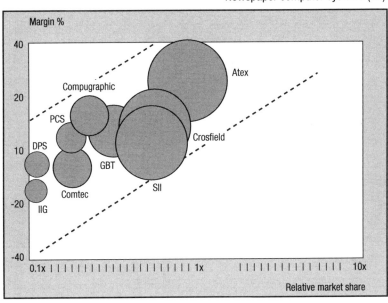

In this way we can achieve higher margins, greater profitability, and thus a better competitive position. Economies of scale imply that a fixed cost is distributed over a large number of units produced. In many cases the advantages of economies of scale in Europe are lost because of the relative smallness of the continent and the traditional tendency of each country to see itself as the served market. This is especially true of the public sector, for instance in government institutions, including such public-service corporations as the post office, railways and telecommunications.

The experience curve lends itself to a range of expressions, a number of which are given below. It was first formulated by an American officer at Wright Paterson Air Force Base in Dayton, Ohio, in 1926. He discovered that unit costs fell by as much as 30 per cent every time the volume of production doubled.

Economies of skill or skull is an expression for the equivalent of economies of scale in knowledge-based companies. In certain skilled industries, for instance in architecture, economies of scale exist in the form of investment in cadcam software and accounting systems. Often, however, the intellectual skills of a company's employees play a considerably greater role in its success.

The effects of the experience curve are not based on a natural law, so it is necessary to understand the causes that produce the effects. The cost reductions which are a consequence of the correlation do not occur automatically; the possibilities must be appreciated and actively exploited. The underlying phenomena overlap and are closely interrelated, but nevertheless they can be distinguished:

- **Labour efficiency:** when workers repeat a given task, they do so with progressively greater efficiency. Wastage is reduced and productivity increases. This process can be accelerated by training and good personnel management policies.

- **Organization of work:** adjustment of work organization may manifest itself in two ways. The degree of specialization may increase with rising volume, or the organization may be restructured to match the flow of production more closely. In the former case this means that each worker performs fewer tasks. In the latter, both management and the division of work can be more effective.

- **New production process:** inventions and improvements in the production process can play a significant part in reducing unit costs, especially in capital-intensive industries.

- **Balance of labour and capital:** as a business develops, the balance between labour and capital may change. If wages rise, for example, money may be diverted from wages to invest in robots. This has happened in countries with high labour costs like Japan, Sweden and Germany.

- **Standardization of products:** The benefits of the experience curve cannot be utilized to the full without standardization of production. Ford's production of the Model T in the 1920s is an example of how standardization can lead to a dangerous lack of flexibility. Thus standardized mass production tends to inhibit innovation in a company.

- **Technical specialization:** as the production process develops, specialized equipment may be procured. This results in more efficient production and thus reduced costs.

- **Redesigning:** as experience accumulates, both customers and manufacturer acquire greater knowledge of the relationship between price and performance. Through value engineering, products can be redesigned to save material, energy and labour whilst maintaining or improving performance.

- **Economies of scale:** from the analytical standpoint, economies of scale are actually a separate phenomenon that may occur independently of the experience curve. Economies of scale imply that a fixed cost is distributed between many units.

A company with a high volume of production can not only derive greater benefit from economies of scale, but can also move along the experience curve farther and faster than smaller companies in its industry as a result of the sheer volume effect. It is important to be aware of competitive advantages based on the E-curve and economies of scale if we are to identify where our competitive strength lies. Excessive demand after World War II meant that the customer experience, measured in terms of utility function and quality, was given little attention. This was certainly also due to the fact that the supposed certainties of the economies of scale concept appealed more to economists and engineers than vague market-analytical initiatives.

The experience curve is of significant importance in some industries, while in others it is less relevant. It is important to understand the background to the experience curve if it is to be applied correctly, particularly in view of the imminent integration of European states, which by all accounts will entail a redefining of served markets and analyzes of economies of scale contingent on this.

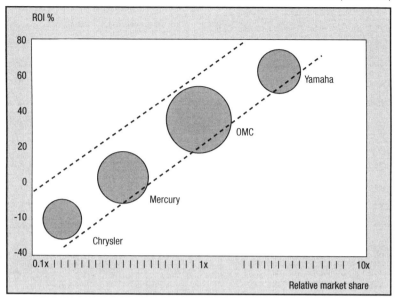

Outboard motor market (worldwide)

The reasoning can be given as:

1. The experience curve gives cost advantages as a result of accumulated production volumes.

2. Over a period of time it is possible to predict the rate of price reductions.

3. Large market share is good to have in order to have high accumulated production and the experience that goes with it.

4. If the cost advantages of the experience curve are exploited, large production volumes will result in high margins.

5. High margins can either be used to create a price umbrella and consequently greater profits in comparison with the industry average, or can be used to reduce prices, gaining further market share and thus greater volumes.

In a competitive market prices fall in a way that is predictable over time, regardless of whether companies find they can reduce their costs. Competitive pressure increases as substitutes come on to the market, which means that profitable companies continually have to work on their unit costs. Price levels are therefore something that management have only a very limited control over: price trends are driven by competitors, substitutes and the willingness of consumers to pay.

Costs, on the other hand, must be reduced by determined management action. Managing the cost mass calls for determination, insight and often the courage to make unpopular decisions. The creation of customer value is one thing but a completely different mentality is called for when productivity-promoting management is necessary. The former is often associated with positive decisions, while the latter implies the ability to say no, cut capacity, personnel and other costs. We could say that the price curve is driven by the market dimension, while a company's cost curves are determined by its management.

The experience curve also applies to service-producing companies in principle, although its relevance diminishes as the focus on knowledge increases. Service companies which base their production on a certain amount of repetition follow the dictates of the experience curve. It is actually the degree of repetition in the service offering which determines the extent to which the experience curve applies.

A company which has to control the effects of the experience curve in a competitive market must be aware of the following six points:

1. Price trend curves are market driven, while E-curve costs are controlled by management.

2. The E-curve can be applied to service companies. The degree of applicability increases with the degree of repetition.

3. Working with the experience curve is no guarantee of quality. Quality can be impaired when costs are reduced.

4. The sudden appearance of substitutes or technological innovations can upset the E- curve, so they should be identified as soon as possible.

5. When experience curves are established for subordinate organizational functions, the parameters governing the development of these curves will be revealed.

6. The competitor with the greatest accumulated experience has the potential for the highest margins.

We can say that the experience curve has three dimensions: time, price and the competitor. By analyzing the relationship between volume and costs for different functions, we obtain a very sound basis to tackle questions of productivity, costs reduction and therefore, effectiveness.

RECOMMENDED READING

David B Montgomery and George S Day, Experience Curves: Evidence, Empirical Methods and Applications.

External environmental analysis

When we speak of the external environment we mean everything outside a business that is capable of affecting the survival or success of the organization. Everything from global macro-trends to new stakeholder developments can be included in the external environment. Our competitors are a part of an industry which itself is part of the external environment.

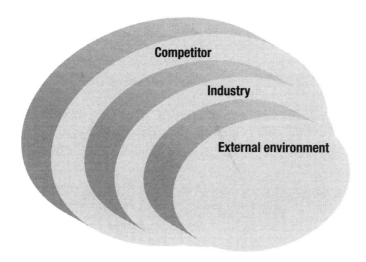

External Environmental Analysis, as do so many terms in management, means different things to different people. Some think it means 'business intelligence', the knowledge useful to a business that exists outside its boundaries. Others think of the gathering of what is written and said about competitors and their own company. The term itself is usually qualified as *strategic* external environmental analysis or *operative* external environmental analysis. The former seeks to identify long-term developments in the external environment that will affect the business, while an operative monitoring of the external environment attempts to find factors which will have a direct effect on the business and which therefore must be dealt with immediately.

Regardless of the form analysis might take, the identification of trends and elements is important for a business as it can prepare itself for what might be threats or opportunities.

PEST is a model used to scan trends and developments in four areas:

- Political/legal trends such as those found in legislation, treaties, ordinances and political stability, or the lack of it.

- Economic trends such as those found in economic development, levels of interest, access to venture capital and the labour market situation.

- Socio-cultural trends such as those found in demography, differences in income, ethnical groups, changes in life-style, levels of training, and attitudes to work and leisure time.

- Technological trends. National and supranational investment, technological change, technological maturity and new discoveries.

Different models can be used to act on trends once they have been identified. Trends are commonly evaluated by means of a risk map, in which a trend's probability is plotted against the magnitude of the effect that it is likely to have on the business.

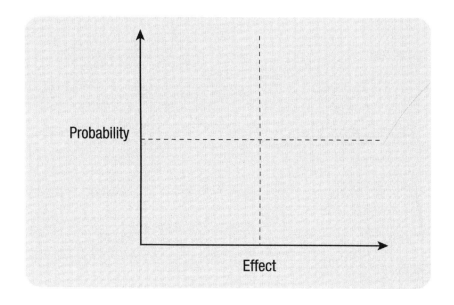

Trends with a large element of probability and a probably significant effect are natural candidates for some form of action. It can also be important to monitor trends with a doubtful element of probability but with a significant effect were they to materialize. Once trends have been identified the following questions can be answered:

1. What can the trend lead to? Describe what the trend is based on, how it has been identified and what qualifies it to be a trend.

2. What kind of effect can the trend have on the business? Threats and opportunities are identified at this stage.

3. How do we react to the trend? What level of preparedness do we have for it? Should we be doing something already?

4. How will we monitor the development of the trend? What indications can we follow up to monitor its development?

The above is a relatively simple trend analysis that can be done quickly, but trend analysis is an important field in its own right. Experts can spend the greater part of their time identifying and describing trends, many of which could affect all businesses.

A useful exercise can be to match the strategies that a business has with the different trends that it has identified. Is the direction of the business vindicated or contradicted by developments in the external environment?

Extreme results for different trends can be combined in different ways to visualize future scenarios. What for example would be the outcome if a business's trademark were to get a very high profile at the same time as consumer power rose dramatically? (See also *Scenario*.)

Many businesses could profit by systematically carrying out external environmental analyzes where information was gathered, evaluated, prioritized and marked for possible action.

RECOMMENDED READING

1. Larissa T Moss and Shaku Atre, Business Intelligence Roadmap: The Complete Project Lifecycle for Decision-Support Applications.

2. Kenneth G McGee, Heads Up: How to Anticipate Business Surprises and Seize Opportunities First.

3. Michael E Porter, Competitive Strategy: Techniques for Analyzing Industries and Competitors.

Facilitation

Facilitation is a term used for helping a group of people, as efficiently and as pleasantly as possible, to pursue goals which they have set up together.

The role of facilitator is one of the important roles in the process of change, both in its entirety and in the various stages (for example, at a workshop). A facilitator enables the process to flow, acts as a catalyst, encourages commitment among the participants and is largely responsible for seeing that goals are agreed on and reached. The role of facilitator subsumes the role of expert, in that s/he appears as an expert in some industry or in a particular subject and controls the content of the process.

A facilitator is an expert in the process of strategic planning, and will know how to put the skills and experience of participants to good use. Simple tasks, such as time-keeping and documenting results, are also part of the facilitator's role. This role is summarized in the following five points.

- Leader of the process
- Partner in dialogue
- Question-master
- Ideas man
- Quality controller

Apart from juggling the above roles, a facilitator has to be good at dealing with group dynamics and conflicts that might arise within the group. The following points, based on our experience and that of others in the field, are success factors in effective facilitation.

- The ability to think on several levels – the current stage of strategic work, as well as the next step and the process in its entirety. While the strategic group is focusing on a particular point in the work, it is the facilitator's job to be a step ahead, planning for the next step in the process.
- The ability to be 'one of the gang', while at the same time an external and objective observer.

- The ability to juggle a consultant's advisory role while being leader of the process.

- The ability to stimulate discussion, being devil's advocate when necessary, and to summarize results.

Facilitation is largely about being flexible, and through experience and the use of various methods, being prepared for any eventuality. No matter how carefully a meeting has been prepared, it is impossible to be one hundred per cent certain of how it will turn out. The group may have new insights along the way so that arrangements have to be changed; participants may have appointed substitutes unfamiliar with the goals of the group; acute operative problems can pop up and cause a loss of concentration among participants – the list is long. This does not detract from the importance of well thought out preparation, but the facilitator must be ready to adapt along the way. A facilitator learns through experience when it is the right time to move forward with the material s/he has prepared, and when it is time to change direction.

For readers interested in facilitation, the authors recommend the following works on *Displayed Thinking and Teambuilding*.

RECOMMENDED READING

1. Bob Abernathy and Mark Reardon, Hot Tips for Facilitators: Strategies to Make Life Easier for Anyone Who Leads, Guides, Teaches, or Trains Groups.

2. Edward De Bono, Lateral Thinking: Creativity Step by Step.

3. Fran Rees, How To Lead Work Teams: Facilitation Skills.

4. Roger Schwarz, The Skilled Facilitator.

Fair process

Economic theories often take it as given that people will maximize their utility, supposedly a condition that is primarily reinforced by coolly calculated self-interest. It is natural for people to care about achieving results, but they are at least as interested in the process along the way. Results are important, but no more important than the integrity of the processes leading up to it.

The idea of *fair process* has even more importance today, when success in business and commerce is increasingly geared to a knowledge-based economy. Here, the creation of value is depending more and more on ideas, creativity and innovation. Fair process profoundly affects how people act and behave, and is fundamental in performance of a high standard.

Writers, philosophers and researchers through the ages have been intrigued by the idea of a person with complete integrity. Meanwhile, the first systematic study of fair process appeared in the middle of the 1970s when two social psychologists, John W Thibaut and Laurens Walker, got together to examine the psychology of integrity in a study on processes. They tried to understand the mechanisms that lead us to rely on legal systems and submit to legislation when we are under no compulsion to do so. Their research revealed that people care just as much about the integrity of the process that culminates in a result or judgement, as they do about the judgement itself.

Other research has shown how the power of fair process has had an effect across cultures and social conditions. In their study of strategic decision-making in multinationals published in the 1980s, Kim and Mauborgne discovered the importance of fair process in progress development. Many top managers in these companies were baffled and frustrated at the actions of some of the managers of their subsidiaries. How could these people so often fail to inform the top management of their ideas? Why would they choose to sabotage the plans which they themselves had agreed to carry out?

Research carried out on 19 companies found a thread that ran through processes, attitudes and behaviour. Managers with a positive personal experience of company processes showed a high degree of trust and commitment which in turn led to active cooperation. On the other hand, plans were sabotaged and leaders kept ideas to themselves if they felt that their company's thinking was flawed or difficult to understand.

The idea of fair process answers a human need in each and every one of us, regardless of our position in the company. We want to be valued as people and not simply as personnel, assets or resources. We want to be treated with respect as intelligent beings and in a way that shows that our ideas are being taken seriously. In addition, we need to understand the causal relationship that puts a particular decision into perspective. People are sensitive to signals they pick up in decision-making processes which, by and large, reveal the degree to which an organization is ready to rely on them, seek their creative input and make the most of their ideas.

Kim and Mauborgne list three premises for an efficient process, to which we have added another three. These six mutually beneficial principles are described below:

1. Engagement
2. Explanation
3. Clear expectations
4. Collective learning
5. Raized ambition level
6. Loyalty

Engagement

A consequence of *engagement* is that people become involved in decisions and are able to influence them by coming forward with their own ideas and opinions. An idea is rated in respect of its intellectual content and relevance to a situation, and not on the basis that it is so-and-so, whose idea or opinion it is. Through engagement in a process, management can express its view of an individual's ideas. Because everybody accepts that no dishonour lies in the rejection of an idea, the number of good ideas is narrowed down, resulting in deeper collective insight. More qualitative decisions are made as a result of engagement, and the people involved are more likely to be committed to implementing decisions.

Explanation

The explanation principle implies that the reason for a decision is communicated to everyone involved, including those affected by the decision. People will accept a decision when they understand the reasoning behind it and know that management has considered all views and made the decision without bias and in the interests of the company. Once explanations have been given, co-workers and managers alike will be aware of the good intentions that underlie a decision, even if the views of some individuals may have been discarded. The important thing is that all opinions will have been given due respect.

Clear expectations

The principle of clear expectations proposes that management should make clear all new goals, ambitions and rules that are to apply. Those involved in a fair process will understand the rules under which they will be assessed and how responsibility is allocated, so that essential matters can receive the attention due to them. All too often, people do not realize that changes are expected of them. Decisions may have been made on the basis of certain conditions, without taking into account internal politics, various compromises, or the need for different skills or behaviour.

Collective learning

The point of collective learning is that people go through an intellectual journey together and thus share the same information. The same input is made available to everyone and through discussion becomes shared knowledge. We can assume that people in a group will have different opinions and levels of understanding. The process allows everyone to assimilate certain elements of information and add to this.

The result is a high-quality decision based on collective knowledge and, perhaps more important, an energized process and all-round improvement. Collective learning and the innovation process are especially important in the work of strategic planning and can produce qualitative decisions, all-round agreement and a motivating energy.

Raized ambition level

Almost without exception, a process with a raized ambition level will not only result in higher quality decision-making, but also in a raized ambition level in the group taking part in the process. The effect is for the group to want to achieve more than otherwise would have been the case. Higher ambition levels bring more energy into an organization in a way that both stimulates and motivates management and co-workers.

Loyalty

When we speak of loyalty, we refer to two things: loyalty to the work of change, including decisions already taken, and loyalty to the company or organization. A more or less conscious opposition to some process may sometimes materialize in a company. Fair process is intended for just this situation. If people can be allowed to give their opinion, it is very probable that they will support the decisions made by management.

RECOMMENDED READING

W Chan Kim and Renee A Mabourgne, Fair Process: Managing in the Knowledge Economy (Harvard Business Review).

Functional strategy

Functional strategy is the direction followed by an organization's function or department that has no responsibility at the organizational level. A functional strategy (a general definition of strategy is a pattern of decisions and actions in the present to ensure future success) must then be formed in line with the overall orientation of the larger organization. Strategies for government agencies and other public bodies also fall into this category, where the challenge is to form a strategy on the basis of political directives, for example, an official document assigning grants. Some of the areas in which functional strategies can be found are:

- staff functions (marketing, personnel, IT, information, etc).
- competence groupings (competence pools lacking responsibility at the organizational level).

- Processes (management and support processes, possibly main processes, depending on how responsibility is allocated in the organization – see the section on Processes).

Functional strategy is becoming more and more important in organizations because of two factors; these are:

1. New organizational divisions such as programs and processes mean that more and more people are being given strategic responsibility.
2. A wave of decentralization is putting greater pressure on innovation and development in the above functions.

A number of questions must be considered when a functional strategy is being drafted:

1. What is the role of the function in the organization and are there conditions that favour development?
2. In what way does the function contribute to the main business (or political goals/directives)?
3. Who are the function's important stakeholders, and what needs or expectations of the function do they have?
4. What will the function produce and what is the target group for its products?
5. How is the function's efficiency evaluated? How do we know that we are doing a good job?

It should be clear from the above points that it is most important for the main business of the organization to be kept in mind when a function's strategy is being formed. There is a danger that a function's growth and the resulting area of responsibility become a goal in itself. Managers of functional units can also be in danger of seeing in their department's expansion their only means of showing initiative and drive.

Business strategists can get a quick picture, and often a cruelly realistic one, of management success by taking a look at the profit and loss statement. Competitors also put pressure on a company to raise its ambition level and undertake rationalization. But functional strategists cannot make use of competitors or profit and loss accounts – far from it. Functional units are generally kept to budget and often have a performance model that promotes inefficiency and lowered ambition level. If, for instance, a unit reduces its costs, its budget for the following year is reduced correspondingly.

However, benchlearning can prove to be a valuable substitute for the stimulation provided by forces at the organizational level. Instead of competing with their company's competitors, units can compare themselves with similar functions in their own organization or in other industries, and in so doing have its efficiency and potential for improvement validated. For more on this see *Benchlearning*.

It is not unusual for well-organized functions to gradually develop into separate business units. A company may perhaps notice that its IT function is highly skilled and offers services that are not to be found on the market and in this see business potential. The outsourcing trend of recent years has meant that many a function has been acquired by companies with the function in question as their core business. This has been the case with Ericsson's IT business, for example. Or a function may be companized and run as a business unit within the company, which for example has happened to Volvo IT at the time of writing.

Companization of internal functional units normally occurs because of the following motives:

1. The function has a large number of external deliveries.

2. It is a step prior to being sold.

3. The function is perceived as being inefficient and the organization is able (and prefers) to purchase equivalent services from the outside market.

4. The core business is subject to restrictions that can be evaded by setting up a separate company.

5. A tactical move in bargaining with unions

6. Personal ambition and prestige: somebody wants to be a managing director instead of a department manager. This may seem trite, but as a possible motive it should not be forgotten.

7. The function's co-workers feel that they are neither getting enough opportunities to develop nor the appreciation from the organization that they deserve.

Perhaps the most common way to raise the performance of an in-house delivery function is to allow it to compete with players under the same conditions that exist in the outside market for the orders of its own organization. When this happens management must ask itself why the unit in question should remain an internal function.

More information on functional strategy can be found under *Strategy and Strategic Process*.

RECOMMENDED READING

1. Jim Collins and Jerryl I Porras, Built to Last: Successful Habits of Visionary Companies.

2. Gary Hamel and C K Prahalad, Competing for the Future.

Gap analysis

Gap analysis is a name generally given to identifying, specifying and taking action on the gap between a situation as it exists and the situation as we would like it to be. In management this kind of analysis can be used to find strategies to close the gap between the current situation and the vision. In marketing, a gap might be the one between customer satisfaction as it now stands and the company's goal for customer satisfaction; or there may be a gap between a company's competence now and the competence it needs to unfurl certain strategies.

A process for carrying out a gap analysis is described in the following six steps:

1. Define the area for analysis (for example internal efficiency, competence, or performance of information systems).

2. Describe the existing situation. Supplement this with metrics if necessary.

3. Describe the desired situation. Set up measurable goals if this can be done.

4. Specify how the desired situation differs from the present one.

5. Decide on measures to close the gap.

6. Follow up and where necessary carry out corrective action.

A common approach in gap analysis is to set up a *gap matrix*. The first step is to identify the factors comprized by our gap analysis (step 1, above). These factors are then placed against each other as in the matrix overleaf.

The present situation and the desired one are described for each factor and the actions needed to close the gap are described where these coincide in the matrix. Alternatively, the factors, gaps, actions and goals can be tabulated:

FROM TO	Customer satisfaction Description of current situation	Co-worker satisfaction Description of desired situation	Profitability Description of desired situation
Customer satisfaction Description of desired situation	Increase in SCI by investment in customer service		
Co-worker satisfaction Description of current situation		No gap identified	
Profitability Description of current situation			Desired profitability through streamlining costs purchasing and logistics

Factor	Gap	Actions	Goals and metrics
Customer satisfaction	Raise customer satisfaction from 3, 5 to 4	Investment in higher service level	Reduce number of customer complaints by 50 per cent by next year

Goals

We use goals to indicate what should be achieved within a given period of time. Researchers and business leaders have found it convenient to differentiate between different kinds of goals. There are strategic goals, tactical goals, principal goals, sub-goals, performance goals, and so on.

A rule of thumb for the designation of a goal is that it should be:

- **S**pecific (It should be clear what the goal concerns and what effects it is expected to have.)
- **M**easurable (It should be possible to measure a goal without too much effort.)
- **A**cceptable (A goal should be understood and accepted by those who are expected to achieve it.)
- **R**ealistic (A goal should be achievable as well as challenging.)
- **T**ime-framed (There should be a date by which time a goal should be achieved.)

The observant reader will have realized that the above list forms the acronym **SMART**, which represents the usual framework for the quality assurance of goals. Sometimes an extra parameter is added – 'ambitious' for instance, to indicate that improvements are called for.

Goals can be divided into three main categories:

1. Economic goals
2. Quantitative goals
3. Qualitative goals

Economic goals often have to do with the company balance sheet, while quantitative and qualitative goals strive for a behavioural change and improved performance, which in the long-term lead to an organization's improved financial position (quantitative and qualitative company goals are often called its *leading indicators*). For more on the distinction between leading indicators and lagging indicators, see the entry under *Performance management*.

With the entry of the balanced scorecard it is now common to formulate goals on the basis of a particular set of perspectives, the following ones for instance:

- Co-workers
- Customers
- Finance
- Processes/efficiency
- Innovation and development

See also *Balanced Scorecard*.

Goals often represent a breakdown of the overall intentions of an organization. A model that can be used for this purpose is the goals/means hierarchy, which is based on the principle that the means at one level is a goal at a level below. Using the means/goals hierarchy we can arrive at a level to formulate goals that are meaningful for us. This is illustrated by the example below where the main goal of 'greater profitability' has been broken down to the organization of a sales contest. A 'smart' goal can then be formulated including time constraints for the contest and what it is intended to generate in terms of increased sales volume.

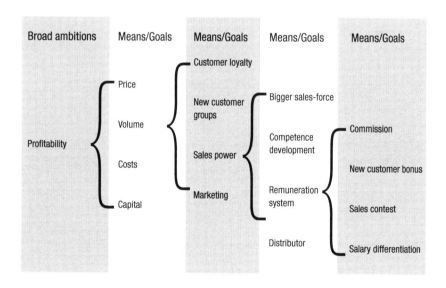

Criteria for a worthwhile goal:

1. Fight *for* something, not *against* something (don't use the word 'not' when formulating a goal).

2. Based on current knowledge (we know what the present situation is).

3. Reasonable yet challenging

4. Quantified

5. Clearly defined

6. Easy to understand

7. Time-framed

8. Clearly addressed (to whom or what does the goal pertain?)

9. Address problems at their source (the illness, not the symptoms.)

Management by objectives is an expression that means setting a performance goal for an individual or unit without specifying the means or strategies to be used in reaching the goals. Management by objectives has become increasingly common, and is a natural tool for managing decentralized organizations. Management by objectives stands in contrast to direct management or management by order, where subordinates are given exact instructions on how to act in specific situations.

A model has been developed for management by objectives. It assumes that a superior and his or her subordinate agree on goals for the subordinate's work within a given timeframe. Here the superior approaches the subordinate in the guise of a consultant rather than a boss.

RECOMMENDED READING

1. Douglas K Smith, Make Success Measurable! A Mindbook – Workbook for Setting Goals and Taking Action.

2. Jim Collins and Jerry I Porras, Built to Last: Successful Habits of Visionary Companies.

Industry

The meaning of the term industry has broadened from the original sense of manufacturing to include any category of organization that produces goods or services.

An industry is defined by a number of variables, of which the most common are:

- a specific need, defined by a set of utility functions.
- a specific type of product or service.
- a specific type of business logic.
- different forms of distribution.
- a public, as against a commercial, organization.

A well-known framework for the analysis of an industry is presented in the section under *Porter's five competitive forces*. In the section under Industry attractiveness and strategic position, we present a model for analyzing a company's role and development opportunities in an industry. Eric Giertz' division of industries according to their business logic is presented in the section on *Business model*.

Interesting discussions can ensue when we try to place a company within its proper industrial classification on the basis of its customer needs satisfaction. For example, does a football team come under 'professional sports' or under the entertainment business? The answer to the question has great strategic importance, as it affects the choice of served market, competitors and what alternative actions the organization might like to take. Should a football team in fact regard other football clubs as competitors for public and sponsorship money, or is it competing against the entire entertainment industry with its theatres, opera houses, cinemas, festivals, and so on? The challenge is to define industrial classification based on relevance to the needs structure, so that it is not so narrow as to be limiting but neither so broad as to be a meaningless classification.

Should Coca-Cola be classed under 'cola drinks', 'soft drinks', 'beverages', or simply the 'industry for the satisfaction of needs'?

For more on this, see the entry under *Needs*.

RECOMMENDED READING

1. Derek F Abell, Defining The Business: The Starting Point of Strategic Planning.

2. *Michael E Porter, Competitive Strategy: Techniques For Analyzing Industries and* Competitors.

Insourcing

Insourcing is the same as *outsourcing* (see this term) except that the insourced function ends up inside instead of outside a company. In many cases economies of scale are created for a particular function by hiving off production from large, highly integrated organizations. Insourcing, then, is a business development opportunity that is gaining in popularity as diversification mania is responding to treatment and traditional value chains are rationalized. Below are some real and inspirational examples of the phenomenon:

1. Hi-tech consultancy firms suspect that a large number of companies, public bodies and other organizations are running their own planning departments. An analysis has revealed that an astonishing number of such companies have been employing a handful of engineers to run their planning departments with a motley assortment of technology. Hi-tech consultancies are now making offers to take over staff under long contracts which are benefiting both parties. Both productivity and customer value are soaring.

2. A large training enterprise with traditional employment training as its basic product, wishes to ensure its survival and expansion by utilizing its expertise in in-company training. The training needs of a number of companies are established and an insourcing concept is drafted whereby the training company takes over a number of basic courses which can be produced at a lower cost and give higher customer value.

3. A finance company connected to a bank discovered through an experience curve analysis that unit costs for handling leasing

contracts fell with higher volumes. The finance company came up with an insourcing proposal which meant that the sellers of capital goods did not have to handle their leasing contracts themselves, as the finance company was able to produce them at a lower cost.

4. A steelworks is a huge consumer of energy. A large supplier of energy made a proposal to the steelworks to take over their entire supply of energy, including operations and maintenance of the steelworks, energy stocks, etc. The supplier was able to absorb a certain percentage of employees at the steelworks, which was able to get rid of a function that did not belong to its core business but took up much management time.

Many companies could profit from outsourcing's edifying mirror image in a business-to-business context. Unsurprisingly, a familiarity with outsourcing can often be enormously helpful in making an attractive offer to a prospective business partner. Remember, too, that managers may have to be reminded of such factors as have escaped their attention; these can be dealt with in an offer description.

Here are some essential activities in connection with insourcing/ outsourcing:

- *An understanding of all aspects of the problems involved* is fundamental if the management receiving proposals are to be confident that they really have been well thought out.

- *Clearing up doubts* is often vital, as such fundamental changes can give rise to doubts and anxiety on the part of employees (see also Change Management).

- *Quality assurance of product and its delivery* is fundamental if your prospective business partner is to feel confident in the knowledge that such things as quality control and complaints are going to be dealt with properly.

- *Securing a long agreement* is good business sense as it makes for continuity.

- *Effectiveness in respect of the customer* is essential in what concerns both cost levels and quality. Think carefully of how rationalizations, like improvements in quality, could benefit your customer.

- *Psychology in relation to the partner and its employees* means that their co-workers, from being an unimportant part of just another business now become a fundamental part of your core business while the partner's management energies are focused on the right things, i.e. your core business.

RECOMMENDED READING

1. David Hussey, Outsourcing – Insourcing.
2. Mary Cecelia Lacity and R A Hirschheim, Beyond the Information Systems Outsourcing Bandwagon: The Insourcing Response.
3. Robert B Chapman with Kathleen R Andrade, Insourcing After the Outsourcing: MIS Survival Guide.

Intellectual capital

Intellectual capital was a management concept that attracted much attention in the latter half of the 1990s. The underlying idea was that there were values in an organization that could not be expressed by traditional metrics. Such values were collectively called intellectual capital and together with an organization's book value constituted its total value. Synonyms for intellectual capital are invisible value, soft values, hidden assets, and so on. *Balanced Scorecard* (see this term) is a tool for the control and measurement of both book value and intellectual capital.

Skandia AFS with Leif Edvinsson at the helm were the leaders in formalizing and launching the concept. Skandia defined its intellectual capital as made up of human capital (the value of whatever goes home at 5 p.m.) and structural capital ('the value of whatever remains when the human capital has gone home'). In other words, human capital comprises co-worker competence, skills and relationships.

Structural capital consists of an organization's processes, trademark, patents, culture, customer relations, etc. Skandia continued to divide structural capital into customer capital (the value of an organization's customer

168

relations) and organizational capital. Organizational capital was categorized as innovation (an organization's ability to renew and develop itself) and process capital (the value of internal efficiency).

Leif Edvinsson won the Brain of the Year Award in 1998 as a result of Skandia's analysis of intellectual capital, which is shown in the following model.

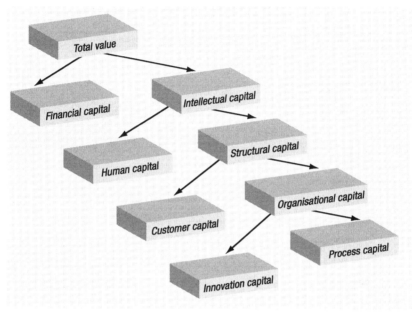

Source: Skandia AFS

The five perspectives resulting from the above analysis constitute the basis for Business Navigator, Skandia's version of the balanced scorecard. The concept of intellectual capital and balanced scorecard are closely related. Intellectual capital describes *what* is important, while balanced scorecard is a tool for measuring and following up what is important (*how*).

One of the positive aspects of the concept of intellectual capital was that it introduced useful language for discussion of invisible values. As with balanced scorecard, it gives us a breakdown of what, beyond the financial accounts, is important in an organization's control and follow-up work. Meanwhile, both models have helped many business leaders to understand how their organization's value is created.

Criticism directed at the concept of intellectual capital has mainly been of two kinds:

1. Connection to market value

The concept was introduced during a period when many companies were experiencing highly inflated stock market values. Intellectual capital was used to explain what investors and speculators saw in a company that did not appear in the balance sheet. The following equation was common at the time:

$$\text{Market value} = \text{Intellectual capital} + \text{book value}$$

This relationship was not found to avail itself of ready explanation, especially when the stock market subsequently took a dive. The whole concept of market psychology and speculation economics was completely ignored. When the hi-tech bubble broke, the reasoning that many had used to introduce and sell the concept fell apart.

2. What is actually new?

The concept's innovation value was also called into question. As are so many other fashionable management concepts, this was one that was highly overrated. A multitude of voices consequently claimed that they had for a long time realized the importance of, and worked on, customer relations, co-worker development, process efficiency, innovation development, and so on. The term 'intellectual capital' was also questioned; it made some people think of intellectuals, i.e. people with a high IQ, rather than a company's human and structural capital.

RECOMMENDED READING

1. Johan Roos (ed.) et al, Intellectual Capital: Navigating in the New Business Landscape.

2. Leif Edvinsson and Michael S Malone, Intellectual Capital: Realizing Your Company's True Value by Finding its Hidden Brainpower.

3. Thomas A Stewart and Tom Stewart, Intellectual Capital: The New Wealth of Organizations.

Internal demand

By *internal demand* we principally mean the demand that a business enterprise has in in-company personnel and service functions. Terrence T Paré argues in an article in Fortune Magazine that large, extravagant head offices have become symbols for what is wrong with big business. The somewhat subversive picture which he and other critics paint of the typical head office, as one of luxurious trappings that puts a strain on competitive strength and consumes a disproportionate amount of resources in relation to value added, may be an exaggerated one or indeed quite false. Nevertheless, many human resource departments clearly fall over themselves in their hurry to offer services that are not necessarily required, instead of satisfying actual demand. Most businesses know very well that it is vital to find out what their customers want and how well their organization satisfies these needs. But internal personnel and service functions all too rarely carry out studies for this purpose.

Power over people and money has for a long time been the most important way of demonstrating success in business but there are signs in today's world that all this is changing. Sales ability, expertise and the ability to develop are examples of success criteria which are becoming increasingly important.

Staff and service functions are seeing themselves more and more as entrepreneurial suppliers of services rather than as consumers of the capital and comforts created by profitable parts of the company. More about the possible consequences of this can be read in the section on *functional strategy* in the entry under *Strategy*.

A simple test can be done to establish internal demand and at the same time evaluate a staff or service unit's contribution in various areas; this is done by answering, together with the customer or recipient of services, the following two questions:

1. What does the customer/recipient think is important to get from their personnel/service unit?

2. How well, in the estimation of the customer/recipient, is the unit doing this?

Once these questions have been answered, it should not be difficult to prioritize investment areas and distribute resources to what the customer thinks is important. Answers to these questions can also serve as a useful gauge of the unit's overall performance.

The staff or service function can also use a Problem Detection Study (PDS) in order to obtain from customers a better indication of where to devote its resources.

In a PDS, customers have to define and weight the problems they have had with the company's departments, for example its IT or information systems. This documentation can then be used to establish the areas which the unit should focus on to attain maximum increase of customer satisfaction. There is more on PDS studies under the section of this name.

RECOMMENDED READING

William E Halal, Ali Geranmayeh and John Pourdehnad, Internal Markets: Bring the Power of Free Enterprise Inside Your Organization.

Investment

Investment means making an economic commitment at the present time in the expectation of receiving revenue in the future. The term investment is traditionally associated with the buying of tangible objects which are capable of generating value for a long time to come and can therefore be listed as assets on the balance sheet.

The term investment, as with most other management terms, is constantly in flux. This partly depends on changing circumstances but also on a misuse of the word to motivate the buying and selling of services. By 'changing circumstances' we mean the declining relative importance of physical capital and the increasing importance of intellectual capital. A large number of services will come to be seen as investments in the light of our definition of investment in spite of the fact that they are taken as a cost in the profit and loss account and not split into periods over the timeframe in which they are expected to generate income.

Modern thinking in VBM (Value Based Management) has through EVA (Economic Value Added) come to regard costs as income generators. Whether costs should then be seen as investment depends on the time horizons for returns. Something that should reasonably be seen as a cost is instead treated as an investment in order to influence price in the long-term.

A term closely linked to investment is *depreciation*. It means that the capital committed to an investment remains a charge against the profit and loss account for a number of years. The sum invested may for example be distributed over a period of ten years. When one-tenth of an investment is written off every year on the profit and loss account, this is called depreciation. Depreciation of inventory is sometimes called write-down.

A couple of points must be clarified to judge the profitability of an investment:

1. How long can the investment be expected to be profitable compared to other possible alternatives? (Economic lifetime.)

2. What gross margin contribution (revenue less variable costs) will the investment give, and how will the cash flow be distributed over the years to come?

On the basis of these two questions, there are several models for investment calculation, including:

1. The present value method, which calculates all cash flows at present value and compares them with the size of the investment.

2. The payback method, which calculates the time it will take until the investment has repaid its own cost.

The meaning of the term investment has been extended to describe all situations in which an extraordinary present sacrifice is made in the hope of future profits. Market investment is an example of this use of the term. In this context it means spending money on special marketing activities over and above the expenditure normally budgeted to maintain the present volume of sales. This meaning of the word often gets debased, being used to describe any money spent on advertising or sales promotion.

Another use of the term investment relates to know-how and human capital. With a growing realization of the importance of human capabilities, people have begun to speak of investing in skills and know-how. Here again it is a matter of an economic commitment made with a view to future gains, although this kind of investment is nearly always booked on the profit and loss account, that is, it is shown on the company's books as a straight cost item.

Bad investments can often be disastrous. A new giant shipyard was opened in Sweden in the mid-1970s at a time when the huge expansion of Japanese and Korean yards were already common knowledge. Investments like the Uddevalla project simply destroy capital.

During the 1960s and 1970s, the countries of Eastern Europe, Poland among them, invested heavily in steelworks, concrete factories and shipyards. Investment in heavy industrial plants was then thought to be a good idea. These investments led to a sharp decline in Polish living standards and necessitated heavy foreign borrowing that crippled the country's economic development for a long time.

The prevailing culture of the civil aviation industry has prompted investment in new aircraft, preferably big ones, as peer-group status symbols. This is probably one of the reasons why the total profitability of all IATA-affiliated airlines has been negative over a twenty-year period.

Investment in know-how can also turn out badly. The rise of big engineering consultancy firms, during the period when Sweden was expanding its infrastructure and information systems, led to a surplus of engineers and IT technicians and to financial difficulties for those firms when the expansion phase came to an end.

Bad investments can likewise be made in product development (the Concorde airplane is the classic case of that error of judgment), and in markets (as when several foreign manufacturers of heavy goods vehicles tried to break into a Swedish market dominated by two domestic manufacturers, Volvo and Scania).

Industries with a heavy capital base, irregular demand and great price sensitivity experience a special set of investment problems. Examples are airlines, hotels and telecoms operators. Rapid development is often accompanied by high rates of investment to create 'first mover advantage', where early expansion and inducements to an expectant market are meant to create an early opening to a high yield customer base delivering good profits. Unfortunately all the other players usually follow the same logic, which as a result leads to overcapacity, mergers, poor returns and bankruptcies. In an established industry with this kind of structure the ability to work creatively and proactively with revenues is one of the conditions of existence. The upshot has been the concept of yield management.

It is received wisdom that high capital intensity leads to low profitability. There are three main reasons for this:

1. High capital intensity leads to harder competition, especially when sales are sluggish and capacity is not fully utilized. That kind of situation, more than any other, tends to result in price-cutting and market wars.

2. Closing down a manufacturing operation involves such heavy losses that companies tend to struggle on for too long.

3. Margin pricing is common in situations of high capital intensity.

If a business decides to make a heavy investment in manufacturing capacity, its productivity per employee must be increased to avoid a drop in profitability.

Companies with high productivity combined with a low capital-to-turnover ratio are generally much more profitable than others with low productivity and high capital commitment.

The technique of relating tied-up capital to value added offers interesting opportunities for making comparisons between companies, not only in the same industry but also between companies in different industries.

We can recommend the concept of *added value* as a model and tool for measuring productivity. The concept considers changes in capital and costs, depreciation and interest, outsourcing of business as well as the exchange of work for capital. For more on added value, see *Efficiency* and *Productivity*.

RECOMMENDED READING

1. Aswath Damodaran, Investment Philosophies: Successful Strategies and The Investors Who Made Them Work.

2. Aswath Damodaran, Investment Philosophies: Tools and Techniques for Determining the Value of Any Asset.

3. Jonathan Mun, Real Options Analysis: Tools and Techniques for Valuing Strategic Investments and Decisions.

Just-In-Time, JIT (efficient production)

Just-In-Time, which we will abbreviate to JIT, has its origins in Japanese management philosophy and comprises approaches and methods to activate resources so that waiting times are minimized, transit times optimized and efficiency improved. JIT is also called lean production or layerless production. The essence of JIT is to have the right thing in the right place at the right time.

The motor-car industry was the first, with Toyota Motors in the vanguard, to adopt the JIT philosophy. It was popularized in the West by Deming and Juran, the Total Quality Management (TQM) experts, and both Ford and General Motors began to use the system at an early stage.

The driving forces that underlie JIT can usually be found at work in one or more of the following factors:

1. Reduction of set-up times in the organization.
2. Improvement of the ordering system.
3. Shorter lead times and more efficient processes.
4. Ability to produce small batch sizes.
5. Reduced production costs.
6. Reduction of overcapacity.
7. Less need for safety stocks.
8. Reduction of the frequency of defects occurring in production.

When organizations take on a JIT project, it is normally carried out in combinations of the following actions:

1. Buy and produce goods in smaller batches but with higher quality.
2. Design more efficient work-flows and eliminate bottlenecks in time and costs.
3. Review stakeholder relationships and how they affect the production apparatus.
4. Build partnerships with important suppliers.
5. Reduce unnecessary work and the number of mistakes.

6. Prevent technical stoppages or whatever can be deleterious to production.

7. Motivate co-workers while encouraging worker participation in the production process.

The work of making production-related work-flows more efficient has revealed a number of points, some of them unexpected:

1. Large stocks do not improve service levels. Flabby systems and a want of precision mean that stocks – and this goes against conventional wisdom – do not improve service levels.

2. Productivity increases as resources are minimized. Greater precision leads to an improvement in timekeeping and quality, and to greater effectiveness.

3. Motivation and job satisfaction go up when greater demands are placed on precision and timekeeping. This may come as a surprise.

4. Quality improves. The reason for this is that defects in a JIT system can have serious consequences; as a result, defect detection improves dramatically.

5. Consumption of resources goes down, not only because less capital is bound up in production, but also because the cost of defects drops and productivity, as was mentioned previously, goes up.

Mass production in the manufacturing industry is the largest catchment area for JIT. A result is that stock-keeping often receives less attention in the sub-supplier integration chain. The JIT system is most effective when the following conditions are present:

- Easily predictable volumes per unit of time
- Short lead times
- Relatively large quantities
- Steady sales
- Repetition of work tasks

By way of concluding, we give some of the criticism that has been levelled at the JIT concept. Michael Cusumano of the MIT Sloan School of

Management has revealed a number of limitations to the system which many companies today have experienced.

1. On-time deliveries have caused enormous service problems. Factory workers stand idle while they wait for the parts they need for production.

2. When Japanese companies undergo expansion to other countries they cannot always find suppliers who can satisfy the high standards of JIT, for which perfect supplier relations are necessary.

3. Shorter product life cycles and greater demands for variation in production cause problems in JIT, which can experience difficulty in dealing with flexibility in choice of supplier and the constant restructuring that is often necessary.

RECOMMENDED READING

1. James P Womack and Daniel T Jones, Lean Thinking: Banish Waste and Create Wealth in Your Corporation.

2. Steven M Bragg, Just-in-Time Accounting: How to Decrease Costs and Increase Efficiency.

3. Yasuhiro Monden, Toyota Production System: An Integrated Approach to Just-In-Time.

Kaizen – continuous improvement

Kaizen, according to its founder Masaaki Imai, is just as much a philosophy as it is a method for the development of organizations. As well as applying to the workplace the concept can – and according to its founder, should – be applied to private life among family and friends.

Kaizen is composed of two Japanese signs: *kai,* which means 'change', and *zen,* which means 'good' as well as 'wisdom'. The term can be roughly translated as 'changes for the better' and this is what Kaizen is about: continuous improvement that helps to achieve long-term success and does not require large investments. It is also very important for management and co-workers to participate in the work of improvement.

According to Imai, Kaizen changes the way people think and work. Kaizen is a close relation of TQM (see the section under *Quality*). It is said that Imai launched Kaizen when he realized that the concept of Total Quality Management (TQM) was being abused by mainly western companies. His first book on business management, published in 1986, was called *Kaizen – The Key to Japan's Competitive Success.* Kaizen also focuses on process development and in this respect has much in common with the PDCA wheel (see this term).

According to Imai, Kaizen can be regarded as a collective term for a number of contemporary trends; among these are:

- TPM (Total Productive Maintenance)
- TQC (Total Quality Control)
- Suggestion schemes
- Quality circles
- Customer Orientation
- Robotization
- Automation
- JIT (Just-in-time production)
- Zero defects
- Small group schemes

- Quality improvement
- Employees as partners of management
- Work discipline
- Improvements in productivity
- Product development
- Kanban (planning system involving two control cards for JIT systems)

Kaizen has come to play a leading part in many management systems, among them the standards set up in the ISO family. The concept has also come to play an important role as a counterweight to Business Process Re-engineering (BPR) and other more drastic ways of effecting change, by emphasizing the importance of co-worker participation and small, continuous improvements in the production process.

Kaizen has come in for some criticism, a summary of which is now given here.

1. Small, continuous improvements are not enough in today's business climate and changing world.

2. Kaizen was a product of the Japanese manufacturing industry and could be difficult to apply to service companies. However, this has been contradicted by many service companies who say they have been working successfully with the concept.

3. Kaizen is vague and woolly-minded; it apparently applies to everything but in so doing becomes meaningless.

4. The concept was developed to explain Japan's superior business achievements. If things go badly for Japan it will lose its attraction.

RECOMMENDED READING

1. Masaaki Imai, Kaizen: A Commonsense Low-Cost Approach to Management.

2. Masaaki Imai, Kaizen: The Key To Japan's Competitive Success.

Knowledge Management (KM)

Knowledge Management (KM) is a term that has become popular since the middle of the 1990s. Much promoted by systems development companies, it has often come to be equated with building systems and databases to handle different kinds of information flow in organizations. Experience shows that the technology part of effective KM is relatively small, however important.

In the middle of the 1990s, after the heyday of concepts like Business Process Re-engineering (BPR) and Total Quality Management (TQM), many academics and practicing managers began to be interested in the importance of knowledge where organizations were concerned. One of the pioneers in this field was Karl-Erik Sveiby, now professor of Knowledge Management at the Hanken Business School in Helsinki. As early as 1986, Sveiby published The Knowledge Company (*Kunskapsföretaget*), which was voted Management Book of the Year in Sweden. He published Knowledge Management (*Kunskapsledning*) four years later. Other pioneers in the field are Peter F Drucker, with his ideas on the knowledge society, James Brian Quinn and his concept of the intelligent enterprise, and Ikujiro Nonaka and HirotakaTaakeuchi with their theories on knowledge-creating companies.

In speaking of KM we should be clear about what we mean by 'knowledge' and how this differs from 'information' (and how knowledge management differs from the earlier and very popular concept of information management).

Gardner (1995) has provided a nexus of conditions on the theme of knowledge as applied in business:

- Know what information is required (know what).
- Know how information is to be used (know how).
- Know why certain information is required (know why).
- Know where information for a particular purpose can be found (know where).
- Know when certain information is required (know why).

A taxonomy which distinguishes between data, information, and knowledge is this one:

- Data are symbols that have not been interpreted or put into meaningful context.

- *Information* is data that has been given a meaning.

- *Knowledge* is what makes it possible for human beings to create meaning from data and thereby generate new information.

A simple definition of knowledge used by many is: *knowledge is information that has value.*

A classification of knowledge that is often applied in KM distinguishes between explicit and tacit knowledge. This classification has met with criticism; why, people ask, should the term information be used at all if knowledge can be codified into explicit and tacit knowledge? However, this debate does not concern us here. Codified knowledge, then, is knowledge which in some way can be expressed and communicated, whether it is in the form of documented experience of a project or success factors relating to past improvement work. Tacit knowledge comprises what cannot be codified and communicated between individuals. The Hungarian physicist and philosopher Michael Polanyi has given some thought to tacit knowledge. To quote Polanyi, "We know more than we can express". What we are able to express is codified knowledge. What we know but cannot express is tacit knowledge.

Polanyi uses swimming to exemplify the tacit side of knowledge. It is impossible to learn to swim by merely following the instructions from a book or manual. The strokes must be coordinated with breathing, which can only be learnt by the act of swimming itself. The serve in the game of tennis can also be used to illustrate the meaning of tacit knowledge. Again, we are confronted with the necessity of coordinating a whole range of conscious movements and unconscious reflexes. Certain principles of the serve can be codified and communicated: "one foot in front of the other", "throw the ball up high", "follow up your swing", etc, but the more subtle motor actions must be practiced. Training in the serve together with someone who has already mastered the art and can offer advice to correct our serve in purely physical terms, can accelerate learning.

A basis for many KM initiatives is the axiom that further knowledge is generated when knowledge is transformed from tacit to codified knowledge and back again. Theories based on this theme have been developed by Nonaka and Taakeuchi, among others. The transformation of tacit knowledge to tacit knowledge generates new knowledge through dialogue, reflection and learning, which can be comprehensively termed *socializing*. This kind of transfer of tacit knowledge can take place without the use of language, for example when we study, observe or imitate an 'expert' in a learning situation. The transformation from tacit to codified (explicit) knowledge implies expression, e.g. in the form of a manual; this enables the resulting knowledge to be available to others and creates opportunities for more interaction where new knowledge is formed (this is called *externalization*). The transformation of codified knowledge to tacit knowledge implies that someone interprets and assimilates codified knowledge by for example, reading a book and reflecting on what has been read (this is called *internalization*). The final transformation to be considered is from codified to codified knowledge. We may wonder whether knowledge really can be transformed in this way without the need for human intervention but it could be argued that this kind of transformation occurs when two databases are combined (this is termed *combination*). The above transformations have been summarized in the following matrix which is based on the one used by Nonaka and Taakeuchi.

FROM	TO: EXPLICIT	TO: TACIT
Explicit	Combination	Internalization
Tacit	Externalization	Socialization

It is possible to distinguish two main streams of thought in KM and these have this in common: the knowledge available to a business must be handled properly if the business is to be flexible and use its reorientation abilities to the fullest. The one school of thought focuses on how databases are used and how companies can employ them in strategically effective ways. The other school of thought focuses on how knowledge is organized and disseminated *within* an organization. In this connection, ideas on the transformation of one form of knowledge to another are extremely important.

If we now return to the distinction between information management and KM, it can be said that information management focuses on how codified knowledge is handled, transferred and made available through systems and databases. KM focuses instead on the creation of the right conditions for the interpretation and development of both tacit knowledge and explicit (codified) knowledge. In this respect, KM has much in common with *learning organization* (see this term).

Benchlearning (see this term) is another concept the aims of which are closely related to KM. Benchlearning is a method for the structured transfer of knowledge and learning between groups and individuals. Here the right conditions are created for transfer of knowledge both in its codified form and face-to-face, thus facilitating the transformation of tacit knowledge.

We conclude by offering a few words of wisdom from businesses which have worked more or less successfully with KM:

1. Avoid an immediate focus on technology; technology should be an enabler rather than an end in itself.

2. Think in terms of demand: what knowledge do co-workers need and when do they need it? Making all information available to everybody, turned out to be less successful.

3. Encouraging co-workers to actually look forward to sharing their knowledge was an idea that proved successful, while 'defending one's territory' was an obstacle to effective KM. The review of management culture and ideas was often seen as an important success factor.

4. Do not talk too much about Knowledge Management, just do what improvement work you have to do. Act first, communicate later and do not complicate things unnecessarily.

5. Set up clear goals for your initiative and decide how and when progress is to be measured; then review developments.

RECOMMENDED READING

1. Georg Von Krogh et al, Enabling Knowledge Creation: How to Unlock the Mystery of Tacit Knowledge and Release the Power of Innovation.

2. Ikujiro Nonaka et al, The Knowlede-Creating Company: How Japanese Companies Create the Dynamics of Innovation.

3. Karl-Erik Sveiby, The New Organizational Wealth: Managing & Measuring Knowledge-Based Assets.

Lean production

Japanese production philosophy began to attract much attention at the beginning of the 1980s. At first there was a focus on employment conditions.

The Japanese were rumoured to have permanent employment and Western leaders wanted reasons for their spectacular industrial advances.

The concept of lean production gradually emerged as one of the reasons for Japanese success. Lean production can be said to comprise two elements. The first has to do with productivity and coming to grips with the management of work to give lower costs per unit produced. The second element underlying the concept of lean production has a more benign character: a striving for continuous improvement, or Kaizen (see this term), which means that people are encouraged to take a new approach to their work and the opportunities that it offers.

Interest in this philosophy increased significantly in the latter half of the 1980s when Japanese *transplants* began to operate in the West. (By transplant we mean a Japanese company in a Western environment.) In 1987 MIT presented a study of productivity in Japanese factories situated in the West and staffed with a Western workforce. It showed that productivity was almost as high as in the parent factories in Japan, or 40% greater than equivalent factories owned and operated in the West. Of course these Japanese transplants enjoyed favourable conditions. They were often established in regions with high unemployment and were able to get unions to accept their agendas surprisingly easily. It can be said in passing that Western-owned plants had the same opportunities.

 MIT's five-year research project pointed to a different approach in the following areas:

- Worker responsibility
- Flexibility
- Subcontractor relations
- Quality
- Minimized stock-keeping
- Frugality in all ranks

Among the distinguishing elements of lean production are:

1. Short changeover times
2. Minimal stock and buffer stock
3. Small batch sizes
4. Minimal staff
5. Flexible personnel
6. High machine evacuation rates
7. Zero-defect manufacturing
8. Active quality work
9. Continuous improvement – Kaizen
10. Elimination of productivity losses
11. Elimination of unnecessary tied-up capital

Through this production philosophy everyone becomes involved in continuous improvement.

Some of the above points deserve special attention. One is the requirement for a flexible workforce. A flexible workforce can help out where it is most useful, something that naturally occurs in many situations at work, especially in small businesses. In fact, it is one of the big advantages that small businesses have over larger ones. In small companies people help out where it is necessary, while in large companies employees might refuse to carry out tasks other than those for which they have been employed.

An emphasis on time in the form of set-up times and transit times is another prominent element of lean production. A number of these have of course been adopted in the West. Many people may be acquainted with the literature on time competition and projects such as T50 (so called because it reduced product lead time by 50 per cent) in the Asea Brown Boveri Group (ABB). In many cases the time factor can serve as an excellent approximation of productivity, i.e. cost per unit produced.

Another very important factor is Kaizen, which strives for improvements in both productivity and quality. In Japanese commerce and industry, quality became a matter of pride after the long period following World War II when their products were considered to be inferior. The Japanese were determined to show the world that their industry could produce high-quality goods. This must be one of the reasons for their aspiration to high standards of quality.

Japanese industry and lean production have come to be the standard-bearers of the ambition to achieve optimal quality. As an aside we might mention the obvious pleasure that those involved in lean production derive from their work. Many studies have shown that lean production has given fresh meaning to the working lives of many people. This discovery has in fact triggered a debate in the West on the working man in the production line. Theories on the bio-psychological conditions of the workplace and the importance of motivating people through information, leadership, commitment and development, have come to stand out as important elements in the debate on leadership. Business leaders have become more interested in men and women as working people capable of personal development, rather than just as tools to carry out a given function.

Meanwhile, the philosophy of lean production is in crisis in its founder nation. Its methods are felt to be hard and remorseless and are leading to high staff turnover. It is becoming harder to motivate young people and sing the virtues of lean production, which is seen by many as part of an ascetic culture based on self-sacrifice.

RECOMMENDED READING

1. James P Womack and Daniel T Jones, Lean Thinking: Banish Waste and Create Wealth in Your Corporation.

2. Michael N Kennedy, Product Development for the Lean Enterprise: Why Toyota's System is Four Times More Productive and How You Can Implement It.

3. W Edwards Deming, Out Of The Crisis.

Learning organization

The concept of the learning organization became popular largely through a book by the MIT professor Peter Senge. Called *The Fifth Discipline,* it was published in 1990 and built on current research on the ability of organizations to learn, in particular on Chris Argryis' ideas on double and triple loop learning. Organizations must "learn how to learn". Senge added his own system of thought to previous theories and made organizational learning accessible to a wider public. He proposed that the following five *disciplines* should be characteristic of a learning organization:

1. **Systems thinking**. Organizations are complex systems of interrelationships. We must learn to see the patterns in these relationships and uncover the problems inherent in them. Senge developed a number of system archetypes to help organizations identify typical problems and obstacles to learning.

2. **Personal mastery**. The individual's importance to the learning organization is stressed. While working on common goals, individuals should have aspirations of their own, not merely in the business sense, but also in the sense of personal development.

3. **Mental models**. This basically refers to company culture and the theories and different mindsets which form the framework for the functioning of the business. A learning organization is conscious of these models and curious about the effect they have on organizational development. See also *Company culture* and *Values*.

4. **Shared vision**. A learning organization has a common vision anchored in its co-workers. Senge stresses the importance of blending together personal aspirations and goals with the company's vision. See also *Vision*.

5. **Team learning**. The importance of dialogue and discussion in groups. In order to facilitate team learning we must learn to transcend barriers and reach beyond agreement to genuine alignment and effectiveness. Benchlearning (see this term) is one method which has proved to be conducive to team learning.

Many researchers and practicing managers have thought about the connection between organizational learning and organizational structure, and the detrimental effect on learning of lengthy decision procedures and the bureaucratization that often results from them. Process orientation and the resulting discussions of functional boundaries ought to favour organizational learning, if indeed fresh knowledge is created when current knowledge is questioned. The right conditions for learning can be created by bringing together co-workers with different backgrounds and expertise in a culture based on openness and curiosity. It has been said that coffee breaks provide the right environment, a suggestion not unworthy of serious consideration. The diversity afforded by competence, gender and cultural background is also said to be important for organizational learning.

Many people find it difficult to understand how the theory of the learning organization can be put into practice. In many cases there are good intentions and that is as far as it goes. However, the current trend has led to much insight into learning at all levels, as well as the tools we have at our disposal to promote learning.

RECOMMENDED READING

1. Bengt Karlöf, Kurt Lundgren and Marie Edenfeldt Froment, Benchlearning: Good Examples as a Lever for Development.

2. Chris Argyris and Donald E Schön, Organizational Learning II: Theory, Method, and Practice.

3. David L Dotlich, Action Learning: How the World's Top Companies are Re-Creating their Leaders and Themselves.

4. Peter M Senge, The Fifth Discipline: The Art & Practice of The Learning Organization.

Make/Buy analysis

Should a staff restaurant be run by SAS Catering?

Should a County Council occupy itself with chemical analysis?

Should Saab manufacture its own engines?

These are all questions that a *make/buy analysis* attempts to answer. Make/buy analysis is one of the many instruments a business can use to improve its effectiveness.

The theory of why companies or businesses emerge in a market economy was first formulated in 1937 by Ronald Coase in his article, "The Nature of the Firm". Coase, who was awarded the Bank of Sweden Prize in Economic Sciences in Memory of Alfred Nobel in 1991 for this article, established beyond doubt the importance of transaction costs. A cost is associated with availing oneself of an open pricing mechanism, i.e. the market, just as there is a cost for holding together and utilizing a business or organization. To put it simply, a cost consists in the resources that must be sacrificed to create all the agreements or contracts which are necessary in a free market. If all the elements involved in production can be brought under one management by means of long agreements or contracts, then a cost reduction is achieved, as compared to the case where production elements have to be sought out on the free market and contracted one-by-one, time after time.

Make/buy analysis was conceptualized in the 1950s mainly in the engineering workshop industry. The term was used to indicate the choice which had to be made between producing a component oneself, on the one hand, and having it produced by contract, on the other. With the passage of time the term *outsourcing* (see this term) has come to express the same phenomenon.

RECOMMENDED READING

1. David R Probert, Developing a Make or Buy Strategy for Manufacturing Business.

2. Maurice F Greaver, Strategic Outsourcing: A Structured Approach to Outsourcing Decisions and Initiatives.

Management systems

A complaint that we often hear in business is that it is easy to say, not so easy to do. Goals and plans of action are often formed in the right spirit but somehow seem to fizzle out. A problem in businesses of a certain size is how to control everything that happens in the organization. Management systems are tools to help with these problems.

Large organizations can be more efficient by implementing a system for formulating goals, one that indicates how goals are to be communicated throughout the organization; what documentation is to be used; what the areas of responsibility are and who is to be involved; how progress will be measured and when and by whom measuring will be done. When it functions properly, a good management system can give insight into how the business works.

Management systems were given a big boost with the introduction of the ISO 14,000 and ISO 9,000 standards, management systems offering certification in the environment and quality, respectively.

Introduction of a management system can cause problems, especially if the ISO standards are used as a model. The business can become unwieldy, even paralysed, when it simply becomes too difficult to change anything. If this happens, the object of introducing the management system in the first place, namely to stimulate the work of constant improvement, will have been lost.

A management system should answer the following questions:

- What management documentation does the business have (strategy plan, budget, operative plans, marketing plan, quality programme, balanced scorecard, policy documents, etc)?

- What do the different documents contain?

- How are they inter-connected?

- In what forums and when is documentation drafted? When and where are decisions taken?

- How is reporting and review organized?

- How effective are the lines from organizational goals and strategies to individual employee goals and plans of action?

When used in the right way, a management system can be an excellent tool for keeping everything in order and ensuring that the plans of the business are carried out.

Some success factors for viable management systems are:

- Keep the management system simple and easy to understand. Ask yourself what the business needs in order to function well.

- Use only one management system for all organizational matters (for example, quality, the environment, development of trademark, IT, etc).

- Management must feel that it is the owner of its management system.

For more on this, see *Planning chart*.

RECOMMENDED READING

1. Derek F Abell, Defining The Business: The Starting Point of Strategic Planning.

2. Stephen G Haines, The System Thinking Approach to Strategic Planning and Management

3. Walter J Salmon, Harvard Business Review on Corporate Governance.

Market

A market can be defined as an organized meeting for trade, originally a town square where sellers could find buyers and vice versa. Today, the term market is an abstraction, a collective term for a group of customers who may be united either by geographical location or by common needs that generate demand. The use of the word market in both these senses often causes confusion, so a more detailed explanation is called for.

In the geographical sense, the term market can, for example, be applied to a country or region: the Norwegian market or the European market. Here the term is applied to all customers in a given geographical area, regardless of what products they buy or how they use them.

Bankers speak of the private market and the company market, and manufacturers of hand tools speak of the DIY (Do-It-Yourself) market and the pro market. The bankers are of course referring to those of their customers who are private individuals and companies respectively, while the toolmakers are talking about people in a geographical area who buy tools for private use in the home and for professional use at work. In these two examples, the term market is really an abbreviation for market segment. A segment is a part of a whole where differences within the part are smaller than differences between that part and other parts.

The use of the term market as an abstraction has sometimes caused large companies to make the mistake of failing to consider individual customers and to learn about their customers' need structures. If we use the term market as a name for broad categories, we run the risk of blunting our sensitivity to subtle differences in the need structures of our customers.

Market orientation means a view of management based on the market and its needs. By identifying the market's needs, the underlying factors that create demand, a company can adapt its resources (its costs and capital) accordingly and thus make itself more competitive. The term market orientation has come to be used as a contrast to the old technocratic view, which was based on the company's resources and strengths and which aimed at persuading the market to want what the company had to offer. Market orientation denotes a more entrepreneurial view; it calls for willingness to listen to the customers we want to serve and for empathy, for the ability to put oneself in the other person's place.

Market analysis is the collection, processing and compilation of data that provides information about the market for a company, product or service. A distinction is made between quantitative market analysis, which refers to the collection of data about numbers of buyers, frequency of buying, seasonal variations, and so on, and qualitative market analysis. The latter covers things like attitude polls, surveys of customer-perceived quality and image studies. Image here means reality as perceived by those around one. Market analysis originated in the customer goods trade, and its industrial applications are not yet fully developed, but its use among the manufacturing and service industries is now growing rapidly. In large corporations, too, it is becoming increasingly common for departments and sections to measure their performance in serving in-house users of their products and services. See also *Market analysis*.

Marketing means the creation of demand, whereas selling means getting orders. In everyday speech the term marketing is used loosely for both processes, for both spreading the word about a product and actually selling it. Marketing is one of the four basic *functions of management* (see this term), by which we usually mean:

- Development

- Production

- Marketing

- Administration

Most industries during the greater part of the twentieth century have experienced a constant rise in demand, which made marketing seem less important than production or administration. The first two decades after World War II, in particular, were marked by a world-wide shortage of goods that diminished the importance of marketing skills. But the shortages gradually gave way to surpluses once most needs were satisfied. This resulted in a sharp upswing of interest in marketing in the early 1960s, when both marketers and market communicators became much more important people in the corporate world. (Today the importance of marketing has been boosted further by the number of companies that are becoming aware of the need to protect and develop their trademarks.)

During this period the marketers tried to extend the meaning of the term to cover both market studies and product development, as well as creation of demand and physical distribution of goods. Note that the term marketing is still sometimes used in this sense, with a definition so broad that it tends to dilute the term to the point of meaninglessness.

In the interests of clarity, it is advisable to distinguish between product development and marketing. Demand is created in radically different ways depending on what kind of product or service we are selling. If we are selling nuclear power stations, we have little need for mass communication in the form of advertising in the daily press, a medium that is very important to sales of fast-moving consumer goods like toiletries or groceries. If you are a lawyer or management consultant selling professional services, your efforts to create demand must be adapted to the channels through which buyers are open to influence, specifically by making them aware of high-quality work you have already done.

Internal marketing is a term to describe measures taken to increase motivation through effective internal communication of a company's visions, goals, corporate mission and strategic course. Many companies have discovered that they can achieve substantial improvements in efficiency by motivating their employees to perform better by putting more of their energy into their work. Employees benefit too, because they come to regard their work as more meaningful and consequently their whole life as richer.

The market dimension

The two polarities of the market dimension

Organized activities are based on satisfying the needs of a number of people. These needs result in a demand for the most favourable offering of goods and services that can satisfy demand and give the highest value. By value we mean the relation between utility and price. For there to be demand there must be a knowledge of the product. There has been plenty of discussion in recent years of how the market dimension should be handled.

One school of thought is represented by customer or market orientation, i.e. it says that goods and services produced should satisfy the needs of target groups: this is plainly the key to success.

The school of innovation orientation on the other hand, says that customers will prefer products and services which outperform their rivals and which, as cost-efficiently as possible, satisfy their needs, i.e. give the best value.

Peter Drucker, the well-known business consultant, once said that the only purpose of a business was to create and keep a customer. Many people have interpreted this to mean that for organizations to be successful they must first establish the needs of their customers and then produce the goods and services that will satisfy these needs.

Thesis: study customer utility

All organized activity is founded on the creation of a value that is higher than the cost of producing this value. This idea may seem trite, but it provides us with the most important parameters for the study of a business. It always boils down to finding the right path to productivity and the creation of value, a search that takes place in a complex world with many different alternatives, whether they are a competitor's product or completely different ways for your prospective customers to use their money.

Here are ten tools that may be helpful in an analysis of customer value and motivate creative thinking in real-life situations:

TOOLS FOR CUSTOMER ANALYSIS	THESE TEN TOOL ANSWER THE FOLLOWING QUESTIONS
1. Market-based quality profile	What quality factors are important to the customer? How do we satisfy these when compared to the customer's alternatives?
2. Relative price profile	What are the product characteristics that the customer is willing to pay for, and how much is s/he willing to pay?
3. Customer value graph	What is our position on a value graph, i.e. one which shows price against performance?
4. Business gained/lost	What are the real reasons for our having gained or lost important business?
5. Customer value compared with principal competitor	How did we do, point for point, compared to our main competitor?
6. Key developments	Has anything taken place that explains market developments? If so, how can this be exploited?
7. What/who matrix	According to the planning chart, who has responsibility for what should be done better?
8. Repurchasing	To what extent have we satisfied our customers? Will they buy from us again?
9. Customer loyalty	How great is the loyalty of our customers?
10. After-sales	How can we continue to look after our customers?

Antithesis: to hell with what the customer says!

Rules and good advice are valuable. The painful truth is that the wisest course is sometimes to do exactly the opposite of what the rules say we should. But first we have to learn the rules – otherwise we won't know when we are breaking them, or why we choose to do so.

There is a risk of becoming 'feedback fanatics', slaves to the supposedly correct information that suppresses the risk-taking that underlies all business activity. Barry Diller, the media guru, once expressed this same thought in the American journal *Fortune,* when he said that we had become the slaves of all manner of studies that made us produce what the figures told us to. We had come adrift from our instincts while our reluctance to take risks was destroying our sensitivity.

Chrysler carried out detailed analytical studies before launching Voyager, their first mini-van. The test panels were appalled when they contemplated what some called a monster vehicle. Voyager went on to become one of Chrysler's really big success stories.

In trials of its new product New Coke, Coca-Cola got the best results for any soft drink in a tasting test. They were so good that Coca-Cola had no compunctions about replacing the old version of the drink with its new wonder product, whereupon the American public proceeded to reject New Coke and the company was obliged to reintroduce the old product under the guise of Classic Coke.

Compaq was openly derided when they launched Systempro, the first computer service for connecting servers to networks. But Compaq stuck to its guns and not for one minute has had cause to regret its decision.

McDonald's carried out trials of a low-calorie hamburger that was launched under the name of McLean. In spite of exceptional test results, the American public continued to put away the good old – and very fatty – Big Mac.

Examples such as these continue to illustrate the two opposites of the market dimension: customer orientation and innovation-driven development.

RECOMMENDED READING

1. Art Weinstein, Defining Your Market: Winning Strategies for High-Tech, Industrial, and Service Firms.

2. Michel Wedel and Wagner Kamakura, Market Segmentation: Conceptual and Methodological Foundations.

3. Bradley Gale, Managing Customer Value.

Market analysis

All organized activity in business is designed to satisfy customers' needs. The main job of market analysis is to study the nature of these needs and the demand expressed by them, as well as who the customers are. Market analysis is a collective term for a number of methods and tools with this aim. More about needs can be found in the section under *Needs*.

Market analyzes can be both qualitative (for example through interviews and focus groups) and quantitative (as in customer surveys and sales information). Common drivers for conducting a market analysis are:

1. To produce documentation for positioning on the basis of customer needs. Positioning can be in absolute terms such as pricing levels and productivity, or in respect of trademark, i.e. how customers perceive the company and its products. Conjoint analysis is a useful tool here (see this term). More information can also be found under *Trademark*.

2. To assess the potential for new and existing products against new and existing market segments. This is often done using a product/market matrix, in which each product or product group is set against its market segment or customer group. Criteria essential to judge the potential of each product/market section are then identified and assessed. For more on this, see *Product/ market matrix*. There is more about customer value in the section under Value.

3. To identify areas for improvement in respect of customers. A common approach here is to begin with a number of qualitative interviews to identify what customers think is important in their relationship with the company. A larger population is then asked through a survey to rank these factors and to indicate how well they think the company is performing in each area. The result can be represented in a diagram with two axes, *importance* and *performance*. Areas ranked by customers as important where they perceive company performance as low, are naturally candidates for improvement. It can also be useful to ask customers about their problem areas and get them to rank them in order of importance. A PDS analysis is an effective way of doing this (see the section under *PDS analysis*).

4. To have a fact base prior to launching a new product. It is not uncommon for products to be test-launched and then evaluated, as it can be difficult to evaluate how a product will be accepted on a purely theoretical basis. It is important to remember that an offering sometimes creates demand: we do not know what we want until we can see it. For more on this, see *Market*.

5. To build customer awareness and get continuous feedback on the market. Many companies find that they need a real dialogue with their customers, which is why they often establish customer advisory boards or reference groups. A customer reference group can challenge the company, make it aware of trends and changes in needs and if necessary, question company decisions and play the devil's advocate. Another way to do this, if not as dependable, is to make use of the possibilities offered by the Internet.

An interesting exercise is to confront the picture of the reality outside with internal perceptions. This can be done by getting salespeople, marketing staff and management to say how they think customers have answered the questions in the positioning analysis. The results and the consequences of these are worth considering (see the example below).

RESULT	POSSIBLE CONSEQUENCES
We have underestimated the importance to the customer of certain factors.	We have failed to stress these factors enough in our sales work and customer care because we did not think they were important.
We have overestimated the importance to the customer of certain factors.	We thought that these were the factors that caused customers to buy and stay with us and therefore did not invest time and money where they could have donethe most good.
We have overestimated our position and ability in relation to our competitors.	We were satisfied and did not think we had to bother about our competitors, but this could be disastrous.
We have underestimated our position and ability in relation to our competitors.	We have become passive and won't invest aggressively in the opportunities we get.

Customer loyalty is an important concept in market analysis. It can be measured by looking at customer re-purchase levels. Loyal customers are a vital success factor for many companies and an important condition for organic growth. More about re-purchasing can be found under *Sales Strength*.

The distinction between primary information and secondary information is important in market analysis. Primary information is information that a company collects and collates. Secondary information is information that has been collated by statistics bureaux, research companies and trade associations. The latter kind of information can often be purchased for a much lower cost than it would take to carry out our own studies. Some kinds of market information, for instance demographic variables, can often be obtained through desk research.

In his book *Marketing Communications,* P R Smith has given the following stages in the work of planning and carrying out a market analysis:

1. **Define the problem**. Clearly define what information is needed, why it is needed, if it should be quantitative or qualitative, etc.

2. **Draw up a plan for the analysis**. This should contain:

   a. Analysis techniques: observations, surveys, focus groups, interviews, etc.

   b. Population: size and type (connected to confidence level).

   c. Cost/time plan.

   d. Formulation of surveys, interview sheets, etc.

3. **Marketing actions**. Collection of information.

4. **Analysis**. Sort, structure, weight, evaluate and put together information.

5. **Interpretation and representation**. Interpret information, draw conclusions and present all of this so that it is easy to understand.

6. **Activities**. Act on the basis of the information that has been analyzed.

RECOMMENDED READING

1. Gilbert A Churchill and Dawn Iacobucci, Marketing Research: Methodological Foundations.

2. Philip Kotler, Marketing Management.

3. P R Smith, Market Communications: An Integrated Approach.

Market attractiveness and strategic position

A method for rating market attractiveness and strategic position was developed at roughly the same time by McKinsey & Company and General Electric within the framework of the PIMS model (see this entry). Unlike the BCG matrix, this concept aimed at a more considered assessment of the prospects of individual business units.

The method was presented in the form of a matrix, where strategic position is set against market attractiveness. A matrix of this kind as used by McKinsey is shown below:

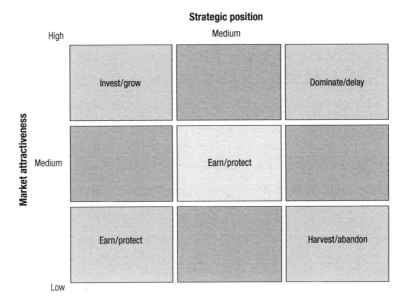

A special and fundamental question is of course in what geographical market the relative market share should be calculated. There are plenty of examples of how misjudgements of market share have led to disastrously bad decisions. Some of the criteria used to judge strategic position market attractiveness are:

STRATEGIC POSITION	MARKET ATTRACTIVENESS
• Relative size	• Absolute size
• Growth	• Market growth
• Market share	• Market breadth
• Position	• Pricing
• Relative profitability	• Structure of competition
• Margin	• Industry profitability
• Technological position	• Technical role
• Image (reality as perceived by outsiders)	– Social role
	– Effect on environment
• Leadership and people	• Legal obstacles

Matrices setting market attractiveness against strategic position have been severely criticized of late. Criticism has focused mainly on the consequences of the recommendations that generally emanate from the use of these matrices.

If a business unit is judged to be in a weak strategic position in an unattractive market, the theory says that it should be harvested, that is, milked for every last drop of capital that can be wrung out of it, and then dropped.

Following this advice has repeatedly proved to be disastrous. In the first place, who wants to be head of a company scheduled for rape and murder? General Electric, where much of this kind of thinking originated, has now radically reappraised such broad recommendations. Business units judged to have weak strategic position in unattractive industries have shown that they can be extremely successful if they go against generally accepted recommendations. Thus, for example, the manufacture and sale of tramcars and underground railway systems have proved to have a great development potential, the simplistic recommendations of the model to the contrary notwithstanding.

RECOMMENDED READING

1.   Gary Hamel and C K Prahalad, Competing for the Future.

2.   Michael E Porter, Competitive Strategy: Techniques For Analyzing Industries and Competitors.

3.   Michael Treacy and Fred Wiersman, The Discipline of Market Leaders: Choose Your Customers, Narrow Your Focus, Dominate Your Market.

Market share

The importance of market share has long been acknowledged, especially in traditional strategic thinking. Relative market share, above all, has been the focus of attention. This is because a high relative market share was believed to offer opportunities for mass production with consequent economies of scale. These economies in turn would mean long runs, low unit costs, high margins and high profitability. (See the entry under *Experience curve*). The value of theories on market share has since been called into question. A large market share is something that cannot be achieved simply by investing in expansion. Neither can a sustained high market share be gained by acquisition. The only way to get a high market share is for a company to earn it, that is by satisfying customers' needs so well that enough of them prefer its product to give it a high market share compared to its competitors.

Sometimes the theory works admirably, but sometimes it gives totally wrong answers. It all depends on the material from which market share is measured. The term can only be meaningful if we define the market in which our company wants to stake a claim, and which is significant to the outcome of competition. This is known as the market served. If we manufacture concrete beams for private houses, the market served will be fairly small, perhaps within a radius of 150 km from our factory. If on the other hand we build airliners or nuclear power situations, our market served is global in extent.

A strong emphasis on a large market share is often justified. It must however be remembered that the conception of the importance of market share originated in the United States, where competitive strategy is heavily focused on rational production and price. Europe, on the other hand, has traditionally attached more importance to segmentation and quality.

In a fragmented market with no advantages of scale and a low level of awareness of available alternatives among buyers, market share is relatively unimportant.

Conversely, market share becomes much more important in concentrated markets with substantial advantages of scale and with knowledgeable customers. The British automotive industry, for example, committed a serious error of judgment by persisting in measuring its market share relative to the British market. By failing to redefine the market it served, it lost sight of potential advantages of scale in both production and, later, development.

Defining the served market

In order to work out our market share, we first have to define the served market, i.e. the geographical scope of our company and the areas that our marketing organization has chosen to target. These territories are of course the same ones on the basis of which we measure our market share.

If we run a chain of bakeries in Stockholm that produces buns, we do not compete with a bakery in Madrid that chiefly produces plain bread. Similarly, a small German construction company cannot be said to compete in Thailand for example. These examples are a little far-fetched but do illustrate the idea of a served market.

Companies can sometimes use too narrow a gauge in defining their served market.

The British automotive industry or Danish bakeries, to name two examples, have restricted their served markets to within their national borders.

When the Japanese found economies of scale in their car production and were able to substantially lower production costs and prices, the British car industry offered feeble competition. When Denmark joined the EU, bakeries in Copenhagen suddenly found that the French were flying in baguettes from Paris.

Determining our served market, i.e. the basis on which our market share is to be calculated, is thus critical for both our business strategy and analysis of the portfolio strategy we opt for. There is a simple theoretical basis for analyzing the smallest served market:

1. A combination of experience curve effects and economies of scale in development, production, marketing and even administration. In passenger car manufacturing, for instance, the economies of scale have shifted from production to development. In the manufacture of artists' colour, too, the work of developing dispensaries is the factor that determines the scope of the served market. Satellites over Europe have provided marketing opportunities and created economies of scale in distribution.

2. The other factor is the ideal delivery capacity for the customers we serve. Value in the form of products and services should be added as long as it increases competitiveness in the business unit. This has to do with *value elasticity* or the way goods or services can affect customer value.

We should not forget that negative value, too, can easily be created in organizations that have become too large. A lack of resolve, flexibility, motivation and coordinating energy in a complex organization can slowly eat away at economies of scale.

RECOMMENDED READING

1. Lee G Cooper and Masao Nakanishi, Market-Share Analysis.

2. Richard Miniter, The Myth of Market Share: Why Market Share is the Fool's Gold of Business.

McKinsey's 7s model

McKinsey's 7s model cannot really be considered as a pure strategy model, but rather as a way of thinking about development or remodelling of organizations. Its name comes from the seven factors that McKinsey found essential in the context of organization development: strategy, skills, shared values, structure, systems, staff and style.

Normally, when a company sets out to change its organization, the seven S's are dealt with in a given sequence. In the first phase the strategy is usually determined. The next step is to define what the organization must be especially good at in order to be able to implement its strategy, in other words, what skills it must develop or otherwise acquire. The final step is to determine what changes are needed in the other five factors to make the change a successful one.

Strategy tells a company how it must adapt itself to its environment and use its organizational potential, whereas the analysis of skills answers the question of how the strategy ought to be implemented.

It is seldom difficult to define five, or maybe even tens skills of fundamental importance. But this is not enough, because the need is to develop winning skills, and this often makes such heavy demands on the organization that it is only possible to develop between one and three skills at a time. These skills represent the link between the strategy and the new era, while at the same time they define the changes that need to be made in the other five S's: structure, systems, staff, style and shared values.

A company's *structure* is perhaps the best known of the concepts relating to organizational change. It refers to the way business areas, divisions and units are grouped in relation to each other. This, too, is perhaps the most visible factor in the organization, and that is why it is often tempting to begin by changing the structure. There are many examples of corporate managements who thought they could reorganize their companies through structural changes alone.

Systems can be defined as the procedures or processes which exist in a company and which involve many people for the purpose of identifying important issues, getting things done or making decisions. Systems have a very strong influence on what happens in most organizations, and provide management with a powerful tool for making changes in the organization.

The *staff factor* is concerned with the question of what kind of people the company needs. This is not so much a question of single individuals as of the total know-how possessed by the people in the organization.

Style is one of the lesser-known implements in the management toolbox. It can be said to consist of two elements: personal style and symbolic actions. Thus management style is not a matter of personal style but of what the executives in the organization do, how they use their personal signalling system.

Shared values, finally, refer to one or more guiding themes of the organization, things that everybody is aware of as being specially important and crucial to the survival and success of the organization. (This section on the 7S model has been taken from Dag Sundström's *McKinsey & Company Inc.*)

RECOMMENDED READING

Thomas J Peters and Robert H Waterman, Jr, In Search of Excellence: Lessons from America's Best-Run Companies.

Mergers and acquisitions

The acquisition, merging and sale of companies often come under the umbrella term of structural business. Mergers have become much more common in the last decade. They have sometimes been monumental and sometimes disastrous. Research into acquisitions and mergers has intensified and the results should be of interest to those who are considering a restructuring of their business.

Below we give a bulleted list of these developments without revealing their sources.

- Generally speaking, no value is created through mergers and acquisitions. Comparisons of share prices and other relevant values before and after mergers showed that both parties came out losers, but the buyer was the loser much more often than the seller. It should be remembered that these results are of a general character and in no way definitive.

- The winner in the bidding always has a tendency to pay too high a price, one which cannot be defended in the new constellation of companies. This is called the 'winner's curse', a sardonic reflection on the buyer's eagerness to conclude a transaction in order to come out on top.

- 64 per cent of mergers and acquisitions reveal a post-costing which is considerably lower than the preliminary costing in terms of the value added to the merged organizations.

- A review of bank mergers all over the world presented the following gloomy picture:

  1. The value of shareholdings did not increase.

  2. Employee wages did not rise, nor did the number of employees.

  3. Customers did not benefit.

- Synergy is often the villain of the piece. Predicted synergies which include higher receipts and/or lower costs usually go unfulfilled. For more on this, see *Synergy*.

These are statistics and may in no way apply to individual cases; but it does not hurt to be careful and well informed.

Acquisition is a common growth technique, with a variegated structure of underlying motives. By buying a business or shares in a company, we can grow in leaps and bounds, whereas *organic growth* is a matter of gradual expansion based on resources the company has generated from its own business operations.

A great deal of research has been done on acquisition as a method of corporate development. It shows that in a great majority of cases, the seller is the more satisfied party, while the buyer all too often regrets the acquisition. The techniques of acquisition and the process of administering the acquired business have been greatly improved in recent years so that buyers nowadays generally manage to avoid the most common traps for the unwary, like extrapolating result curves which are abnormally high due to temporary circumstances.

We sometimes hear of soufflé companies whose profit levels are inflated by a process of cost cutting that cannot be sustained in the long run and will eventually damage business. It is possible to hike profits considerably in the short-term by stopping expenditure on development of products, staff and markets.

Another pitfall connected with acquisition is the buyer's tendency to be in too much of a hurry to remould a going concern in order to match his own business structure, without paying enough attention to the factors that contributed to success before the acquisition. Apart from sabotaging the acquired company's corporate mission, the buyer risks losing its most capable people, in the worst case to competitors.

A considerable trap is the deleterious effect that acquisitions can have on the balance sheet. For one thing, return on invested capital (ROIC) must be calculated for the acquired company. The capital cost and risk premium which together represent the interest costs of the acquisition can turn what looked like a lucrative opportunity into a loss. Because leaders of solvent companies are under pressure from the stock market to reinvest funds, there is a tendency to ignore what happens in the balance sheet.

The acquisition itself is seen as a triumph for the managing director, but the effects taken together are often hidden. Even where a merger by and large leads to a reduction of costs for the new organization, the cost of the merger itself is seldom taken into account. The fusion of two companies often entails considerable extra costs which are often put down as an isolated cost but in fact continue as employees struggle to integrate incompatible system solutions or fight over posts and prestige. The search for greater yield is often an important link in pre-acquisition calculations.

Large mergers are usually expected to result in opportunities for *cross-selling*. When for example America On Line (AOL) bought Time Warner, the companies were expected to sell each other's subscriptions and advertising. Among other things, Time Warner was to deliver AOL services through its cable network. The same expectations were encouraged in the merger between City Corp and Travelers where City was to sell insurance for Travelers and broker services to millions of customers. At the same time Travelers was to sell banking services to its customer. A certain amount of cross-selling does occur, but almost never to the extent expected by the parties to the merger or acquisition.

We can distinguish five motives for acquisitions:

1. To fill a gap in a portfolio
2. To invest a surplus
3. To strengthen a business unit
4. To build an empire
5. Growth and change

It is only recently that we have begun to really understand the psychological forces that lead to structural change in organizations. The motives involved often seem to lack a rational dimension, which is why much structural business can only be understood by adding a large dose of psychology. As a general rule, people want to grow and have more power and influence over other people and have more money into the bargain. This is a natural and often legitimate compulsion. If it did not exist, industrial development over the last few hundred years would have been severely compromized.

Research that resulted in the book *Good To Great*, by Jim Collins of Denver University, showed that companies which had unbroken success over a long period of time had only in exceptional cases undergone structural changes. Mergers and acquisitions make the headlines and put the spotlight on management. Managers of the companies which Jim Collins identified as most successful in the long-term have not been particularly high-profile but their companies have grown organically with time and without spectacular changes. To take a couple of examples, in Sweden, there is Scania which for decades has been the world's most profitable producer of heavy lorries – without structural change – and there is IKEA. The combination of carefully planned operations and organic growth is a recipe for success that is hard to beat.

The difference between being managing director of a company and Chief Executive Officer of a portfolio is considerable, and one that is not always appreciated. The manager of a business unit can work on organic growth and efficiency in the form of product development, improved production methods, cost and capital rationalization, marketing, and so on. When the same person is promoted to lead a portfolio, i.e. is responsible for a group of business units under common ownership, his or her freedom of action can be severely impaired. As portfolio CEO, s/he now has other people in charge of development in the units. But the new CEO can show drive by getting involved in structural business. It makes for headlines in the business papers and leads to interviews and often positive price trends in the short-term. The organization's portfolio strategy has now taken on a completely different character. Group boards should therefore consider the matter carefully before contemplating a merger, acquisition, or sales of a company.

There is a wealth of literature on the subject giving checklists, screening methods and other techniques applicable to acquisition. The latest research offers a good guide to the 'dos and don'ts'. Here are some important questions for consideration:

- **How much profit is the candidate for acquisition expected to generate?** It is becoming common practice to link the purchase price to the growth rate of the candidate's earnings, so that the seller is made to give a firm undertaking. Expectations of future earnings must of course be weighed against the purchase price, so that an assessment of how realistic those expectations are can often be a useful check question.

- **Can a weakness in the candidate be corrected?** Replacing the management is one possibility already mentioned. In other cases the buyer may have noted weaknesses in marketing organization, production or other functions that can be put right immediately and thereby bring about speedy improvement in profitability.

- **Will the acquisition complement the present portfolio and, if so, how?** Advocates of planned acquisition often argue for synergies which are in fact hard to realize. Especially where the real motive is empire building, there is a tendency to camouflage that motive by pointing to synergies of a diffuse nature. It can be legitimate to make such bogus synergies the cover story for public consumption, as long as the buyer is honest with himself and recognizes what the real motives are.

- **How much is the acquisition worth?** An answer to this question can be obtained by proceeding from the top price we are willing to pay bearing in mind the value the acquisition can have for our own company. This kind of reasoning is often very helpful in clarifying the framework of negotiations. Though due deliberation before decision is a virtue as far as acquisitions are concerned, there is seldom much time for it.

The purpose of this entry is to clarify the true motives for acquisition: to offer a few points to ponder and questions to ask. We would like to mention in conclusion that we have known heads of companies who, with very little formal analysis, have made entrepreneurial acquisitions that turned out to be enormously successful.

RECOMMENDED READING

1. Bill Vlasic, Taken for a Ride: How Daimler-Benz Drove Off With Chrysler.

2. Patric A Gaughan, Mergers, Acquisitions, and Corporate Restructurings.

3. Robert J Aiello et al, Harvard Business Review on Mergers & Acquisitions.

Mintzberg's five structures

Henry Mintzberg is one of the organization researchers who have strongly influenced thought, particularly during the 1970s and 1980s. His thinking is based on the proposition that organizations contain a number of forces that interact dynamically to create various contours. The figure opposite shows the five principal structures postulated by Mintzberg and the characteristics of each type.

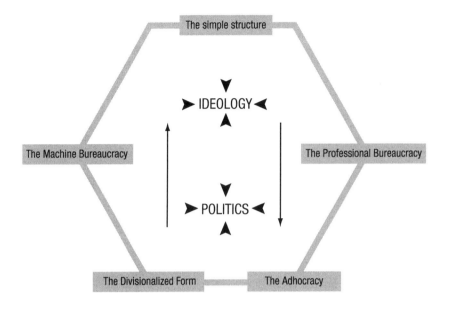

The simple structure

The *simple structure* is characterized above by what is missing in its development. It has little or no techno-structure, few people in support functions, minimum differentiation between units and a low management hierarchy. Very little of its behaviour is formalized and it makes hardly any use of planning, training or communications. It is primarily organic.

Coordination within the simple structure is mostly handled by direct supervision. The top person has power over all decisions. The structure often consists of an organic nucleus with one person in charge.

The environment of the simple structure tends to be both simple and dynamic. A simple environment can be grasped by one person who is therefore able to make all the decisions. A dynamic environment calls for an organic structure, which is one of the characteristics of the simple structure. The simple structure is often a transient phase in the development of an organization.

The machine bureaucracy

A national postal service, a steelworks, and a big car manufacturing company: all these organizations have a number of structural character- istics in common. Their operations are of a routine nature, often simple and repetitive, and result in heavily standardized procedures. These factors produce the *machine bureaucracies* in our society: structures that work like integrated, regulated machines.

The work done by the operative nucleus is here rationalized to the extreme and seldom calls for advanced training. The primary coordination mech- anism is the standardization of work routines.

Because the machine bureaucracy relies so heavily on standardized routines, the techno-structure emerges as the most important aspect of this contour. It is manned by analysts who acquire great informal power, even though they are not part of the line organization, because they are the ones who standardise everyone else's work.

The professional bureaucracy

Organizations can be bureaucratic without being centralized. These organ- izations are characterized by stable operative work that gives rise to predictable, standardized behaviour. But they are also complex and must therefore be under the direct control of the operators who do the work. Because of this, structures of this kind resort to a coordination mechanism that simultaneously embraces both standardization and decentralization – standardization of know-how.

The professional bureaucracy, commonly found in universities, hospitals, school administrations and similar organizations, relies on the skills of its professional operatives. The organization hires highly educated special- ists for its operative nucleus and gives them wide latitude to organize their own work. This autonomy means that the specialist works independently of his or her colleagues, but close to the customers who s/he serves. A teacher, for example, is in sole charge of her classroom and in close contact with her pupils.

The divisionalized form

The divisionalized form is not so much an integrated organization as a number of quasi-autonomous units, linked by a central administration. Its units are usually called divisions (possibly organized as subsidiary companies), while the central administration is known as the *head office*.

Divisions are created to correspond to the markets the business wants to serve, and are given control of the operative functions needed to provide service to those markets. Separation of operative functions makes the units mutually independent, enabling each one to operate as an autonomous unit that is not required to cooperate with the others.

Decentralization in the divisionalized form is fairly limited. It need go no further than the executives appointed to head the divisions, and often stops there.

Some kind of coordination between units is always needed in order to take advantage of central resources. This is done through control of performance; the chief coordinating mechanism, in other words, is standardization of result reporting. See also *Business unit.*

The adhocracy

'Ad hoc' is a Latin expression meaning, 'for a particular purpose at hand'. None of the contours discussed thus far provides an environment conducive to sophisticated innovation or creative problem-solving. The machine bureaucracy and professional bureaucracy are both performance-oriented, not problem-oriented structures. The creation of an environment for problem-solving calls for a fifth and very special type of structure that can bring together experts from different disciplines in smoothly functioning *ad hoc* project groups.

The adhocracy is very much an organic structure with a low degree of behaviour formalization, a high degree of horizontal work specialization based on training, and a tendency to group specialists in functional units for purposes of internal administration but in small market-based project groups to do the actual work. It encourages mutual give and take, which is its most important coordination mechanism. Invention implies the breaking of old patterns, so an innovative adhocracy must eschew any form of standardization.

Mintzberg's strategy analysis

In 1973, Henry Mintzberg wrote a famous article on business strategy entitled 'Strategy Making in Three Modes'. It marked the start of a new approach to issues of strategy, as its publication coincided with the emergence of the new insights into the crucial factors for success in business and industry that began to gain ground in the mid-1970s.

Mintzberg distinguishes between three different kinds of strategy development:

The planning model

1. Strategy determination is a deliberate, fully conscious and controlled thought process.

2. This model views strategy as a planning process. The result is relatively standardized and is usually expressed as a position.

3. This model designates the Chief Executive Officer, supported by a planning staff, as the chief architect responsible for designing the strategy of the organization.

4. The model assumes that strategy implementation will follow strategy determination in a specified timeframe.

5. The planning process will produce fully developed strategies, which will be formulated and communicated in various ways.

6. This classical model assumes the existence of central staffs and aims at a strategic position or portfolio strategies.

Entrepreneurial-type vision model

1. Strategy formulation is a semi-conscious process which takes place in the mind of the entrepreneurial leader.

2. Long experience of trade logic and deep insight into trends enable the leader to formulate a vision, a scenario, of which way the business will have to go in the future.

3. The vision serves as an umbrella under which specific decisions can be made and detailed plans and activities developed.

4. The vision must remain informal and personal to preserve its fertility and flexibility.

Learning-by-experience model

1. Strategy determination is an evolutionary process of a repetitive nature requiring mutual give-and-take.

2. Strategy is a pattern generated by impulses from the outside world received as strategy is implemented.

3. Strategies can arise from the dynamics of an organization; embraced by a large number of people, they can fertilize and infuse the behaviour of the whole organization.

4. The process of fertilization may be either spontaneous or managed. The latter involves a smaller degree of control than that required to identify the emergence of strategies and intervene as necessary.

In the field of strategy, Henry Mintzberg is a member of the group that reacted against the way the planning technocracy, especially in the USA had, so to speak, claimed the exclusive right to formulate strategic issues. According to Mintzberg and others, this had led to the deprecation of visionary leadership.

RECOMMENDED READING

1. Henry Mintzberg, The Rise and Fall of Strategic Planning.

2. Henry Mintzberg et al, The Strategy Process: Concepts – Context – Cases.

3. Henry Mintzberg, Bruce Ahlstrand and Joseph Lampel, Strategy Safari: A Guided Tour Through the Wilds of Strategic Management.

Motivation

Motivation, to put it briefly, is what makes an individual act and behave in a certain way. It is a combination of intellectual, physiological and psychological processes that determines, in a given situation, how vigorously we act and in what direction our energy is channelled.

Herzberg's two factor theory is a well-known motivation theory that was based on a thorough analysis of 200 auditors and engineers. The two 'factors' in his theory refer to sets of hygiene factors and motivation factors, or 'motivators'. If the hygiene factors are not satisfied, employees are dissatisfied and unmotivated. If only the hygiene factors are satisfied, co-workers are not dissatisfied but they are not motivated either. If both factors in the theory are satisfied, co-workers are happy and motivated.

The hygiene factors in Herzberg's theory are:

- company policy and administration
- salary and other forms of remuneration
- level and quality of supervision
- quality of interpersonal relations
- working conditions
- job security

Among the motivators were:

- status
- personal growth and advancement
- recognition
- responsibility
- challenges and stimulation at work
- personal development and self-actualization

According to Herzberg, the important indicators of low motivation in co-workers are:

- low productivity
- low service levels and poor quality

- conflicts (strikes, personal disputes, etc.)
- dissatisfaction with salary or working conditions

Herzberg suggests the following three measures to increase employee motivation:

1. greater responsibility
2. rotation of work
3. job enrichment

The other well-known motivation theory is Maslow's pyramid of needs, which is described in the entry under *Needs*.

There are innumerable classifications of human motives. The reason why motives are so interesting is that they are actually a synonym for needs.

Motives and needs, in their turn, provide the basic key to all organized activity, especially business activity.

In his book *Psychology and Work Organization (Psykologi och arbetsorganization)*, Sven Söderberg cites a classification made by the Danish psychologist K. B. Madsen. Madsen distinguished a number of basic motives, which he divided into four groups:

1. Organic motives

   a. Hunger

   b. Thirst

   c. Sexual urge

   d. Maternal urge

   e. Avoidance of cold (self-protection)

   f. Avoidance of heat

   g. Anal urge (excretion)

   h. Urge to breathe

2. Emotional motives

   a. Fear or security motive

   b. Aggression or combative motive

3. Social motives

    a.   Desire for contact

    b.   Desire for power (self-assertion)

    c.   Desire to perform

4. Activity motives

    a.   Need for experience

    b.   Need for physical action

    c.   Curiosity (intellectual activity)

    d.   Need for excitement (emotional activity)

    e.   Creative urge (complex activity)

The way people act, their buying behaviour for example, is generally controlled by a number of simultaneously acting motivational forces. Motive systems thus arise which are a complex of different motives that in their turn control a certain pattern of behaviour. When motive systems block each other, or are mutually opposed we speak of conflicting motives.

Individual variations in areas of interest are an expression of motive systems. They may comprise physical action, curiosity, excitement, or experience in general and creative activity. The performance, power and contact motives are others that often occur in motive systems. All the components of a motive system are important to the performance of a certain action, a job of work, for example. It is therefore to the benefit of the individual, his employer and society at large if he takes an interest in his work. Interest is a powerful driving force, a motive system in itself, in fact.

Madsen puts it like this:

It is important that the activity motive gets maximum satisfaction from work. In any work situation it is possible to create variation in order to satisfy the motives of physical action, excitement and curiosity. It is also important to satisfy the performance motive. As Frederick Taylor, the American management theorist, once expressed it, it is a matter of putting the right person in the right place, so that all individuals feel they are exercizing their powers to the full. Finally, it is important to satisfy the contact motive. If this is not possible in the actual work situation, opportunities for leisure-time contact must be provided.

The social motives, specifically the performance motive, are present in all of us in varying degrees. Suppose that we could enhance the performance motive in an organization just a little: it would result in a substantial boost to that organization's charge of energy, for social motives can be influenced. They are strongly affected by the environment in which we find ourselves and the things that inspire our confidence.

Well-known names in motivational research, apart from Abraham Maslow and Frederick Herzberg, who we mentioned earlier, are Victor H Vroom and David McClelland. These researchers and many business leaders underline the importance of understanding the driving forces that govern individual behaviour. This is true for an organization in which individual motives should ideally conform to the work assignments that have to be carried out. It is even truer however in relation to a management's understanding of the motive system of the customers it serves. Segmentation, or the division of a market into subsets of customers with similar needs, is built on motive systems.

It is Victor Vroom who has most strongly underlined the importance of relating an individual's motivation and acts to the goals of the organization and of the individual himself. If we understand these relationships, we will also understand why an individual chooses to act in one way rather than another.

RECOMMENDED READING

1. Frederick Herzberg, One More Time: How Do You Motivate Employees?

2. Jim Tompkins, Think Outside the Box: The Most Trite, Generic, Hokey, Overused,Clichéd or Unmotivating Motivational Slogans.

3. Ken Blanchard, Gung Ho! Turn On The People in Any Organization.

Needs

Needs are an expression of underlying motives that control demand. Thus need and demand are not the same thing. Let us take an example. All human beings have a need to feel successful. That is why people often prefer to reduce their burden of responsibility to a load that they can handle successfully, rather than keep on carrying more responsibility that they feel is too much for them.

One way to satisfy the need for success is to display symbols of success.

For a company executive, this may mean acquiring a turbo-charged car or an expensive watch. In this case the underlying need is the desire to feel and display success, whereas the demand can take a variety of forms.

Needs in the most widely differing contexts can likewise express themselves in different ways. The need of a businessman to feel successful by heading a profitable company can express itself in a business development programme, a planned reduction of costs or of tied-up capital through inventory cut-back, a reduction of receivables or the sale of some fixed asset.

Discussions of need and demand are apt to become complicated. There are two reasons for this:

1. Many people do not know the difference between need and demand.

2. It is important to enter the hierarchy of needs at the right level, the one that is relevant to what we want to talk about.

The latter point may seem somewhat cryptic, but if for example we talk about the needs that an air freight service satisfies, it is enough to address the buyers' needs for rational transport to improve the profitability of their own operations.

It is unnecessary to go to the level of a chief executive's need to feel successful by running a successful business. That level is irrelevant to the situation in hand. In the same way it can be relevant for Coca Cola to define its customer need as the need for soft drinks, which in turn may be expressed in a demand for Coca Cola.

A definition of customer need as *satisfaction* would be too broad to be meaningful, while the need of *soft drinks* would be too narrow.

The concept of needs is also treated from other perspectives in the sections on *Business Concept* and *Motivation*.

One problem with needs is that the relevant need structures change with time. The word 'relevant' refers to the needs that are crucial in a business situation. An example of this can be taken from the car industry. The motor trade's analysts long assumed that we motorists choose our cars on the basis of a rational trade-off between price and performance. That was why mass production, the 'world car' and cheap cars were the predominant strategic themes throughout the 1970s. The rational man's weakness is that he tends to ignore the psychological shadings of need structures, and thus falls into the rationality trap.

An understanding of how need influences demand is a fundamental and necessary ability in business. If the consumer co-operative movement fails to realize that shopping for groceries ought to be a pleasant experience that satisfies a need for entertainment, its prospects of capturing new market shares will not be impressive. If it has also fallen into the rationality trap of believing that people look only at price and performance, it will have further demonstrated its failure to understand essential aspects of customers' needs. Another example: a large company selling complicated mechanical equipment had neglected its customers' legitimate need for good after-sales service in the form of spare parts and technical service, at reasonable prices and with quick delivery.

An area of need must be broken down into utility functions to identify all the variables that add up to customer-perceived quality.

Modern, entrepreneurial management is characterized by a strong and genuine interest in the need structures that control customer demand. That is where the key to successful businessmanship often lies.

Theoretically speaking, there are a number of models which seek to clarify our need structures as human beings. The best known of these is Maslow's Hierarchy of Needs, as illustrated by the pyramid below.

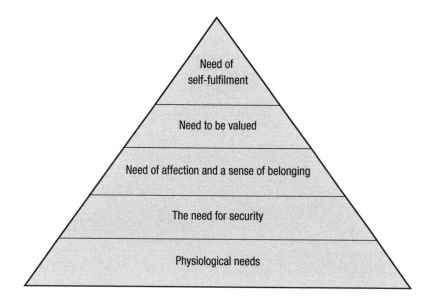

When a relatively primitive need in the hierarchy has been satisfied, a more sophisticated need will be felt. Except for the last stage of self-fulfilment, needs become less important once they have been satisfied.

Some other well-known needs models are given in the table overleaf.

THEORY	NEEDS STRUCTURE	PRINCIPLES
Alderfer	1. Existence 2. Relatedness 3. Personal development	No special emphasis is laid on the order of needs. The importance of a need increases once it has been satisfied.
Herzberg "Dual-factor theory"	1. Hygiene (external factors) 2. Motivation (internal factors)	The lowest level (hygiene) must be fulfilled. Hygiene corresponds to Maslow's lower levels of needs and motivation corresponds to the higher levels.
McClelland	1. Power 2. Intimacy and affiliation 3. Achievement	Key to McClellands model is the notion that needs are learned and can be changed in the relatively short term. The need for power is at the lowest level of needs and the need for achievement at the highest.

RECOMMENDED READING

1. Abraham H Maslow, Maslow on Management.
2. Jill Griffin, Customer Loyalty: How to Earn It, How to Keep It.

Organic growth

The word organic comes from the natural sciences – principally biology and chemistry –and indicates the chain structure of carbon atoms in organic molecules. By analogy, the term organic growth has been adopted in the business world to mean expansion based on an existing corporate structure, as distinct from expansion by diversification or acquisition.

Generally speaking, there are three ways for a company to grow:

1. Organic growth as described here
2. Branching out into other lines of business (diversification)
3. Through structural change, i.e. acquisitions, mergers or disposals.

For the businessman or businesswoman the ability to grow organically is always evidence of strength, because it is proof of their ability to improve business. A company that develops successfully from the base of its own resources has proved that it is competitive, that customers prefer its goods and services to those of its competitors. This assumes that its growth rate has exceeded that of the market, meaning that it has captured market share.

Competition is the driving force in any business. A performance chart compares performance against competitors and shows market share, profitability and growth. A company's organic growth is in fact a reflection of its ability to compete: its ability to develop new products and win new geographical markets or market segments.

 Often, however, managements find the process of organic growth too slow, and try to speed it up by buying companies. This is a risky business, as the odds against success are high. The most important thing to bear in mind in this context, however, is that the risk of failure in acquisition rises sharply if your own business is not already growing.

There are many examples of companies using their financial muscle to make acquisitions. A fat wallet may call for takeover bids or mergers but the consequences of carrying them out may not have been properly thought out. The AOL (America On Line) bid for Time Warner is an example. A booming stock market around the millennium put a high value on AOL, which thought it saw fruitful synergies in the merger. These synergies never fully materialized however.

Successful development in one's own business, which finds expression in organic growth of various kinds, is valuable insurance where mergers are concerned. In knowledge-related industries, growth on the basis of one's own resources is more meaningful than in companies with a physical product, since acquisitions in knowledge companies relates to the know-how of individuals, and people do not necessarily stick with the same company throughout their careers.

One example of organic growth is SAS's development of catering into a separate business unit, Service Partner. Saab has used its experience in military aviation to build passenger planes. Research carried out by Jim Collins, the writer on management subjects, shows that success stories, emerging after companies have been in business for decades, have their basis in organic growth. Businesses like these do not make the headlines with spectacular structural changes. But they do create value, not only for their shareholders, but also for employees and customers. Scania, Nokia and 3M are examples of companies that have systematically nurtured organic development.

Organic growth can be distinguished from other forms of growth:

1. We use the term organic growth in contrast to growth by acquisition, that is, by buying other companies or shares in them.

2. We also use the term organic growth in contrast to ventures into new types of business unrelated to a company's basic operations.

3. Organic growth results from a company's competence in respect of its products and markets, rather than from its financial competence, which is the basis for its structural growth.

4. Competitive strength is closely connected to organic growth.

RECOMMENDED READING

1. Adrian J Slywotzky and Richard Wise, with Karl Weber, How to Grow When Markets Don't.

2. Craig Terrill and Arthur Middlebrooks, Market Leadership Strategies for Service Companies: Creating Growth, Profits, and Customer Loyalty.

Organization

The term 'organization' can be variously interpreted. Meanwhile, the concept of an organization has had an enormous influence on human behaviour, company development and on the development of organizations in general. Many researchers with a background in behavioural psychology have looked at the interplay between people and organizations with a view to creating added value. About 60 years ago, Chester I Barnard defined an organization "A system of consciously coordinated activities or forces of two or more persons."

This simply means that people gather together to perform a task and coordinate their energies with a common purpose. We can think of exceptions to this definition of organization, such as in stochastic organizations as when, for example, three people agree to put a boat out to sea. This operation may have a once-for-all character but if these three individuals decided to put boats to sea on a regular basis, an organization would result. An organization as a concept demands some kind of formal planning.

Edgard Schein, an organizational psychologist and Professor of Management at MIT, has defined four categories of organization:

1. **Coordination** – individuals who gather together and coordinate their mental and physical energies can achieve great things such as the pyramids of Egypt, a cure for Aids, journeys to Mars, and so on.

2. **Common goals** – this is a necessary condition to coordinate the energies of everyone striving for something they all want.

3. **Division of labour** – leads to specialization by dividing up work tasks so that our resources can be used more efficiently.

4. **Hierarchical structure** – means the right to direct the actions of others. It is difficult to coordinate the energy of a group of people without a clear decision hierarchy.

The last point may seem somewhat controversial in the light of the tendency in recent years towards 'flat' organizations. As an organizational theorist once put it, "Hierarchies may at first seem difficult to accept as there is the idea that they smother initiative, suppress creativity and therefore belong to the past. However, twenty years of experience has convinced me that hierarchical organizations are the most effective and natural structures we have."

With the right structure and the right people, hierarchies can release energy and creativity to form an effective organization and improve the working environment.

Organizations are basically structured as follows:

1. **The simple structure** means that there is no formal structure at all. This is common in small companies, where everybody more or less does everything.

2. **The functional structure** is based on the main company functions of production, finance, marketing and personnel.

3. **The divisional structure** means that the organization is divided into sub-groups called divisions which are based on products, services, geographical areas or market segments.

4. **The matrix organization** is a combination of structures which take into account at least two of the following dimensions: product, geography, function and market.

5. **The virtual organization and network** is an organizational model which extends beyond the company itself to include other players.

6. **Intermediary structures** which are simply variations on the above basic structures, or transitional forms between one structure and another.

7. **The process** which comprises a flow of activities to give optimal delivery.

Classical organizational theory is based on a centralized policy function which issues directives to be acted upon. Proponents of this approach, among them Taylor, Fayol and Weber, have based their ideas on the following factors:

1. Far-reaching division of labour

2. Delimited areas of responsibility

3. Hierarchical structure

4. Communication through superiors

5. Formal authority

6. Management by rules and instructions

7. Impersonal contact through formal channels

8. Statutory system of promotion according to years of service, and so on.

In a world that is becoming more and more decentralized, this list would seem to be an anachronism, to put it mildly. A significant swing of the pendulum in the other direction took place in the 1990s, when the blessings of the flat organization were proclaimed. Research has recently shown that a flat organizational structure is by no means always to be desired. In fact, there is nothing to prove that flat organizations are in themselves superior to any other form of organization. Here is a summary of essential factors to be considered in any organization.

Centralized and decentralized

No organization is so simple that work can be arranged to be either centralized or decentralized. There must be a balance between the two, and with this in mind, the following points have been selected to serve as a guide in analytical work.

1. Advantages of scale and skull

2. Strategic sense

3. Need for local initiatives

4. Management overview

5. Advantages of small-scale operations

What we call 'advantages of scale and skull' refers to a company's need to operate on a sound financial basis, where a critical mass of volume and competence forms a basis for effective production.

A car manufacturer cannot deliver a Volkswagen to Germany and a Volvo to Sweden. It has to coordinate a number of factors including careful management of the trademark and research and development, to name just a couple of the elements of a successful strategy.

Processes in sales, service and after sales call for local initiatives. There must be some variation and adaptation to local conditions even if economies of scale can be exploited in the whole organization.

In some cases the demand for uniformity in respect of accounting principles has even been dropped, making the job of the controller impossible, for instance if the costs of network building are entered as a cost somewhere but activated in the balance sheet somewhere else.

Small-scale advantages comprise a number of factors of a behavioural character. The most important of these are:

1. Motivation grows, energy levels increase.

2. Easy communication

3. Immediacy of customer demands

4. Processes can be optimized without being suspended.

5. Economization of resources through thrift

6. Greater flexibility in the work force; people help each other as a matter of course.

The above analysis is intended to produce a satisfactory centralized, as well as decentralized, distribution of work tasks.

The one-man business

When a new company is started with one employee, this person does all the jobs, as in the simple structure. This work is divided up as soon as the company expands ("I will do this and you will do that"). This leads to specialization in work but also creates a distance between functions which has to be somehow bridged. Seen from this perspective, an organization comprises the following elements:

1. Division of work

2. Work specialization

3. Working methods

Gaps that must be bridged will appear between functions once work has been distributed and certain tasks have undergone specialization to raise the level of efficiency. Processes are established and meetings and other opportunities to exchange information are set up to bridge gaps and enable companies to work smoothly.

The larger the organization the greater the degree of specialization, and the more complex the organization's internal structure will be. A disaster scenario is the large organization in which the work of coordinating functions calls for such a dedication of its resources that an increasingly smaller share is directed externally to is customers. The organization is then on the way to becoming a neutron star or black hole, with all its available energy concentrated internally.

Managing dependencies

However, it may be that we human beings often wish we could act independently of others, freely and honestly, so that we would not have to be constantly taking some condition or other into account, a large, complex organization can be seen as a number of situations, each one dependent on the other. Some of the most important factors that give rise to interdependencies in an organization are:

- Products
- Customer groups
- Geographical areas
- Customers' industry classification
- Applications
- Internal specialization units
- Reporting requirements

Large companies often endanger the flow of their operations through a desire to create an organization that takes all of these factors into consideration. Some years ago, an American telecoms company attempted to reorganize itself from a customer perspective on the basis of seven interdependent factors. The team which was finally put together had bigger problems with the company's internal organization than with its customers, problems which seriously compromized its effectiveness. Sometimes we simply have to ignore certain interdependent relationships, giving attention to the most important ones and letting the others become part of the culture, to be dealt with when necessary.

Zero-based solutions

Some years ago we met a middle manager in one of the more rarefied business spheres who did not know who he delivered to, who it was who evaluated his delivery and how what he delivered added to the value of his end-customer, i.e. the external buyer. Group management had so tangled up the organization that intelligent engineers were not able to understand their contribution to the whole.

A zero-base initiative, in which people, investments and relationships are all cast to one side, can in many cases prove to be very useful. We begin with a sheet of paper and a given number of customers with their demand for an essentially given set of goods and services. If a number of things complicating matters can be shut out, we can sometimes approach organizational problems with a fresh outlook and solve them more easily.

Zero-base thinking is especially important as organizational issues are sensitive and can affect the careers of individuals as well as their relationships with others.

From a production economy to customer value

Below is a representation of what is in principle a simple process but in fact a difficult one: the transition from competence and manufacturing preparedness to the satisfaction of customer needs.

It can be useful to see the stage of production competence to customer satisfaction as a number of interfaces that transform effective production into customer satisfaction. Production does not take place on a sound financial basis if everything is adapted to the customer. If, on the other hand, we only cater to the needs of a production economy, we are not satisfying our customers. Toyota was a pioneer when it demonstrated, some 40 years ago, that we could exploit economies of scale in production and at the same time make allowances for the factors that created customer value.

The process perspective

There was a movement at the end of the 1980s and the beginning of the 1990s in favour of the process perspective, i.e. a succession of activities resulting in a product or service. The process perspective was in vogue when most of the world was suffering a recession. The book *Business Process Re-engineering* was published and BPR became synonymous with cutbacks and reductions. As a result, the process perspective got something of a bad reputation.

The process perspective can in many cases be relevant and rewarding. Poor organization can often result in the suspension of processes and sub-optimization, unnecessary work and other discontinuities. An altogether too rigorous application of the process perspective can however lead to models which obstruct the work of the whole organization. The relevance of process orientation depends on which aspect dominates – the customer aspect or the production aspect.

By production aspect we mean the need for optimal work specialization and by customer aspect we mean the importance of a satisfactory delivery to customers. If an airline has a need for heavy industrial maintenance, the degree of specialization called for is such that this function should be carried out by a separate unit. If, on the other hand, a telephone exchange must be installed for a customer, functionality would be such an important factor that the delivery of hardware, software and installation should be seen as a single process. For more on this, see *Processes and Process orientation*.

Virtual organization

In 1992 Ronald Coase received the 'Nobel Prize in economics' for an article ('The nature of the firm') that he had written a long time before. Coase was interested in where a company began and ended, and why it did so in both cases. The concept of virtual organization has emerged in the wake of these thoughts as an expression of the coordination between different suppliers and deliveries to the customer that represent a total solution.

A fundamental rule in strategic planning is that low competitive pressure leads to diversification mania. This implies that traditionally protected industries such as the airlines industry, telecommunications, energy, and so on, themselves carry out work which, when they experience heavy competition, is outsourced to specialized companies. Flextronics manufacturing and service in the telecoms industry is an example of this. The term virtual means 'apparent' or 'illusory', and here indicates an informal organization where internal transactions and a planned economy are replaced by external transactions and a market economy to enable a certain delivery to the customer.

Questions of decisions as against behaviour and competence

Decisions on organizational change often result in changes that may be of academic interest but have no real effect on an organization's effectiveness. It is easy to make decisions to change an organization's structure, but another thing to change the organization's competence and behaviour and achieve the co-worker participation necessary if the changed structure is to be understood and accepted.

Changes not accepted are often sabotaged. The organization's effectiveness suffers, resulting in a fall in customer-perceived utility. In many cases, therefore, it can be better to leave things as they are, even if the organization would be better off with a different structure, rather than to create confusion in the organization with a loss of effectiveness as a result.

Strategy comes before organization

Alfred Chandler, a professor at the Harvard Business School, said as early as the 1960s, that "organization follows strategy". He was referring to the tendency of business leaders to make changes to organizational structure unconnected to strategy. Strategy is defined here as 'a pattern of decisions and actions in the present, undertaken to make the most of opportunities and secure future success'. It is possible to organize structures so that operations are left in their currently efficient state, but whether such changes will have any affect on long-term success is another matter.

A dilemma that business leaders often have is the difficulty of providing for efficient operations in real time and at the same time developing a strategy to ensure future success. There can be significant differences in alignment between management and employees in this connection. The aim of a company's operations is, given a set of conditions, to provide the organization with a sound financial base. The aim of its strategy is to change the conditions that control its operations. For more on this see the section under *Strategy*.

RECOMMENDED READING

1. Henry Mintzberg, Structures in Fives: Designing Effective Organizations.

2. Jay R Galbraith, Designing Organizations: An Executive Guide to Strategy, Structure, and Process.

3. Margaret R Davis and David A Weckler, A Practical Guide to Organization Design.

Outsourcing

Outsourcing is seen by some as a euphemism for cutbacks in staff or capacity. Others see it as an effective way of concentrating on core business by hiving off unimportant parts of a company to a core business somewhere else. This concept used to be called a make/buy analysis (see this term).

Outsourcing has a place in organizations plagued by diversification. If it is regarded by many as a defensive tactic, its mirror image, insourcing, could be termed an aggressive tactic in business development (see *Insourcing*). If for example a company selling capital goods wanted to rationalize its contract leasing business, a finance company could offer to insource the business, thus increasing its volumes and effectiveness.

One of the fundamental questions in strategic planning is the connection between competitive pressure, effectiveness and unwise diversification. The lower the pressure from competitors, the lower effectiveness becomes and the greater the temptation to diversify.

One could say that outsourcing is what happens when internal transactions in a planned economy become external transactions in a market economy.

Four important factors form a basis for consultation and decision in relation to outsourcing. They are:

1. Financial rationalization
2. Psychological aspects for concentration and motivation
3. Flexibility in maintaining the ability to change
4. Political ideology

Financial rationalization

The rational factor has its origins in advantages of skull and scale (skull = cranium, i.e. the repository of competence) and is based on the fact that processes and functions in a company can operate more effectively, i.e. with lower costs per unit or higher customer value, if economies of scale are exploited. This perspective is based on the fundamental principles of work specialization and distribution in organizational theory.

The financial/rational aspects are many and many-faceted. All of these aspects should be considered when an audit is carried out on a candidate for outsourcing. An effectiveness diagram (see *Effectiveness*) can be used for the identification of candidates for outsourcing.

The formula for value-added productivity is an excellent litmus test for outsourcing. This relatively unknown concept is most useful, as it takes both automation and make/buy reasoning into account.

The formula is given here:

$$\frac{\text{revenue} - (\text{purchases} + \text{costs} + \text{depreciation} + \text{interest})}{\text{number of employees}}$$

In outsourcing the denominator decreases because the number of employees goes down. At the same time costs go up for purchases, which then reduces the numerator. The net outcome should be positive if a candidate is worth outsourcing. This formula also takes automation into account. Investment in automation should reduce the denominator (number of employees) more than the numerator (depreciation and interest) to give a positive figure. The value-added productivity formula can be used to make comparisons between industries as well as for comparative studies in the same industry. It can be adapted for use with one's own company in connection with outsourcing.

If an analysis shows that outsourcing is a viable proposition, the difficult divorce proceedings must begin, i.e. the transition from the current situation to the new one with the business outsourced. We recommend that this process should be done in two stages. The first stage is to decide whether the business is a suitable candidate for outsourcing. If the answer is in the affirmative, the problem of how, and in what timeframe, this is to be done, is dealt with next. The first question deals with what has to be done, the second one with how.

Psychological factors in concentration and motivation

Also involved is an irrational factor of a psychological nature, mainly in relation to three things: the advantages of entrepreneurship, management's concentration on its core business and the business unit's career in a new core business as a result of outsourcing. The market economy bears witness to the fact that independent actors are more flexible, work harder and take greater risks than when they enjoyed protected status. These are important drivers for any business but especially for one which is to be outsourced.

The importance of concentrating on the core business – the corporate mission's most important element – cannot be exaggerated. We do not have instruments to tell us the whys and the wherefores, but as things stand we can discern an empirically strong connection between such concentration and success on the one hand, and diffusion and a lack of success on the other.

Small-scale advantages and entrepreneurship both have an importance that may not be evident from a knowledge of traditional business economics. Independent players are more flexible, work harder and take bigger risks than businesses run within the framework of a large company.

Co-worker ambitions for a business that has been outsourced, together with the opportunities presented to further its development, are important drivers. People can experience great anxiety when faced with being outsourced from the parent's reassuring embrace. However, studies show that after a few years these same people look back on their outsourcing experience as a period of enormous excitement and innovation. Instead of doing work that could sometimes seem to be irrelevant or hum-drum, they were now at the heart of a new operation and a most important part of a corporate mission.

An important factor in outsourcing is escape from a situation where buyers are not free to choose what they want to buy. Buyers often become hyper-critical when they are forced to accept the goods and services of an internal unit. They will go to any lengths to find fault with deliveries and the internal supplier. When there is then the freedom to choose other goods or services, the buyer often over-reacts by ordering from any source as long as it is not their old internal supplier.

Flexibility in maintaining the ability to change

The third factor in consultations in respect of outsourcing concerns a management ambition to maintain flexibility. Conditions in the global market in which we now compete are changing so fast that it is worth a lot of money to companies and other organizations to be able to maintain flexibility, and not bind themselves to long fixed undertakings. European labour laws make it especially difficult to hire or keep people in businesses which are irrelevant to the corporate mission and which could therefore be outsourced with some advantage.

Flexibility can be a decisive factor in a company's success and an outsourcing manoeuvre can usually contribute to a company's flexibility both internally and externally.

However, we have to be clear by what we mean when we speak of flexibility. What theoretically can look like flexibility might in reality prove to be an illusion. Long contract periods with hard and fast business rules can work against flexibility, and prove to be as damaging as the worst effects of a planned economy.

Again, flexible contracts can work both for and against a company. Constant changes of supplier can cause suspensions to operations and other discontinuities. On the other hand, a business that is too stable may experience a fall in productivity and customer value. Another factor is sticking to outdated technology. A high level of integration and abundant planned economy can lead to a technological lock-in effect with businesses falling behind as a result. This is analogous to what is generally accepted, i.e. a market economy encourages renewal, a planned economy does not. Opportunities offered by the experience curve must be grasped if there is to be reconstruction, and so on.

Political ideology

Both traditionally right-wing and reformed left-wing parties favour the transition from a planned economy to a market economy and its emphasis on effectiveness. More and more of the production that used to be in the public sector is now under consideration for outsourcing. Where this is not the case the cause is more often a lack of competence rather than political convictions one way or the other.

Outsourcing, then, is a combination of complex financial analysis on the one hand and, on the other, an assessment of psychological factors that can only be noted. The element of uncertainty is sobering. To all of this can be added the difficulties inherent in going from an integrated business to one that is vulnerable to market forces.

A number of pitfalls and success factors are involved in actually carrying out outsourcing. Fixed costs will no longer be able to be absorbed as when the business is run in-company, for the reduction in operating volume resulting from outsourcing means that fixed costs will of course have to be distributed in the remaining organization. An airline which wants to outsource its heavy machine maintenance loses its contribution margins that cover all the common costs for management, administration, IT, etc, and the same thing applies to other functions such as cleaning, telephones, or office services.

RECOMMENDED READING

1. J Brian Heywood, The Outsourcing Dilemma: The Search for Competitiveness.

2. Maurice F Greaver, Strategic Outsourcing: A Structured Approach to Oursourcing Decisions and Initiatives.

3. Simon Domberger, The Contracting Organization: A Strategic Guide to Outsourcing.

PDCA (Plan, Do, Check and Act)

PDCA stands for Plan, Do, Check and Act. PDCA is a simple and popular concept originally used to analyze and develop processes but now applied to many other areas.

The concept was introduced in the 1930s by Walter Shewhart, now called the Godfather of PDCA, who was a statistician at Bell Laboratories in the USA. However, it was W Edwards Deming who came to represent PDCA when he popularized it in the 1950s. PDCA is often called the Deming wheel. Deming was one of the pioneers of quality assurance and his theories exerted a great influence in the reconstruction of Japanese industry after World War II. In 1951, the Japanese Society of Science and Engineering instituted the annual Deming Prize in his honour.

Deming developed the PDCA wheel as an analysis and measurement tool in order to identify deviation from customer demand. The model as used by him can be seen here together with a brief explanation.

The four phases of PDCA are:

Plan

Set up goals for changes that are to be carried out and establish methods to do so.

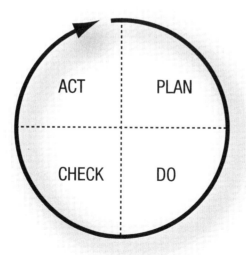

Do

Implement the changes conceived in the previous phase. Measure results and carry out any necessary training.

Check

Evaluate metrics and implementation work and analyze the result. Report to decision-makers if applicable.

Act

Take action on what has been learnt, then return to the plan phase.

RECOMMENDED READING

1. Mary Walton with W Edwards Deming, The Deming Management Method.

2. Walter A Shewhart, Statistical Method from the Viewpoint of Quality Control.

PDS (Problem Detection Study)

Almost all companies have some form of index for measuring customer satisfaction. An index, apart from being of use in marketing, can also be useful as a general sort of barometer. It is not a good idea to use one for improvement work, however. The fact that 85 per cent of customers are satisfied or very satisfied is not a directly useful indication as to what a company should do to become more customer-oriented.

What many companies have done in order to get around this is to begin with the problems which customers experience in their interaction with them. Actions that have the greatest effect on customer satisfaction can then be undertaken. This method is called a Problem Detection Study (PDS).

The PDS process involves starting with a number of in-depth interviews in order to formulate the problems connected with the use of a given product or service. The rough list of problems is then used as a basis for polling a large number of respondents. The results are then analyzed and evaluated.

A rough guide for carrying out a PDS is given in the illustration.

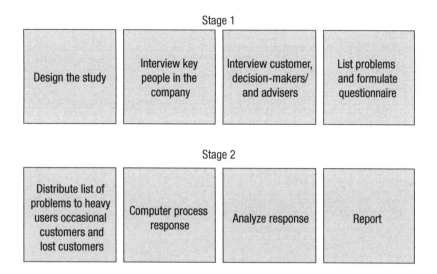

British Telecom carried out a PDS at the beginning of the 1990s. A large customer group was asked to rank the problems they experienced on the basis of a rough list of problem areas. Ten of the most important problem areas were then selected for improvement and action was taken. After about a year BT launched a customer response campaign with the following message:

- We asked you what problems you experienced in your relationship with us.

- The problems you indicated were the following.

- We have now taken action.

- We have listened to you, taken you seriously and corrected our behaviour.

Although this method does not get to the root of the customer need structures, it does often offer a good grasp of the problems that customers experience in using a particular product or service. The results of a problem detection study can often be utilized to make a company more competitive.

One of the best-known problem detection studies was one for dog food carried out in the USA. The three most highly valued characteristics of dog food were established through a number of studies:

- Gives a balanced diet
- Is very nutritious
- Contains vitamins

This information proved to be useless to the makers of dog food. Why?

First, because these characteristics were ones the makers already utilized in their advertising. The study had only given information that the manufacturers had themselves thrown out. Second, because these were things that the dogs benefited from and not so much the buyers of dog food. No dog, not even Rin Tin Tin, buys its own food, so why advertise for them?

According to the PDS, dog owners had completely different priorities. The study found their three biggest problems:

1. Dog food smells.
2. The dog has nothing to chew on.
3. Dog food does not come in different sizes.

To cure the problem of smell, an aromatic substance was inserted under the cover of the dog food tin. It smelt good to both master and mistress and the product was called 'dog stew'.

Dogs were given something to chew on by mixing hard bits into the soft tinned food and were thus fooled into chewing these bits which they then left.

Dog food tins did not come in different sizes in those days. The problem was that when a small dog was given a large tin, food was left over. This was put in the refrigerator and left a bad smell.

Size differentiation solved most of this problem, went on to be an enormous success and was copied by all the other dog food manufacturers in the industry.

In all, the problem detection study had proved a great success.

Performance management

Many companies have some form of system for measuring performance in different parts of the organization, so that business units, departments, managers and working groups can all be assessed.

But there are few successful measuring systems, ones that engender ambition and energy in employees and really raise their sights.

Employees all to often do not feel part of measuring systems and so such systems do not affect their attitudes. They are rewarded for some kind of performance goal that they do not understand and often have not even worked to achieve. Extra money and other rewards seem to be made on an arbitrary basis. It has been said that a leader's most important job is "to set goals and break them down so that they can be understood at the level of the individual".

It is not hard for managers to set performance goals for groups or individuals. However, they can appear to be arbitrary if people do not understand how they hang together with everything else in the company. Goals for the whole organization must be carefully broken down for its units. This is one of management's fundamental responsibilities and is decisive in the work of ensuring the effectiveness of its units, and thus the profitability of the organization as a whole.

Performance metrics often fail in their objectives because leading indicators are confused with lagging indicators. The interplay between leading and lagging indicators is developed below; it basically means that certain measurable goals result from other achievements in an organization. For instance, a measure of return on investment is a lagging indicator or a key ratio, while reduced stock is a leading indicator that in turn affects return on investment. Return on investment cannot be used as a leading indicator, but the amount of stock or the rate of turnover, can. See also the entry under *Goals*.

A general confusion about goals often exists in the public sector and non-profit organizations and it is not unusual to find goals directly conflicting with each other. This often contributes to unhappiness and discord in people who work in such organizations. Intelligent people who can see that goals conflict but cannot reason out why, are often overcome by frustration, turning into cynics or subversive critics of their organization.

It is very hard work to break down an organization's main goals into subgoals. For one thing, the parts must go through the same intellectual journey as the whole if they are to be able to relate to it and set their own goals. We have taken part in many benchmarking projects in which we saw that important parts of the organization did not have performance goals. Benchmarking means that we *must* have goals.

It is important to be acquainted with the goals/means hierarchy. What on one level is a means, on another level becomes a goal. If management has set as a goal to increase volume, and this is mainly to be achieved through product development, then one of the means can be to increase the work rate in this development. If it is decreed that this increase in volume will also take place through a strengthening of the sales organization, this gives the sales organization a goal in terms of number of new recruits, organization and sales results. Not many people can lay claim to this kind of logic; as a result, discussions of goals and strategy often lead to confusion.

Performance goals are often discussed in terms of volume: number of units delivered, revenue, frequency of complaints, customer satisfaction or whatever is important for the business. Attitudes, behaviour and results can all be measured. If the number of sales visits is considered to have a decisive effect on sales volumes, then sales visits can be measured – although what we are really after is greater sales volumes.

Below we give three important concepts in the measuring of performance: cognition, behaviour and results. Let us look for example at salespeople of key accounts in a bank who wish to get better results by achieving greater deposits and advances. Measurement is then done on three levels:

1. **Cognition** – people are agreed that an increase in the number of sales visits will lead to the desired result.

2. **Behaviour** means that the number of sales visits (what will lead to the end result) will be measured.

3. **Result** means that the figure for deposits and advances is measured – which was the result we wanted to achieve.

The goal of increasing deposits and advances gives us a means: increased number of sales visits. This in turn becomes a goal for the sales manager, who finds a way to reward the frequency of visits. In the illustration below is shown the hierarchy of goals and means which in its absence often leads to bewilderment. This is also an excellent exercise in going from key figures to leading indicators.

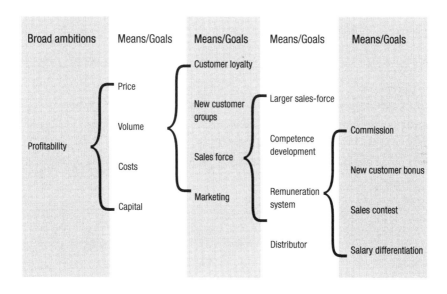

Here we have chosen expansion or increased volume as our main orientation. This is a means to achieve the goal of profitability but becomes, in its turn, a goal for the next level. A number of other means are offered there and we have chosen sales strength. This in turn becomes a goal which can be achieved by different means, of which reward system is one, etc.

Look to the result and not simply activities

It is vital to see that goals are set and that what is measured is the result, rather than the effort put in to achieving that result. It is easy to begin to measure various forms of activities, for example number of sales visits, in the belief that this will lead to the desired result.

Most people know that their company or organization must perform and that they must contribute to this performance. This knowledge is almost as deeply rooted in us as is common sense. No one will protest when we state that it is absolutely vital to focus on performance. In spite of this, it is not every organization that will take on the long and arduous process required to orientate its various parts so that they all work together for the good of the organization. Once we have accepted the idea that we should focus on results instead of activities, the next step is to select the metrics that correspond to the level of performance we want to achieve.

Measuring people

Relationship-oriented people are often disgusted by the idea that people should be evaluated by sets of figures. These people often have a background in behavioural science. They confuse traditionally technocratic key figures with other kinds of performance goals such as improved customer behaviour, faster lead times, increasing the percentage of newly developed products in total sales, etc.

We cannot escape the hard facts of business. Success in business is measured in figures, whether we like it or not. Everything else is a flight from reality. This is illustrated by the events in a variety of young, mostly IT-related companies, where the ability of intellectual capital and a humanistic approach has somehow been expected to lead to success and long-term prosperity, but, as we know, this is not a sound basis for a company's existence.

Management must look for ways to measure effectiveness in all organizational functions in order to secure the company's continued existence. Many people may suppose that consistent measurement is carried out purely to sustain mental agility. This is unfortunate and goes some way to explaining the virulent opposition to measuring. The world is full of de-standardized key figures, mountains of wasted endeavour that never had any effect whatsoever on business decisions. Measurement is not just a question of figures.

Proactive business leaders must try to focus on achieving greater effectiveness, because that is how value is created and with it the continued existence of their companies. Anything else is just wishful thinking. Concepts such as competence, intellectual capital, tacit knowledge, and so on, are all the means to the end of creating value for customers, employees and owners. The better all of this can be measured, the better a company will be run and the safer people's jobs will be. There is no getting around this simple truth.

Balanced perspective

Any evaluation of a company's performance must include financial terms like revenue, costs, profits and profitability. This is how businesses in an open market are evaluated, which should come as no surprise. Sophisticated methods have been developed to control and measure these figures, which are lagging indicators of other organized activities. In the 20th century simple features from the balance sheet and income statement have been developed into a complex web of financial indicators like share value, earnings per share, cash flow and share price in relation to sales.

The surest way to make your key figures worse is to concentrate purely on them. Modern measuring systems must take customers and employees into account and not merely owners, as all three are equally important. We do not need to know which stakeholder is the egg and which one the chicken or the hen. These stakeholder groups reward each other if the relationships between them are handled in the right way.

This is shown in the illustration.

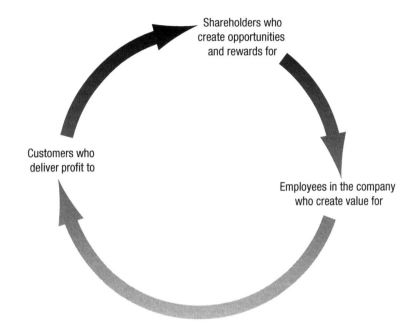

Shareholders who create opportunities and rewards for

Employees in the company who create value for

Customers who deliver profit to

Customer satisfaction and job satisfaction give financial gains. Take the way we use petrol, for example. We do not turn to an economist if we want to economize on petrol. Instead we ask people who know something about improving car performance, a garage for instance. A mechanic can adjust the engine timing, etc, so that our car gets more kilometres per litre of petrol. But apart from this we may have to change the way we drive, avoiding sudden acceleration and braking, and so on. We should know something about the workings of the internal-combustion engine but do not need to be able to understand a balance sheet.

An understanding of stakeholder needs and the relationship between leading indicators and lagging indicators is essential for all performance measurement.

RECOMMENDED READING

1. Bob Frost, Measuring Performance: Using the New Metrics to Deploy Strategy and Improve Performance.

2. Darryl D Enos, Performance Improvement: Making It Happen.

3. Peter F Drucker et al, Harvard Business Review on Measuring Corporate Performance.

PIMS (Profit Impact of Market Strategy)

PIMS stands for Profit Impact of Market Strategy and was developed as a result of a collaboration between the General Electric Group and the Harvard Business School during the 1960s and 1970s. At first PIMS was applied to assess and develop different businesses in the diversified portfolio that General Electric was running even then.

The idea underlying PIMS was based on certain general circumstances conducive to a company's long-term success, much as there are indicators in medicine for treating a sick person that lead to a correct diagnosis. A person's pulse, blood pressure or white blood cells all give indications of his or her state of health, so that different kinds of action can be taken to improve it if necessary. PIMS is given out to be a strategy methodology. We would agree with this up to a point, although we would stop at the diagnostics, which in itself is extremely useful.

PIMS has been given much attention by academics because of its thorough analytical structure. However, PIMS should be supplemented with other methods if a strategy agenda is to be given a reasonably sound base.

PIMS can be briefly described as follows:

1. There are general conditions that control an organization's profitability.

2. These conditions are independent of industry.

3. Strategic conditions that affect profitability explain about two-thirds of a business's results. The remaining third is explained by other factors relating to management skills.

4. There are about 35 generally applicable parameters forming the basis for a classification of business units.

5. A database covers data for about 3,000 business units, which makes it possible to compare a business unit with the average in the database for every one of the 30 strategic variables.

The main principle of the analysis is shown in the diagram.

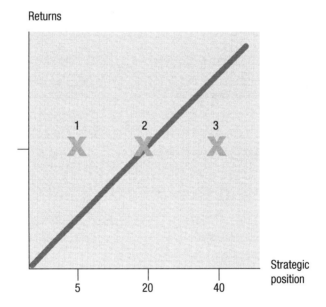

The diagram shows the main principle in a PIMS analysis. Business 1 shows better results than can be expected from its weak strategic position. Business 2 shows a normal result, while business 3 has low returns in relation to its strategic position.

Of the 67 per cent of a business unit's results that are explained by the roughly 35 parameters, five of them explain as much as 50 percentage points of the 67. These five variables are:

1. **Capital intensity**. A company with high capital accumulation has high fixed costs. Businesses with high fixed costs are most exposed to competition. An industry tends to operate on volume and as a result, marginal prices, which is why profitability is squeezed.

2. **Relative quality.** Quality relative to competitors is of great importance in all businesses and together with price determines a customer's choice of supplier.

3. **Productivity**. The PIMS concept of productivity is the amount of added value per employee. The greater the capital per employee, the higher the demands placed on value added per employee.

4. **Capacity utilization rate**. Capacity utilization is real production in relation to the highest possible production. Normal shift-work in the business is taken into consideration as well as the bottlenecks that can be removed most easily through investment.

5. **Relative market share**. This means that a company's own market share is viewed in relation to the market share of its three biggest competitors.

PIMS has the ambition to answer the following questions:

1. What factors explain the differences in return on investment and cash flow of different businesses?

2. What profitability is par for a business unit, independent of industry, in a particular strategic position?

3. What are the possible changes in profitability in relation to strategic position?

4. What strategic actions should then be undertaken to affect return on investment and cash flow?

The diagnostic areas included in PIMS which can have a positive or negative effect on profitability are:

Market growth

- Productivity is most important in fast-growing markets.
- Fast introduction tempo of new products in markets with good growth damages profitability.
- Quality is very important in markets with little growth.

Life cycle

- A narrow product line in a young market is unprofitable.
- Small market share in a young market is unprofitable.
- Low quality is unprofitable in a young market.

Market position

- Large relative market share gives high profitability.
- It is most important to have large market share in industries that are integrated backwards.
- High production costs in relation to sales reduce profitability regardless of market position.
- High levels of organization (unions) limit the advantages of large market share.
- Patents do not help companies with large market shares.
- Large R&D investment is damaging to companies with small market share.
- Small market share is not as unprofitable if a company sells customized products.
- Capacity utilization is most important for companies with small market share.
- Intensive marketing is not profitable if market shares are small.

Quality

- Higher quality in products and service gives greater profitability.
- High marketing investment hurts profitability if quality is low.

New products

- Fast product-launching tempo counteracts the effects of inflation.
- High costs for marketing new products lowers returns.
- New products lower profitability considerably if quality is low.

Capital

- Profitability falls as investment intensity rises.
- Intensive investment and marketing give low profitability.
- High productivity is most important when investment intensity is low.
- High investment intensity and small market share is a recipe for disaster.
- A broad product line is most important in a capital intensive business.

Vertical integration

- A low integration level means that quality becomes more important.
- Diversified companies profit most from vertical integration.
- Businesses with low integration find it difficult to satisfy many customers.

R&D

- R&D is most profitable in mature, slowly growing markets.
- Fairly high R&D invested in product quality seems to give the best profitability.
- High R&D together with high marketing costs lowers returns.

PIMS is an excellent instrument for providing metrics for business units in a diversified portfolio. PIMS has also attempted to evaluate value creation in synergic portfolios, or *clusters*.

The refinements of a PIMS analysis can lead to a wild goose chase. Proponents of PIMS tend to be sectarian and seem to think that PIMS suffices for all strategic questions and that it has the answer to everything. We believe – and many share our view – that PIMS is a useful and effective instrument in strategy analysis but that it does not take into account the importance of creativity and synthesis in the formulation of a strategic agenda. If a business produces good returns in spite of a mediocre product or high capital intensity, then this is valuable information but in no way does it automatically indicate a pattern of action for other businesses. Highly analytical intellects have not always understood the great importance of creative processes where business activities are concerned. By creativity we mean the ability to combine different elements in completely new ways.

PIMS uses capital yield as a general yardstick, but this is not always useful in service businesses, especially not in high-profile knowledge companies.

PIMS is a product of the industrial world but an increasingly greater part of the modern economy is to be found in the public sector and non-profit organizations in which strategy is of the utmost importance but where the strategic parameters differ.

RECOMMENDED READING

Robert D Buzzell and Bradley T Gale, The PIMS Principles: Linking Strategy To Performance.

Planning chart

An organization's work for the year can best be seen using a planning chart. This chart can be used as an aid to planning work and for communicating different stages of a business's planning to the larger organization. When planning is systematized in this way it should not be made too bureaucratic or formal, i.e. it is meant to help and not hinder the business. This should be remembered when using certificated management systems such as those of the ISO family.

A simple framework that can be used to show how planning work is systematically carried out and followed up can be given two axes. The vertical axis describes the actors who are involved in and affected by planning work, and here the whole organization, including possible stakeholders closely connected to the business, should be included. The horizontal axis is temporal and comprises one year. Every event occurring during the year is then associated with an actor and a time. The illustration gives a general example of this. In the example, the process begins when owner directives are formulated and communicated in a plan to group management. Planning work is initiated on the basis of these directives, resulting in a strategic plan presented at a vision and strategy seminar in August. The strategic plan is established by the Board and is the signal for marketing analyzes and planning work of business units to begin.

Business plans are finalized in October and processed with relevant departments before they are decided upon by group management. In January a planning conference involving all co-workers is held to begin the integration of planning work into the plans of businesses and individuals.

In the strategic plan at the bottom of the illustration can be seen the management documents produced at the different stages in the process. The example is fictitious but is based on the internal organization of an American market subsidiary.

A chart, such as the one in the example, can be useful to small companies as well as large, complex organizations. It clarifies the work of planning so that it can be seen at a glance, sorting out different areas and making for more effective planning.

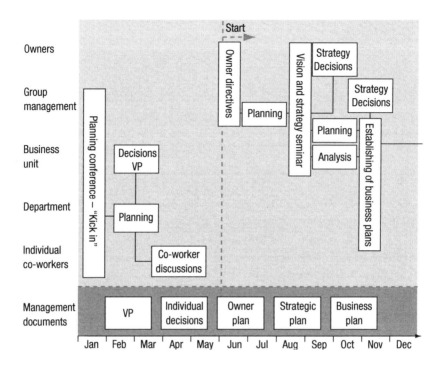

Much time and energy can be wasted in establishing who is doing what and when in the work of planning if the process is not clearly defined.

Obviously, planning work is not just what comes between points distributed over one year. It includes what came before and is still to come and as such has often been described as a cycle or 'planning wheel'.

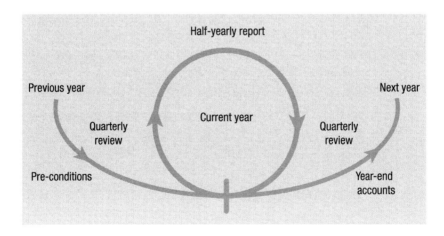

The above example shows the review and revision of established plans. The illustration was inspired by the planning cycle for Gothenburg University.

RECOMMENDED READING

Rod Napier et al, High Impact Tools and Activities for Strategic Planning: Creative Techniques for Facilitating Your Organization's Planning Process.

Policy

A policy is an organization's position on a particular question or for a particular area. An organization will usually have a number of main policies which are then clarified in a range of more detailed policies or guidelines. A policy can describe everything from an organization's general outlook on quality to its view on the acceptance of gifts from suppliers.

Policies are most effective when they are clear indications or directives on subjects that are well anchored in an organization and familiar to its work force. However, policies can cause confusion, and worse, when they are documents which management uses to avoid responsibility for the actions of their organization. A policy, like other documents offering guidelines, is not worth much unless it is communicated to the whole organization and understood and accepted by it.

There is a great deal of confusion concerning the terms used in policy governance.

A breakdown that is commonly used is shown in the illustration.

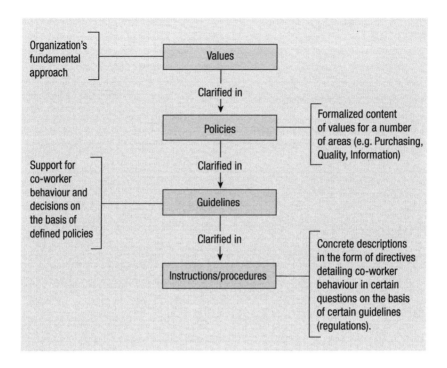

RECOMMENDED READING

John Carver and Miriam Mayhew Carver, Carver Guide: Basic Principles
of Policy Governance.

Porter's competitive analysis

Thanks to his writings and his ability to spellbind an audience, Michael
Porter, a Professor at the Harvard Business School, has been a powerful influence even in those areas which are simply compilations of prior
knowledge.

That category includes competitive analysis, which occupied a prominent
place in the strategic planning that was so strongly favoured in an earlier
era. Running a business was often viewed in terms of game theory, which
conjured up analogies with warfare, chess and other phenomena that lend

themselves to overview. The protagonists were regarded as pieces in a game, and the job of management largely consisted of trying to assess how other players were thinking and evaluating the situation.

Components of competitive analysis

The objective of competitive strategy, according to Porter, is to position your own company in such a way that it can exploit its advantages to the full. From this it follows that an in-depth analysis of the competition is an important element of strategy formulation. The purpose of the analysis is to gain an appreciation of what changes in strategy our competitors are likely to make:

1. What are our competitors' chances of succeeding?

2. How is a given competitor likely to react to conceivable strategic moves by other companies.

3. How are competitors likely to react to the many changes in the industry and the outside world that could conceivably occur?

4. Who do we want to challenge in the industry, and with what weapons?

5. What does a competitor hope to accomplish by his strategic move, and how should we view it?

6. What areas should we steer clear of to avoid provoking countermeasures that might cause us pain or expense?

Competition analysis, like any other kind of strategy analysis, is hard work.It demands extensive research and many of the facts we need are hard to unearth.

According to Porter, there are four diagnostic components of competition analysis:

1. Future goals

2. Current strategy

3. Assumptions

4. Capabilities

With a fair understanding of these four components, we can make predictions concerning the response profile of our competitors. Such a profile is defined by the key questions in the figure.

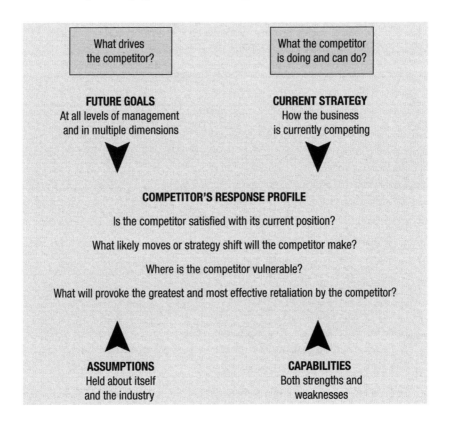

We will now comment on Porter's definitions of the four components.

Future goals

Knowledge of goals makes it possible to predict how satisfied a given competitor is with his current position and financial results. On this basis we can judge the probability of that competitor having to change his strategy and react to events that affect him.

Knowledge of competitors' goals can also help us to predict responses to changes in the strategic picture. Some such changes may threaten a particular competitor. Diagnosis of competitors' goals should further include qualitative factors such as market leadership, technological position and social status.

Assumptions

Assumptions, again according to Porter, fall into two categories:

1. The competitor's perception of himself.

2. The competitor's assumptions concerning the industry and the other companies in it.

Every company operates according to certain assumptions concerning its own circumstances. It may for example regard itself as the leader in its field, a low-cost manufacturer, the company with the best sales force, or whatever. Such assumptions often influence the way a company behaves and reacts to events.

Current strategy

Porter says that a competitor's strategy ought to be defined as the operative programme laid down for every functional area of the company and the way in which he tries to coordinate the various functions. A strategy may be explicit or implicit, but is always there in some form.

Capabilities

Competitors' capabilities complete the diagnostic puzzle. Their goals, assumptions and strategies all affect the probability, timing, nature and intensity of their responses. Porter then goes on to discuss strengths, weaknesses, opportunities and threats.

He holds that on the basis of competitors' future goals, assumptions, current strategies and capabilities, we can begin to ask the key questions that give a picture of competitors' likely responses to various situations.

RECOMMENDED READING

1. Michael E Porter, Competitive Strategy: Techniques For Analyzing Industries and Competitors.

2. Michael E Porter, Michael E Porter on Competition.

Porter's five competitive forces

Michael Porter has identified the five competitive forces that determine profitability in an industry:

- Entry of new competitors into the arena

- Threat from substitutes based on other technology

- Bargaining power of buyers

- Bargaining power of supplier's

- Competition between companies already established on the market

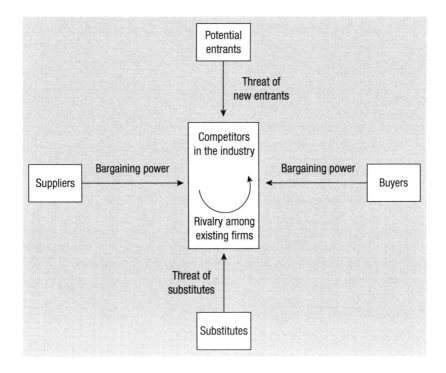

Competitive strategies (business strategies) are derived from an understanding of the rules of competition that govern an industry and determine its attractiveness. The ultimate goal of competitive strategy is to influence those rules in our own company's favour. The rules of competition can be described by the five competitive forces shown in the figure.

Potential entrants

The establishment of a new company in an industry implies an increment of capacity. This can result in price-cutting, or inflate the cost structures of companies in the industry and reduce their profitability. According to Porter there are six major obstacles to would-be entrants:

1. Economies of scale, which mean that the unit cost of a product or service falls with rising volume per unit of time. The economies of scale deter new entrants by forcing them either to start out on a massive scale, which calls for heavy investment, or to risk crushing retaliation from established companies in the industry.

2. Differentiation of production, which means that established companies hold recognized trade marks and enjoy brand loyalty as a result of marketing efforts or tradition. The new entrant must spend a lot of money to break down existing loyalties.

3. Need for capital, which makes it difficult to get started in cases where it takes a large capital stake to be able to compete. This hurdle naturally grows higher with the uncertainty factor. Capital may be needed not only for production but also to extend credit to customers, build up stocks and cover initial losses. Rank Xerox set up an effective barrier to new entrants in the office copier business by renting machines instead of selling them, thereby upping the capital ante for potential competition.

4. Conversion costs, a one-off expense for buyers who switch suppliers. These costs may include retraining of personnel, new production equipment, need for technical service, new production design and risk of production stoppages.

5. Lack of distribution channels, which may make it impossible for new entrants to establish a foothold in the trade. New players must resort to cut-price offers, subsidizing advertising and other inducements to persuade established distributors and outlets to accept their products, thereby cutting into their profit margins.

6. Other cost obstacles unrelated to the economies of scale may, according to Porter, arise from advantages enjoyed by established companies in the industry. These include:

- Patented product technology
- Access to raw materials on favourable terms
- Advantageous location
- Priority claim on government subsidies
- Lead in know-how or experience

Competition among existing companies

Competition among existing companies follows well-known procedures for gaining a more advantageous position. These include tactical exercises like price offers, advertising campaigns, product launches, customer service and warranties.

Rivalry arises, according to Porter, when one or more competitors are in a squeeze or see an opportunity to improve their position. The intensity of competition in an industry can range from the polite or gentlemanly to fierce or cutthroat. Porter points to a number of factors that determine the intensity of competition:

- many competitors or competitors of compatible strength.
- slow growth rate in the industry.
- high fixed manufacturing or inventory costs.
- no differentiation (no conversion costs).
- quantum leaps in capacity.
- competitors of different kinds.
- high strategic value.
- high exit barriers

Substitutes

All the companies in a given industry compete, in a broad sense, with other industries that deliver substitute products. Substitutes limit the profit potential of an industry by putting a ceiling on the prices that companies in the industry can ask without losing profitability. To identify substitutes, we must look around for other products that can perform the same function as our own. This can sometimes be difficult, leading the analyst into areas that are apparently far removed from the industry concerned.

Bargaining power of buyers

Buyers compete with an industry by exerting a downward pressure on its prices, negotiating for higher quality or better service, and playing off one competitor against another, all at the expense of an industry's profitability. The strength of each of the industry's most important groups or buyers depends on a number of factors that characterize the market situation.

A group of buyers is powerful if it meets the following criteria:

- It is concentrated, or buys large volumes in relation to the volume of suppliers' sales.
- The products it buys from the industry represent an important proportion of its own costs or volume of purchases.
- The products it buys from the industry are standardized or undifferentiated.
- It is not sensitive to conversion costs.
- Its profit margins are small.
- The industry's product is not crucial to the quality of the buyers' own products or services.
- It is well informed.

Bargaining power of suppliers

Suppliers can put pressure on the players in an industry by threatening to raise the price or cut the quality of the goods and services they deliver. Suppliers in a position of strength can thus reduce the profitability of an industry that is not in a position to cover cost increases by raising its own prices. The factors that make suppliers powerful tend to reflect those that make groups of buyers powerful.

A group of suppliers is powerful if it meets the following criteria:

1. It is dominated by a few companies and is more concentrated than the industry it sells to.

2. It is not forced to compete with substitutes for the products it sells to the industry.

3. The industry concerned is not one of its most important customers.

4. Its products are crucial to the industry's business.

5. Its products are differentiated.

6. It poses a credible threat of forward integration, that is, of establishing itself in the industry.

According to Porter, a company can identify its own strengths and weaknesses in relation to its industry by analyzing the forces that affect competition in the industry and their underlying causes.

RECOMMENDED READING

1. Michael E Porter, Competitive Strategy: Techniques for Analyzing Industries and Competitors.

2. Michael E Porter, Michael E Porter on Competition.

Porter's generic strategies

In *Competitive Strategy* (1980), Michael Porter presents three basic generic strategies for improving competitive power. A company that wants to achieve a competitive edge must make a strategic choice to avoid becoming 'all things to all men'.

The three basic strategies are:

- Cost leadership
- Differentiation
- Focusing

	Lower costs	Differentiation
Broad	1 Cost leadership	2 Differentiation
Narrow	3A Cost focus	3B Differentiation focus

Areas of competition

To achieve cost leadership, a company must keep its costs lower than its competitors'. To achieve differentiation, it must be able to offer something that is perceived as unique of its kind. By focus, Porter means that a company concentrates its efforts on a specific group of buyers or a specific segment of a product group or a specific geographical market.

Cost leadership is perhaps the most distinct of the three generic strategies. It means that a company aims to be the low-cost producer in its industry. The company has a broad scope of delivery and serves many segments within its industry. This breadth is often a key factor in its cost leadership. The nature of the cost advantage varies according to the structure of the industry; it may be a matter of economies of scale, superior technology, or access to raw materials.

Low-cost production involves much more than just moving down the experience curve. A low-cost producer must find and exploit every opportunity to gain a cost advantage. The commonest situation is one where a producer is selling standard products with no added values, where staple goods are involved and where the distribution chain is strong.

Porter goes on to point out that a cost leader cannot afford to ignore the principles of differentiation. If buyers do not regard the product as comparable or acceptable, the cost leader will be forced to discount prices to undercut his competitors, thereby losing his cost advantage.

Porter concludes from this that a cost leader must be on a par with his competitors, or at least within reach of the principles of differentiation.

Differentiation means according to Porter, that a company strives to be unique in its industry in some respect that is appreciated by a large number of buyers. It selects one or more qualities that many of the industry's customers consider important, and positions itself to satisfy customers' needs. The reward for this type of behaviour is that the products command a higher price.

It follows from this line of reasoning that differentiation variables are specific to each industry. Differentiation can be sought in the product itself, in the method of delivery, in the method of marketing or in some other factor. A company that goes in for differentiation must therefore always seek ways to achieve cost-effectiveness, because otherwise it risks losing its competitive edge through a disadvantageous cost position.

The difference between cost leadership and differentiation is that the former can only be achieved in one way, that is through an advantageous cost structure, whereas differentiation can be achieved in many ways.

Focus is the third generic strategy. It differs radically from the other two in that it is based on the choice of a narrow field of competition within the industry.

Focusing consists in choosing a segment within an industry and adapting our strategy to serve that segment more efficiently than our competitors do. By optimizing the strategy for selected target groups, the focuser tries to achieve a competitive edge in respect of the selected group.

There are two kinds of focus strategy. With the cost focus approach, a company tries to gain a cost advantage in its chosen segment. With *differentiation focus*, on the other hand, it tries to set itself apart from other companies in its industry. In this way the focuser can gain a competitive edge by concentrating on exclusive segments of the market. The breadth of the target group is naturally a question of degree rather than kind, but the very essence of focusing lies in exploiting a narrow target group that differs from the rest of the industry's customers. According to Porter, any one of the three generic strategies can be used as an effective means of acquiring and keeping a competitive edge.

Firms that are stuck in the middle

The following is an extract from Michael Porter's *Competitive Strategy*:

"The three generic strategies are alternative, viable approaches to dealing with the competitive forces. The converse of the previous discussion is that the firm failing to develop its strategy in at least one of the three directions – a firm that is 'stuck in the middle' – is in an extremely poor strategic situation. This firm lacks the market share, capital investment and resolve to play the low-cost game, the industry-wide differentiation necessary to obviate the need for a low-cost position, or the focus to create differentiation or a low-cost position in a more limited sphere.

A firm stuck in the middle is almost always guaranteed low profitability. It either loses the high-volume customers who demand low prices or must bid away its profits to get this business away from low-cost firms. Yet it also loses high-margin business – the cream – to the firms who are focused on high-margin targets or have achieved differentiation overall. The firm stuck in the middle also probably suffers from a blurred corporate culture and a conflicting set of organizational arrangements and motivation systems.

The firm stuck in the middle must make a fundamental strategic decision. Either it must take the steps necessary to achieve cost leadership or at least cost parity, which usually involve aggressive investments to modernize and perhaps the necessity to buy market share, or it must orient itself to a particular target (focus) or achieve some uniqueness (differentiation). The latter two options may very well involve shrinking in market share and even in absolute sales.

Risks of cost leadership

A cost leader is under constant pressure to keep its position, which means that it must invest in modern equipment, ruthlessly discard obsolete assets, resist the temptation to widen its product range and stay alert for technical improvements. Cost reductions are by no means an automatic consequence of large volume, nor is it possible to enjoy all the advantages of economies of scale without constant vigilance.

There are several hazards to beware of:

- Technological advances that negate the value of existing investments and know-how

- New competitors or followers who gain the same cost advantage by imitation or investment in modern equipment

- Failure to detect the need for changes in the product or the market as a result of being preoccupied with cost issues

- Cost inflation, which erodes the company's ability to maintain a big enough price differential to offset competitors' goodwill or other advantages of differentiation

Risks of differentiation

Differentiation has its own hazards:

- The cost gap between the differentiated company and its low-cost competitors may be too wide to be bridged by the specialties, service or prestige that the differentiated company can offer its customers.

- The buyer's need for the differentiated factor may diminish; this is apt to happen as buyers grow more knowledgeable.

- Imitation may blur the perceptible difference, a common phenomenon in maturing industries.

The first of these risks is so great that it merits a special comment.

A company can differentiate its product, but the differentiation can only overcome so much difference in price. So if a differentiated company lags too far behind in cost due to either changes in technology or sheer inattention, a low-cost company can get into a strong attack position. Thus Kawasaki and other Japanese motorcycle manufacturers were able to attack differentiated producers of heavy motorcycles like Harley Davidson and Triumph by offering substantial cost savings to buyers.

Risks of focusing

Focusing involves risks of another kind:

- Increasing cost differentials between broadly-based producers and the focusing company may eliminate the cost advantages of serving a target group with a narrow market base, or outweigh the differentiation achieved through focusing.

- The difference between the kinds of products and services demanded by the strategic target group and the market at large may diminish.

- Competitors may find target groups within the focused company's target group and succeed better with their new venture.

Many business leaders consider Porter's theories far too general to be of real explanatory value in a real-life situation. Nevertheless, it remains true that the balance between the creation of customer-perceived value and price is a central question, and that is what Porter's theory of generic strategies is all about. (See also *Value*.)

RECOMMENDED READING

1. Michael E Porter, Competitive Strategy: Techniques for Analyzing Industries and Competitors.
2. Michael E Porter, Michael E Porter on Competition.

Portfolio

The most usual meaning of the term portfolio in a business context is the collection of securities that we own. By extension, the term has also come to mean a group of business units under one roof. It derives from the term share portfolio, which refers to a stock market investment comprizing shares of a number of different companies (spread investment).

By analogy, the term portfolio as used in business has come to mean a more or less variegated group of business units or firms under the same ownership, together constituting what in legal parlance is called a group of companies. Other common terms are corporation, concern or conglomerate.

Portfolio structures can also be found outside the commercial sector. The local authority for instance, constitutes what could be called a diversified portfolio. It comprises a range of organizations unrelated to each other, such as care for the elderly, schools, an engineering department, and so on. The same thing applies to county councils and a host of other government agencies, as well as to non-profit organizations. Again, trade union organizations often operate publishing businesses and training programmes.

A portfolio can come into being in many ways. Sometimes a new corporate mission arises out of an auxiliary function. Other business portfolios are the offspring of a customer-supplier relationship; this is also called *vertical integration*. A shipyard may buy a steelworks to make its structural steel (backward integration), or it may buy a banana plantation or a coal company to secure cargoes for its ships (forward integration).

A car manufacturer may buy a chain of dealerships or the factory that makes its back axles. An airline may buy into the travel agency business, maintain its own engines and operate hotels.

Yet another way in which portfolios can arise is through development of related business to satisfy customers' needs better. In the data consultancy business, groups of business units have developed in symbiosis, each satisfying one kind of need and thus finding more ways to reach customers. One example is e-learning.

A portfolio may thus be either diversified or synergistic. Intermediate forms also exist, of course. In good times there is a tendency to overrate synergies and cite them as a motive for acquisitions, even though the true motives may be quite different.

Portfolios often become diversified because synergies, with time grow, diffuse and eventually, meaningless. This means that a change in ownership may have to be considered. A common pattern is that a portfolio which has grown up on a basis of synergies in production gradually loses its synergistic connections. Market relations are evolving into an entirely different business situation. An example of this is the publishing industry, which originally included ownership of presses, binding departments, typesetting, etc. Commercial connections in business have gradually become blurred to the extent that a daily newspaper, for instance, may only be one of the owners of its printing press.

Managing and developing a portfolio is a matter of working with business structures rather than business strategies. The chief executive of a company or corporation that contains a large number of diverse business units is in fact in the business unit industry. Since a company almost always contains more than one business unit, its management must be able to:

- buy into new industries.
- strengthen business units, for example by acquisition
- withdraw from unwanted industries
- sell business units that can be better managed by others
- allocate resources in the form of capital and costs
- ensure that individual business units are strategically managed
- take advantage of synergies in the form of greater business strength or more efficient operative management of business units.

When a company consists of several units with little or no synergy, discussions of corporate mission are apt to be long and complicated.

Some thinkers have dubbed an intermediate form 'business areas' by which they mean synergistic portfolios where market synergies or similarities of customers' needs make it possible to find some sort of common trade logic.

If we are managing a portfolio that consists of a number of business units with different corporate missions, one of our main problems will be that of dismantling structures that do not fit. Entrepreneurial managers will disinvest without a qualm, but power-oriented managers seem to balk at selling business units.

There are of course logical and justifiable reasons for the existence of portfolios of disparate business units. These reasons include:

1. The dynamics of the business have generated organic growth, as in the case of the Volvo Bus Corporation in the Volvo Group.

2. Technological skills have lead to the development of business areas related to the original one only by technology.

3. The main business area has been highly profitable but offered no opportunities for new investment.

4. It is desirable to spread business risks.

5. Strong links exist between business units in terms of customer needs or technology.

6. Costs or capital structures can be shared.

Mixtures of legal structure (companies or units with the same owner) and business structure often occur. It is important, therefore, to recognize the difference between legal and business structures.

A company's portfolio strategy usually depends on cyclical conditions in the market. In bad times companies want to reduce investment, whether in products or staff, which generally means that the value of its business units goes down. This might apply to both operating companies and administrating companies such as property companies or investment companies.

It is unfortunate for the many portfolios which develop quickly during the good times that market prices fall when the economic situation worsens. People involved in fast-growing portfolios may feel that it is unfair to suddenly see the market value of their group reduced to perhaps a tenth of what it was just a short time ago, when it was racing away from projected performance.

At one moment everyone wants to buy and nothing is for sale; almost at the very next, everything is for sale and nobody wants to buy. Many players accustomed to moving in the fast lane are suddenly taken by surprise when markets collapse.

Seen over longer periods, it is possible to say that intensive accumulation of capital during periods of healthy profits creates pressure on management to invest in good business opportunities: management preferences tend towards breadth and depth in business.

Thus the value of business units, in the same way as with real and moveable estate, tends to fluctuate wildly from the development curve, depending on the need to satisfy demand or the pressure to supply. Some spectacular examples of market price shift were offered by the 2002 change in the economic climate.

Portfolio strategy

Two lines of thought are especially worthy of attention in respect of portfolios:

1. All business is legitimate (except when it is strictly illegal, as in the case of drug dealing), whether it is manufacturing, the production of services, or trade.

2. The dangers inherent in moving from businesslike reasoning to speculation are not generally noticed.

The first statement can seem trivial. Yet it is interesting because at certain times it has been much easier to make money through speculation – in fact, trading – than through the hard work of producing goods or services. It has not been the thing for economists and engineers to go into industrial production, as it has been so much easier to be successful in company trading, property, shares or options. A phrase like 'fast buck' has led to the debasement of the transaction economy, at the same time as it has represented the height of fashion for many years: an expectation that prices would rise or fall has been a basis for trading since time immemorial. Still, it is a good idea to distinguish this from distribution, a term that indicates a knowledge of suppliers and customers, of utilizing economies of scale and capital rationalization by optimizing batch sizes from supplier to consumer.

A typology for business activity is given below (see also *Business model*).

Extraction and cultivation	Production of goods and services	Distribution	Speculation (Trade)	Production of services	Knowledge

All business is legitimate (except in such a strictly illegal activity as drug-dealing) but the importance of different kinds of business activity may vary from one time to another. The production and extraction of natural resources have obviously had their golden age; trade and speculation reached their latest peak in the 1990s, and 'knowledge business' is now gaining ground.

Many business leaders do not realize it when they abandon business logic for speculative thinking. This lack of insight means that they are unprepared for the risk factors involved with speculation where the object in question is concerned, whether it is shares, property or whatever. Although mistakes may lead to financial difficulties or bankruptcy, it is not necessarily speculative thinking that is at fault but rather the lack of insight into the different conditions and underlying risks that are inherent in such thinking.

Business units in a portfolio are run according to two ways of thinking, exactly as the shares in a share portfolio:

1. Industrial logic in terms of net worth and profits, as represented by fundamentalists.

2. Speculative logic based on assessments of future prices, such as ticks (price movements).

Let us point out two problems that are very likely to lead to financial risks which players may not be aware of:

1. Diversification generally occurs in times of prosperity.

2. There is usually a transition from business logic to the logic of speculation.

Diversification seems to be a knee-jerk move in good times. The boundary between diversification and synergic acquisition is the same one that separates what on the one hand does not give customers added value and what on the other, does. The mood of business leaders at the peaks and troughs of long periods of prosperity or recession tends to produce a certain kind of behaviour that intensifies the amplitudes of trends.

When we speak of synergy we usually mean the benefit of shared costs or greater value for customers. Synergy is actually a special case of other concepts that we can group under the umbrella term 'complementariness', i.e. the extent to which different business units complement one another. See also *Synergy*.

In upturn periods we tend to exaggerate our company's capital many times over, a psychological frame of mind that impels us to speculate. Business leaders who in one industry turn into success stories overnight often find it difficult to assess the risks when investing speculatively in other industries. Such people may be consummate managers within a certain business framework but often find themselves ill equipped to make the decisions called for in a portfolio comprising units from different industries. The jump from being a unit manager to managing a portfolio is much greater than they might have imagined. This can be reduced to the simple question: what differentiates a company manager from the manager of a portfolio?

RECOMMENDED READING

1.   Michael S Allan, Business Portfolio Management: Valuation, Risk Assessment, and EVA Strategies.

2.   Robert D Buzzell and Bradley T Gale, The PIMS Principles: Linking Strategy To Performance.

Positioning

The term positioning has become increasingly popular. It has its origins in advertising agency jargon, and its meaning lies in the boundary zone between marketing, portfolio strategy and business strategy. On occasions, it has played an important part in focusing the resources of a corporation and thereby guiding its strategic course. Positioning is often a way of gaining a competitive edge over the competition. The examples of Volkswagen in the USA (Small is Beautiful) and of the Long Island Trust, which successfully positioned itself as the bank for Long Islanders show how positioning can help to attain a strategic focus and lead to success.

The purpose of positioning is to:

- make a company's capabilities known.
- improve performance.
- explain a many-faceted whole with organic links.
- secure a place for the product in the minds of stakeholders.

Positioning is thus primarily a matter of changing attitudes, and only secondarily of changing the product. Positioning further implies a comparative rather than superlative form of expression. The company and its products are related to the world around them, for example, to competitors or to other products on the market. The idea is not to ascribe superlative qualities to the product that strain credulity and compromise its acceptance.

The Volkswagen Beetle was viewed as a small car, a position that was deliberately affirmed by the message 'Small is Beautiful'. By establishing itself in the public mind as the strongest contender on the small-car market, it automatically gave its marketing a boost.

Another aspect of positioning is that it reinforces attitudes already held by stakeholders. The object is not to change attitudes, but to conjure up latent associations. You can do this, for example, by making it clear what you are not: "Seven-up, the non-cola".

Positioning, then, involves manipulating mental associations. The trick is to find a window in the consciousness and latch on to something that is already there, to reinforce rather than create, by confirming associations.

Positioning is most nearly related to the concept of image, which is the way the public perceive reality, and is an expression of customer-perceived quality, of the way a company is viewed in the light of a number of need-related variables.

Positioning is also a way of achieving distinction, of staking a claim to be best in some particular segment, that is in a sub-set of a need area or of a total market.

Some guidelines for effective positioning are:

- Concentrate on the recipient of the message. How will the customer react to our message and offering?

- Associate with what is already in peoples' minds.

- Keep the message simple.

- The easiest and best positioning technique is to be first to occupy a position.

- A position once taken must be consistently and persistently held.

- An anti-position (what we are not) is often easy to communicate.

- Never try to adopt a head-on position in relation to the market leader.

- The main objective of a positioning programme should be to strive for leadership in a special area.

- Find a hole in the market. Is there a vacant position anywhere?

The idea of positioning is not, of course, the answer to all problems of communication or strategy. In some cases, however, it can be an excellent aid for thinking. In the first place, we can privately consider the question of what position our company and its products occupy in the minds of our market. In the second place, we can sometimes use positioning terminology as a focal point for choosing a strategy and achieving a competitive edge. The term positioning merits a promising place in modern management thinking alongside others like customer-perceived quality or the need orientation of the product.

A company's *trademark* (see this term) often functions to project and communicate its product's position. For more on this, see *Industry attraction* and *Strategic position*.

RECOMMENDED READING

1. Al Ries and Jack Trout, Positioning: The Battle for your Mind.

2. Jack Trout, Differentiate Or Die: Survival in Our Era of Killer Competition.

Price

Price can be defined as a 'predetermined payment for a certain perform-ance' or a 'cost to be paid in the event of purchase'.

Price is one of the fundamental variables of businessmanship in that it is an expression of the sacrifice the customer must make to get the utility that a product represents.

Historically, price has played a key part in business theory. The Price Theory treats the significance of price in terms of demand, ignoring the value vari-able on the assumption that products have equal value.

During the post-war period up to the mid-1970s, price adjustments were made rather callously. Little attention was paid to how price related to value given, because most industries were supplying excess demand or, to put it the other way round, because there was a general shortage of goods. In most cases, prices were increased as soon as costs went up.

An imbalance prevailed in many European countries in the second half of the 1970s, in the sense that utility, generally speaking, did not match price levels. As a result of rates of exchange and cost levels pushed sky-high by massive wage increases, prices had reached a level where those countries were losing market share on the world market.

We might say that customers were not getting utility for the money they were expected to pay. Many companies were then forced to start rethink-ing their policy of automatically raising prices whenever their costs increased.

For many years, up to the mid-1970s, organizations regularly compensated their cost increases with price increases. It is possible to do this when:

- competition is low.
- demand exceeds supply.
- a company enjoys a position of virtual monopoly.

In the situation that has prevailed since the second half of the 1970s, it has been necessary to handle the price instrument with much greater delicacy. Some companies began at an early stage to use price as an instrument of control in the implementation of their strategies.

In a strategic context, a decisive importance has always been ascribed to price ever since the discovery of the *experience curve* (see this term), which says that unit costs fall by about 20 per cent every time output is doubled. Many parallels have been drawn from this correlation in various situations. One example is the thesis that a large market share makes mass production possible at low cost, which in turn makes it possible to cut prices and thereby gain more competitive power.

A cost is what a company actually spends, at the time or over a period of time, on producing a given article or service. A price is the stipulated sacrifice a customer must make to get the article or service s/he wants. The price, multiplied by the number of units sold, must in the long-term cover costs and yield a return on capital. If the price is related to the value of the product, and if that value is high, the profit can be substantial.

If we look worldwide, we find that the relationship between the price of an article or service and its utility is not constant. In the USA, for example, price is regarded as more important in relation to utility than it is in Europe. It is not a coincidence that nearly all manufacturers of passenger cars in the exclusive car segment are to be found in Europe. This category includes Mercedes, Volvo, Saab, BMW, Audi and Jaguar.

Air travel offers another example where high quality in the form of service or whatever is clearly more important than price to people living in economies with a high standard of living and a high growth rate.

Price sensitivity is well illustrated by the events of the Gulf War and the recession of 1991. Sensitivity to utility functions in the form of service, etc., diminished in favour of price. People simply changed their position on the value graph to strike a different balance between utility and price. The importance of price in the context of travel is also undergoing a long-term change in Europe, where the civil aviation industry, like many others, is in the throes of deregulation.

Price sensitivity is an expression of the extent to which consumers switch suppliers in reaction to a change in prices. Price elasticity of demand, on the other hand, is a measure of changes in total consumption (see below). Airline deregulation and market fluctuations offer good illustrations of both price sensitivity and price elasticity.

Price differentiation is the technique of charging different or variable prices according to what customers are willing to pay. Their willingness to pay depends in turn on their respective need structures and the demands thereby arising.

Price elasticity of demand measures how the volume of demand is altered by a change in the price of an article or service. It is defined by the following formula:

$$\frac{\text{Percentage change in volume of demand}}{\text{Percentage change in price}}$$

Price elasticity is always expressed as a positive number. When the percentage change in volume of demand is less than the percentage change in price, elasticity is smaller than 1 and demand is said to be inelastic. When the percentage change in volume of demand is greater than the percentage change in price, elasticity is greater than 1 and demand is said to be elastic. A demand curve does not normally have the same degree of elasticity along its whole length.

Price elasticity of demand is an essential factor in the formulation of company pricing policies, because volume multiplied by price determines the seller's total gross earnings. If demand is elastic, total earnings increase when prices are cut, whereas a price increase reduces total earnings. Conversely, if demand is inelastic, total earnings rise and fall with prices.

This correlation, on which the economic reasoning of price theory is based, is very important in connection with business strategy decisions. Some pioneering work with price elasticity was done in Sweden with Jan Carlzon's introduction of the 100 kronor flight when he was Managing Director of Linjeflyg, the Swedish airline, in 1978.

Then there was Volvo's astonishing cut in the price of its passenger cars in the second half of the 1970s.

Both cases involved investment in new production structures that were implemented. In the case of Linjeflyg, the company had exchanged its fleet of propeller-driven Convair Metropolitans for the Fokker F28 series and thereby almost doubling production capacity. It was obviously important at the time to impose the new production structure on a revenue basis.

In a similar situation, Volvo had in the early 1970s invested in the capacity for an extrapolated demand curve involving the production of 600,000 vehicles. Volvo and Linjeflyg were both dependent on their capital structures, and so it was understandable that they should look to the price elasticity formula for inspiration.

Many attempts have been made to divorce price from the underlying cost structure and from customers' scales of value. The trouble with this is that the strength of the underlying needs that govern demand can never be measured. One example is the cost of medical care in Sweden, where prices have been set so low that demand would seem to be infinite.

We can imagine three frames of reference, all of them important, as a basis for pricing:

1. The cost base is used to calculate the lowest price we must charge to operate at a profit.

2. Value to the customer is based on how much customers are prepared to pay for a given utility function.

3. Competitors' prices often determine the level of prices which it is possible and necessary to charge.

To sum up, we can say that price as an instrument of business has become more important now that businessmen have begun to weigh customer-perceived value more carefully against the customer's sacrifice in the form of the price s/he pays.

RECOMMENDED READING

Thomas T Nagle with Reed K Holden, The Strategy and Tactics of Pricing: A Guide to Profitable Decision Making.

Process orientation

Many organizations choose to be process-oriented, the basic idea being to focus on the customer and avoid sub-optimal solutions and lack of coordination between organizational units. Process orientation often results in the establishment of a matrix organization in which co-workers are included in competence units, product areas, etc, with business processes superimposed over them. An indication of a typical process-oriented matrix organization can be seen in the illustration below.

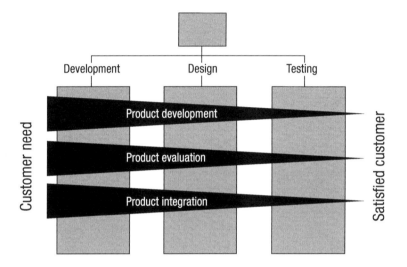

The illustration gives the example of a company with the corporate mission of developing, evaluating and integrating products for its customers. These three functions are thus the three main processes in respect of the customer and there are three competence areas: development, design and testing.

A process-oriented working approach is developed with a focus on the customer in order to make delivery as effective as possible. The question is: how can we utilize our competence in the three areas as effectively as possible (i.e. to deliver a result that satisfies the customer)? Just as the main processes can run across competence areas, it is also common in large organizations for them to run across geographical regions. The question then becomes: how can we exploit our knowledge in different countries as effectively as possible to make a global delivery to the customer?

As the reader no doubt understands, there are always processes in organizations, whether they are articulated or not. Coordination across competence boundaries in the process of delivering to the customer surely must be a question of survival for most companies.

When an organization orientates its processes clearly, it simplifies its structure and makes it easier to explain to both customers and its own co-workers. Articulated processes facilitate a gradual (see *Kaizen*) or a drastic (see BPR) improvement of its structure. It also makes it easier to identify bottlenecks in process flows and to know exactly where costs go.

There are pitfalls and disadvantages in relation to process organization:

1. A danger that the distribution of responsibility may be unclear, resulting in a reluctance to make decisions. What would happen if the owner of the product integration process and the design department manager in our example, had a difference of opinion? Who would have the last word?

2. Uncertainty in where responsibility for the result lies. Is it the owner of a process who should have ultimate responsibility, the line managers, or all of them together? The last-mentioned solution is common and can exacerbate the problem named in point 1.

3. Process-oriented organizations often have higher costs because of a proliferation of managers.

4. This added complexity may cause an organization to move in the opposite direction to the one it had intended, which was to be customer-focused. The organization instead becomes focused on sorting out its internal uncertainties.

We will conclude with a simple pedagogic model used by Evert Gummesson, Professor of Business Economics at Stockholm University, to explain process orientation in companies. (*Relationship Marketing: From 4P to 30R. Liber Ekonomi 1998, p 284.*)

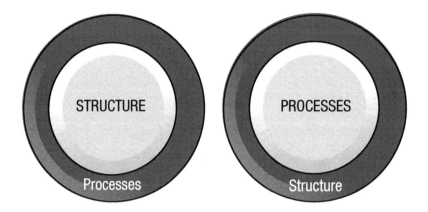

From a situation where the line organization's structure is at the centre with supporting processes, to one where customer-oriented processes are at the centre with the structure in support. For more information, read the section under *Organization* in this book.

RECOMMENDED READING

Michael Hammer, Beyond Re-engineering: How the Process-Centered Organization Will Change Our Work and Our Lives.

Processes

A process comprises a series of refining activities that are carried out within a delimited area. A particular input and output are specified for the whole process as well as each sub-process (stage of the whole process). A simple description of the process of painting a wall might look as follows:

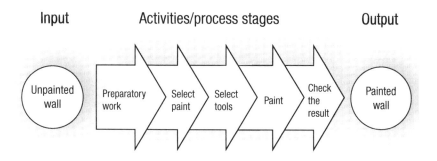

The input of one process is often the output of another. If we were to continue with the above example, 'painted wall' might initiate a 'picture hanging process'. The processes involved in businesses are of course more complex but the basic principles are the same. *Procedures* are often connected to processes; a procedure is a kind of process but described in greater detail. For instance there may be procedures for how the work of painting is to be carried out, the criteria used for choice of paint, and so on. The processes of a business are usually divided into three different categories:

1. **Management processes**. Management processes are used to orientate and develop a business. They exercise a controlling function over the other processes of the business.

   Common management processes are the strategy process, business planning process and the budget process.

2. **Main processes** (also called business processes or core processes). Main processes comprise those processes which are directly connected to the principle aim of a business, and are often described in the business concept/corporate mission. A corporate mission usually identifies a customer need so that a satisfied customer will pay for it. In commercial environments, these main processes describe a company's business, i.e. what it will make money from.

3. **Support processes**. Support processes are processes which facilitate the efficient functioning of main processes. Common support processes are personnel-related processes, IT processes and administrative processes.

Some success factors for processes are:

- Avoid 'paralysis through analysis' – describe processes at a sensible level.

- Somebody should be the 'owner' of the whole of a process.

- Specify how a process is to be developed (process goals), measured and followed up.

The following factors are considered when processes are analyzed:

- Sluggish sections of the process flow. Are there activities or connections in the process which slow it down?

- Redundancy. Are there unnecessary activities in the process that can be eliminated?

- Deficiencies in quality. It can be useful to review processes, especially those involved in production, to look for things that impair quality.

- Cost drivers. Which activities generate the most costs? Can these activities be made more efficient?

RECOMMENDED READING

1. H James Harrington et al, Business Process Improvement Workbook: Documentation, Analysis, Design, and Management of Business Process Improvement.

2. Roger T Burlton, Business Process Management: Profiting From Process.

Product life cycle

Product life cycle is one of the most widely used models for analysis of the successive stages in the development of a business activity, a line of products, or an individual product. It is usually visualized as a sales curve extending in time from the date of launch until the product is taken off the market. The product life cycle is usually divided into five stages:

1. Launch
2. Early growth
3. Late growth
4. Maturity
5. Decline

The usual explanation of the product cycle is that it originates with an innovation. During the launch phase the management works hard and purposefully to make potential customers aware of the product's competitive advantages, but reaches only a few of the potential customers. Gradually others become interested, and sales take off at an accelerating rate. The product is now in its early growth phase. In the late growth phase, sales continue to increase, but at a slower rate. Eventually the product reaches maturity, a plateau where the growth rate slows to zero and the volume of sales is dictated by the need for replacements. Finally, new substitute products begin to appear on the market, attracting customers away from the existing product, and sales begin to fall off. The decline continues until production is discontinued. The development of sales volume in the five phases can be seen in the diagram opposite.

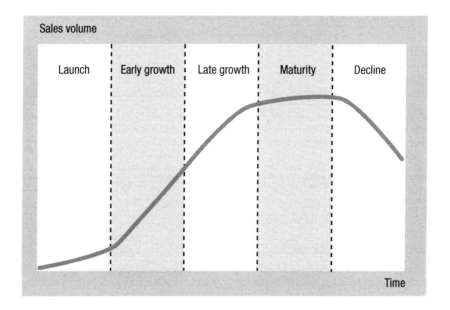

The product life cycle can be developed in a matrix model of four rows representing the different stages of a product's life cycle.

The four stages are:

1. *The idea stage*. The product is not yet out on the market at this stage. The product perhaps exists as a developed idea or prototype. The focus at this stage is on prioritizing, packaging and launching products.

2. *The growth stage*. At this stage we find products which have rapidly increasing demand and which have not reached their full potential. Product at this stage should be marketed and offered to a larger target group.

3. *The Maturity stage*. Stable products with a mature market can be found here. Repurchasing probably accounts for most sales. Here we find established products perhaps lacking in future prospects but providing good yield for business. The focus at this stage is on streamlining delivery.

4. *The transformation stage*. Demand for products at this stage is beginning to fall and they no longer play a developing role for the business. The focus at this stage is either on reworking or

developing the product so we return to the idea stage, or on phasing it out (arrow pointing away from the diagram).

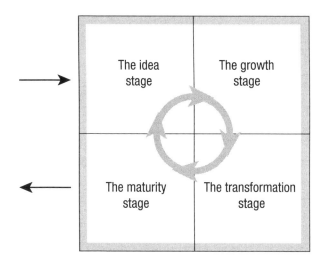

The matrix can be used for analysis of a company's products or services, or as documentation for competence or customer information.

RECOMMENDED READING

Antti Saaksvuori and Anselmi Immonen, Product Life Cycle Management.

The Product/Market Matrix (PM Matrix)

The Product/Market Matrix, often called the Product/Market Certainty Matrix is a classic model in strategy development; its origins cannot be definitely identified.

The matrix is a practical tool for sorting products and markets (read customer categories) with reference to the degree of uncertainty as to sales potential or the possibility of penetrating a given market with a given product. Experience says that it is much harder to sell completely unrelated products to existing customers than it is to sell products linked to the existing range. Products in this context means both goods and services.

In the same way, experience tells us that it is easier to sell an existing range of products to customer categories close to those who are already buying than to sell to entirely new markets. An example is IBM's attempt to establish itself on the office copier market and Rank Xerox's attempt to establish itself on the personal computer market.

In advanced applications, the squares of the matrix can be assigned probabilities that are multiplied by potential sales volume. This serves to quantify a planned situation with regard to sales or business development.

The PM matrix is also used to subdivide a business into markets and market segments or products and services. The sorting process and its results can provide valuable clues to the orientation of business: which categories of customers to concentrate on and which to ignore, and what parts of the product range ought to be developed or cut back.

	EXISTING PRODUCTS	NEW BUT RELATED PRODUCTS	COMPLETELY NEW PRODUCTS
Existing market	90%	60%	30%
New but related market	60%	40%	20%
Completely new market	30%	20 %	10%

Meteoric careers in business often give rise to situations where an executive does not know enough about the types of customer to whom different items in a product range are sold. In that kind of situation the sorting process itself is of great value. The matrix also offers a means of keeping track of trends in markets/market segments and products/groups of products.

The tabulation of products with customer categories can also be used to prioritize market contribution. We should first ask ourselves: what are the important criteria for matching a given product with a particular customer category? Such criteria may include profitability potential, fast probable growth in a customer segment, our competence in a certain area and that it could be fun, etc. Criteria are assessed and attractive product combinations are then prioritized in respect of selected customer categories.

Igor Ansoff, Implanting Strategic Management.

Productivity

Productivity in its simplest form can be defined as the number of units of output per unit of input. The most common formula for measuring profitability is:

$$\text{Man-hour productivity} = \frac{\text{Number of units produced}}{\text{Number of hours worked}}$$

Measurement of productivity in man-hours, however, does not make allowances for input of other resources like materials and capital. The word 'productivity' is unclear, among other things because it has different meanings depending on whether we are looking at business economics or at economics as a science. In the science of economics it is an expression of the value of everything that is produced – in which case it could be correctly assumed that we could put up all our production for sale and find buyers for it.

In business economics, productivity is more an expression of how we rationalize our production of goods and services but it does not take into account value for our customers' or the recipients of those goods and services. We have therefore chosen to look at productivity in the light of efficiency (a word with the same root as effect), which indicates value for the recipient of goods and services.

Productivity is an expression of the generative element in production, while efficiency is a function of value and productivity. The productivity of steam engines in a company can be very high but if nobody wants to buy steam engines, the efficiency of the company will be zero. A company can be inefficient in two ways. Either it produces products for which buyers are willing to pay a certain price but which are more expensive to produce, in which case the problem is primarily one of productivity (certain car manufacturers could serve as examples here); or it has a high productivity of goods and services but nobody is willing to pay for them, as with companies with internal suppliers or parts of the public sector that supply services which people are not willing to pay for. An example of the latter can be taken from the entertainments industry, where a ticket to the opera is subsidized to the tune of 180 euros.

The distinction between efficiency and productivity is thus more than just a question of semantics; it is one of great importance. The idea of efficiency is in fact central to all business economics and should be clearly understood. There are different kinds of productivity:

Total productivity is a measurement that takes account of all the resources consumed in production: capital, labour and materials. To be able to compare these various resources input of all of them must be expressed in terms of a common standard of value, for instance money.

$$\text{Total production} = \frac{\text{Number of units produced}}{\text{Costs}}$$

Capital productivity is measured as the ratio of units produced to the market value of the total assets required to produce them.

Value-added productivity is a quotient derived from value added and the number of hours worked or sometimes the number of persons employed. Once we know the value of what has been sold, we can obtain an expression of the value added produced by each employee.

Value added per employee may differ widely between industries. Stockbrokers, investment bankers and management consultants have produced the highest added value per employee in the last decade. Added value is of special importance in knowledge companies, where it is expressed in different ways, salary being one of them.

The definition of value added per employee (or per hour) is based on the following factors:

1. Revenue = operational revenue.

2. Input costs = purchasing costs of a direct character.

3. Personnel = all employee costs, including fringe benefits, social welfare, etc. Bought- in services, for whatever purpose they are intended, should not be included.

4. Overheads = costs of an operational character, including those for purchased services if they have not been accounted for under input costs.

5. Number of personnel = the average number of personnel in the period.

Value-added productivity can be defined as:

Revenue – input costs – overheads.

Number of employees

If we change the number of employees by buying products or services from outside, the denominator in the formula changes, but this is matched by a reduction in the numerator because the buy-in cost rises.

Changes in value-added productivity are thus an important parameter in make-or-buy analyzes.

The classical make-or-buy analysis (closely related to outsourcing) is based on industrial production, i.e. manufacturing, but now has to be gradually adapted to the provision of services. An essential component in this respect is to identify the internal part of production that is not demanded, or the value of which is low. The purchase of services externally tends to lead to a build-up of bureaucracy in the form of unnecessary service production.

Important too is the ratio of capital to labour through investment in automation. If the number of personnel in a company is reduced because a particular step in their work has been automated through investment in machinery, then this should be reflected in the value-added formula to give evidence of the resulting profitability.

The following modified formula makes these relationships clearer:

$$\frac{\text{Revenue} - \text{buy-in} - \text{Overheads} - \text{Depreciation} - \text{Interest}}{\text{Number of employees}}$$

Investment in machinery implies one of the following three things:

1. Profitability can be improved by reducing personnel.

2. Investment is of a strategic nature and is a condition for future competitive strength.

3. Volumes can be increased to produce more profits in spite of the fact that value added per employee is falling.

We can consider the effects of replacing labour by capital when value-added productivity is expressed as in our modified version. This analysis is of prime importance.

The concept of productivity causes many sore heads, even in academic circles. We have read articles by professors of productivity who have sometimes used the term to mean efficiency and sometimes to mean what we call productivity. For further reference, see *Profitability* and *Efficiency*.

RECOMMENDED READING

Will Kaydos, Operational Performance Measurement: Increasing Total Productivity.

Profitability

The concept of profitability, which is basic for the existence of any company, has changed in character over the years. During the 1990s and the early part of the present century, the idea of profitability was set to one side in that many business leaders believed that while profitability was essential for a company over a period of time, it should not be the main reason for injections of capital. Some trends in profitability can be given briefly:

1. Profitability is defined as return on invested capital. This traditional idea of profitability arose in the 1900s.

2. There has been a focus on cash flow in recent years. A company's long-term profit is no longer seen to be as important as the cash flow that can be generated, however this may be done. Large

organizations have favoured cash flow over profitability and sometimes made some dreadful business decisions.

3. Time horizons have become increasingly more important. Managements have been rewarded for short-term improvements to profitability that have often proved detrimental to their companies in the long-term.

4. Shareholder value has for a long time been in the spotlight. Employees and customers, the two other main stakeholders, have been left in the shade, while 'value- based', as in value-based management, has become the new catchword (see *Value and EVA*).

5. The term profitability is not confined to the world of business. It has been extended to indicate utility for consumers in relation to costs.

The term profitability is traditionally used in industry as a synonym for return on investment (ROI).

Return on investment is calculated by the following formula:

$$ROI = \frac{Revenues \% costs}{capital}$$

ROI, however, is less meaningful as a criterion of the profitability of companies with a knowledge base. The return on capital invested in, say, a data consultancy firm, says very little about that firm's performance, because its assets generally consist of the office furniture, computers and perhaps company cars. In assessing the profitability of companies that produce services, we must use other yardsticks like profit margin, that is the ratio of profit to turnover, or some other appropriate criterion. The ROI formula does however apply to companies that depend on capital invested in fixed assets and/or inventory to carry on their business.

A holistic view of management generally involves the ability to manipulate all the components of the ROI formula:

1. Revenues are simply price multiplied by quantity, whether we are selling goods or services. The price that can be charged depends on customer-perceived value. Marketing skills, together with quality and price, determine the quantity that can be sold.

2. Costs are of two kinds. First there are fixed or capacity costs, which remain the same no matter how many or how few units are manufactured or sold. The second type of costs are variable or unit costs, which are incurred only when units are manufactured or sold.

3. Capital consists of fixed assets, receivables and inventory. Capital is interesting because it occurs in both the numerator and the denominator of the ROI formula, appearing in the numerator as interest and depreciation costs. The effects of a reduction in capital are therefore doubled.

A key question that has yet to find a theoretical answer is how to judge the profitability of non-financial capital such as individual skills and know-how. Most service companies depend on both non-financial and financial capital.

The importance of intellectual and knowledge capital was brought to the fore in the 1990s. The observation has been made that fixed assets have little value without the know-how to exploit them. The part played by industrial production in the gross national product (GNP) generally in the world has diminished. In Sweden it has currently dropped to 17 per cent. Great chunks of industrial service producing units have been outsourced. As a result the ROI formula is of less value and to some extent has acquired a different meaning. Not only the traditional yield on capital but also the returns on intellectual capital are called into question. How do you evaluate and keep revenue from intellectual capital? These are some of the important questions that have come to affect the ROI concept (see *Intellectual capital*).

Strategic development aims at long-term profitability, while operative management aims at short-term profitability. Timeframe is a key consideration in business management. What sacrifices do we need to make today to assure future profitability? Long-term development of a strategic nature is usually booked as a cost, reducing the profit recorded in the year-end accounts. Yet the return on such investments takes a long time to become apparent. The best leaders naturally strive for both short-term and long-term profitability, though the latter may conflict with their emoluments, career prospects, etc. Setting the timeframe for profitability is a tough problem.

Value-added productivity is a model that sometimes makes an excellent tool for making decisions on outsourcing, the compensation of work with capital, etc. Value-added simply means that from a company's total revenue we deduct all purchases and costs and divide by the number of its employees. In this way we obtain an expression of the value added that each employee generates. The formula for value-added productivity is:

Value added =

$$\frac{\text{Revenue} - (\text{purchases} + \text{overheads} + \text{depreciation} + \text{interest})}{\text{Number of employees (possibly, the number of hours)}}$$

If a business is outsourced, the number of its employees should be reduced in the denominator while the services procured appear as purchases in the numerator and make this figure smaller. If work is automated by investment in machines this should be reflected by a smaller denominator due to a reduction of employees, while the numerator is deflated by depreciation and interest. Net added value should be positive if profitability is to increase. Profitability, in both the literal and metaphorical sense of the word, is becoming increasingly important as an expression of an organization's existence and efficiency.

RECOMMENDED READING

1. Adrian Slowotzky, The Art of Profitability.

2. Robert S Kaplan and Robin Cooper, Cost x Effect: Using Integrated Cost Systems to Drive Profitability and Performance.

Quality

Deming and Juran, the quality management theorists, were pioneers when during the 1950s the concept of quality was introduced and made a steady impact. Their theories were adopted by the Japanese who, as a nation, suffered because of the bad reputation of their goods during this period. An intensive programme of quality work began, with quality circles, quality assurance, zero-fault quality control and quality development.

Originally, quality was measured in terms of number of defects, a measure of the number of faults per unit produced. The term functional quality, which came into use later, meant that products were assessed in terms of their ability to perform the function the customer wanted to use them for; and when we speak of quality today, we mean customer-perceived quality, in which has been included a number of factors.

The latter definition therefore represents a substantial broadening of the meaning of the term. Quality then needs to be carefully defined in relation to the context in which it is used. Within the broad meaning of the word quality we can distinguish two principal senses in which the meaning of the term can be discussed.

The first is production-related quality: zero defects, lean production, etc. The second is customer-perceived quality, which influences the frequency of repeated purchases, and so on. The figure below illustrates how these two senses of the word quality affect a company's profit and loss account.

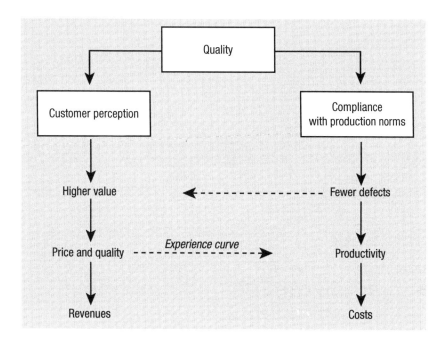

Organizations tend to overrate the importance of product-related quality at the expense of service-related quality. The diagram below, which comes from PIMS research (see the entry under this PIMS) shows how suppliers of a product attach more importance to product-related variables than do the buyers of the product.

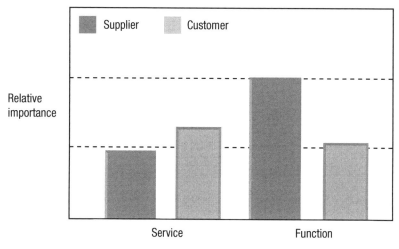

Quality development all over the world has led to different kinds of awards for excellent quality. One of these is the Malcolm Baldridge National Quality Award in the USA and USK (*Utmärkelsen Svensk Kvalitet*), the Swedish Quality Award, which was founded by the Institute for Quality Development (SIQ) in Sweden in 1993.

The basis for the Swedish award is that there should be evidence of 13 fundamental criteria throughout companies considered for awards:

1. Customer orientation
2. Leadership
3. Full participation
4. Competence
5. Long-range outlook
6. Public responsibility
7. Process quality
8. Preventive actions
9. Continuous improvement
10. Learning from others
11. Fast response
12. Management by fact
13. Partnership development

More recently, quality has increasingly come to be associated with the ISO 9000 quality standards. ISO stands for International Organization for Standardization and 9000 is the number series that was chosen for quality (the 14000 series for example was chosen for the environment). The standard was first published in 1987 and has been revised several times since then. The intention from the beginning was to use the standard as a basis for agreements between customer and supplier. But nowadays many organizations choose to carry out quality reviews in order to get a quality certification, where an authorized third party examines whether the provisions of the standard have been observed.

The ISO system is often criticized for generating bureaucracy and impeding progress. This is especially true when a company chooses to introduce a quality management system in order to get a certificate, which its customers might want, rather than from a real desire to improve customer-perceived quality. A trend these days is to integrate quality management systems into structures and management systems already in place, so that extra administration costs can be avoided. For more on this, see *Management systems*.

Another framework for quality work has been provided by the European Foundation for Quality Management (EFQM), which was founded in 1988 through an initiative by business leaders in Western Europe. The European Quality Award was created in 1991 by EFQM in coordination with the European Organization for Quality and the European Commission. The European Quality Award is given to the company which is judged to best represent Total Quality Management (TQM) in Western Europe. The first to receive the award was the Rank Xerox organization, in 1992.

We conclude this section by giving Dr W Edwards Deming's definitions of quality, total quality and total quality management (TQM):

1. Quality is continuously meeting customers' needs.

2. Total quality is continuously meeting customers' needs at the lowest possible cost.

3. Total quality management (TQM) is meeting customers' needs at the lowest possible cost through an organization's full participation.

RECOMMENDED READING

1. Joseph M Juran and A Blanton Godfrey, Juran's Quality Handbook.

2. W Edwards Deming, The New Economics for Industry, Government, Education.

Rationalization

By rationalization we mean the measures to achieve either the same production with less consumption of resources, or increased production with the same consumption of resources. By resources we mean capital, overheads, materials and personnel.

Development work was at one time closely associated with cost rationalization through economies of scale. Thinking on the subject of high market share was based on the need to produce large quantities in order to reduce the cost per unit. Rationalization of the cost mass is a necessary everyday phenomenon that occasionally requires an extra effort to prevent degeneration of a company's profitability.

The true meaning of economy is 'management of scarce resources'. The term economy thus implies a continuous demand for rationalization, that is, orientation towards shrinking resources. All economic activity is based on 'doing more, better and faster with less resources'.

The difference between economy and business is that economy is concerned solely with utilization of resources, while business also includes the creation of value for customers, as well as an organization's innovative strength. The pendulum principle makes it easy to swing too far to one extreme or the other, for example by underestimating the value of rationalization to long-term profitability. Rationalization is apt to be forgotten in periods of rapid development.

The term operational efficiency refers to the management of resources in current business. It is actually a synonym for continuous rationalization, expressing how efficiently we make use of the structure of competence, machinery, buildings, or whatever we work with. The problem that is apt to arise in trying to achieve operational efficiency is that it is easy to neglect our company's strategic aims and customer-perceived value.

Productivity in day-to-day operations often conflicts with the concept of value to customers. This is troublesome and a challenge and touches the very heart of businessmanship. For businessmanship is the art of considering both customer-perceived value and the rational use of resources, and striking an optimum balance benefiting the development of business in the longer term.

Sometimes a distinction is made between:

- strategic level
- tactical level
- functional or operative level

Generally speaking we ignore the tactical level, which lacks instructive value. Then again, the terms functional productivity and operative productivity are often used synonymously. This is not generally a problem. Meanwhile the following distinction may be valuable:

Operative efficiency calls for the ability to 'do things right' with a minimum input of resources.

To give a trivial example, moving a person from Manhattan to Kennedy airport (whether s/he wants to go there or not).

Continually working to achieve constant improvement is a fundamental aspect of businessmanship but it is often overlooked. In Japan this is termed Kaizen (see this term). When we speak of constant improvement what we actually mean is rationalization on a daily basis. The intention is to stimulate creative thinking, look beyond routine tasks and identify areas that call out for improvement. The constant repetition of tasks tends to make us dull and unable to identify things for improvement. Constant improvement also means to combat monotony and inject a little inspiration into our work. The work of rationalization is in fact one of the most common 'sins of omission' of business management.

To simplify somewhat, we could say that operative control is control of the activities of an organization within given terms of reference, while strategic control concerns itself with stating these terms of reference.

Rationalization is related to a number of other concepts. Some of the most important are:

1. The concept of efficiency is fundamental to companies operating on a basis of planned economic relations.
2. The concept of productivity as a special case of efficiency. For further information see both of these terms.
3. Cost reduction as an expression of economy of resources.

4. Capital rationality in organizations where a return on investment is a measure of profitability.

5. Businessmanship as an expression of the relation between customer value and productivity.

6. Relative cost position, which is an expression of our own consumption of resources in relation to our competitors or other players we compare ourselves to.

RECOMMENDED READING

Masaaki Imai, Kaizen: The Key To Japan's Competitive Success.

Relative cost position

This term is often abbreviated to RCP. It states the cost of a business unit or function in relation to those of its competitors or to other points of reference. RCP is usually expressed as an index obtained by dividing the costs of a given business unit by the average costs of each of its competitors. An index of 1.0 thus means that the costs of a business unit exactly match those of its competitors. An index of less than 1.0 indicates a cost advantage, while a figure above 1.0 indicates a cost disadvantage.

RCP can be analyzed for a single product, for a product line, for a business unit, for a company as a whole, or for some function within a company, for example, the in-flight service in an airline or the marketing department in a manufacturing company. The costs included in the analysis may comprise variable costs, total costs, or some combination of elements in the cost structure of the business.

Cost position is especially important in the concept of *efficiency* (see this term). A planned economy operates within the framework of an organization taken as a whole. That is to say, its business units supply departments that do not have a free choice between different suppliers and the supplier unit enjoys a monopoly for its products. It can therefore be useful to see cost position in relation to efficiency and the idea of functional strategy (see *Functional strategy*). An organization's competitive strength rests with a number of units, the total costs of which constitute the cost mass of the whole organization. By means of *benchlearning* (see this term) or other methods, the RCP can be established for whichever units management sees fit in order to take appropriate action.

RCP is one of the two cornerstones of competition analysis. The other is analysis of customer-perceived value. Businessmanship is a combination of an ability to create value for customers and the persistent and painstaking management of resources. Or to put it another way, the two cornerstones of competition analysis are the customer's perception of value and RCP in the guise of a comparison between one or more competitors.

A large, international, mechanical engineering corporation recently carried out a study of customer-perceived value. It revealed that the corporation was inferior to its chief competitor on the after-sales side, i.e. in spare part prices, spare part delivery times and price and promptness of technical service.

Concurrently with the development of strategies to improve the after-sales situation, the company mounted a study of its relative cost position. What this study relates to is the one competitor that the corporation meets on all its major markets. The results of an RCP analysis showed that:

1. Production costs expressed as hourly wage rates were higher than the competitor's because production was based in a high-cost environment (Holland), while the competitor did most of its manufacturing in a low-cost environment (Greece). Production costs, in the form of labour and capital costs, accounted for about one-third of sales value. Calculated on this basis, the wage cost disadvantage came to about 4 per cent compared to its main competitor.

2. Components were bought from all over the world and through analysis it was shown that there was no significant difference in this area. The index for this factor was thus 1.0.

3. Central administrative costs were managed much more efficiently than by the company's main competitor. The company in question was of Scandinavian origin, which meant that it had a slimmed down central administrative apparatus with few staff and effective computerized systems for both accounting and logistics. The

analysis showed that administrative efficiency gave a relative cost advantage of 1.5 per cent of total sales value.

4. An analysis of marketing costs pointed to definite inefficiencies in the company in question. A large number of sales companies had been established all over the world and these had grown somewhat bureaucratic. The productivity of the head office marketing organization and sales companies was low compared to the competitor's and the figures revealed a relative cost disadvantage of as much as 5 per cent of sales value.

The foregoing simple analysis shows how an RCP analysis can be built up. The difficult part is not the theory behind the analysis, but getting hold of competitors' cost figures.

This is often easier in businesses like civil aviation or consultancy. In the airline business, for example, we may choose to compare our position with that of a company with which we have little direct competition. SAS can freely exchange information with Quantas or Japan Airlines and a consultancy firm can compare its administrative structures with a company of similar composition in another country.

RCP should by its very definition be compared to something else, perhaps a company's own experience curve, i.e. the development of costs over a period of time in relation to something. A company's RCP can also be related to other similar organizations through *benchmarking* (see this term). One point of reference is zero-base (see this term), i.e. starting with the assumption that nothing exists and then building a new entity, justifying every step of the process. A fourth reference point may lie in the future through scenario building, where an imagined position worth striving for is used as a reference point as well as a goal (see *Scenario*).

The figure below shows how the different concepts can be inter-related.

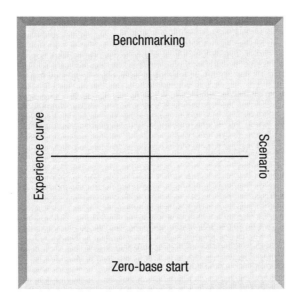

RECOMMENDED READING

1. Michael E Porter, Competitive Advantage of Nations.

2. Bengt Karlöf Kurt Lundgren and Marie Edenfeldt Froment, Benchlearning: Good Examples as a Lever for Development.

Resources – costs, capital and people

The heading summarises the three main kinds of resources we usually speak of, namely costs, capital and people. All of these three kinds of resources can suffer from a surfeit: there can be too much of a good thing. For a better understanding of what they mean, however, we need to break them down into their components.

Capital is composed of:

- bills receivable from customers.
- fixed assets.
- inventory.

The cost mass can be similarly broken down into some main cost categories:

- personnel costs
- capital costs
- material costs
- overheads

People are designated both as a cost and a resource in that they provide the work force and solve problems. The following classification of people was introduced recently:

- People who solve problems and make decisions about what is to be done.
- People who carry out tasks that have been given to them when problems have been solved and decisions have been taken by other people.

The rational use of resources is one of the two chief areas of businessmanship; the other one is *creation of value* (see *Value*).

Management of resources used to be the main object of strategy. Advantages of scale and economies through mass production were key concepts for two-thirds of the last century when demand generally exceeded supply. At first, much less attention was paid to capital than to costs, the reason being that capital costs were small on account of low interest rates. That aspect, as well as much else, changed in the mid-1970s, and much has been learnt about the use of capital since then.

The relationship is most simply expressed by the return-on-investment formula:

$$ROI = \frac{\text{Revenues \% costs}}{\text{capital}}$$

Revenue here represents the creation of value for the customer, while costs and capital stand for the use of resources. A holistic view of business involves the ability to strike the right balance between these three basic elements of business management.

There is a close correlation between the terms capital and investment. Capital is shown on the asset side of the balance sheet under the headings of fixed assets (production equipment, buildings or whatever), inventory (raw materials, work in progress and stocks of finished goods) and bills receivable, which are administered by techniques known collectively as cash management.

The close connection between investment and capital is gradually disappearing as an ever-increasing part of resources consumed are being recorded as costs instead of being activated in a balance sheet. A definition of investment is: a financial sacrifice made in the present in expectation of future profit.

As more and more investment is being recorded as a cost, a conflict is arising between the modern idea of investment and traditional accounting methods. Knowledge capital, also known as intellectual capital, has become a subject of much interest and is one resource that cannot be found in the balance sheet. Intellectual capital is the principal asset in many companies today, and the way it is handled calls for special skills (see *Intellectual capital*).

The term *resource control* has come to mean primarily the utilization of resources in the form of capital and costs to guide businesses as effectively as possible to a position of competitive strength. Two dilemmas have been pointed out in the foregoing: the book treatment of costs as an investment, and the appropriation of human intelligence as intellectual capital.

Resource control calls for special management skills. The market dimension has been largely responsible for the increasing number of prizes and volumes dedicated to the subject. Meanwhile, resources still have to be managed by executives. We know of countless examples of management success stories in times of prosperity; but these managements have not necessarily been able to control their resources in difficult times.

We refer the interested reader to the terms *Productivity, Rationalization and Relative Cost Position.*

RECOMMENDED READING

1. Dave Ulrich and Norm Smallwood, Why the Bottom Line ISN'T: How to Build Value Through People and Organization.

2. David J Collis and Cynthia A Montgomery, Coporate Strategy: A Resource-Based Approach.

3. Jonathan Mun, Real Options Analysis: Tools and Techniques for Valuing Strategic Investments and Decisions.

Risk analysis

Every decision entails some kind of risk, whether it is an environmental risk, the risk of making a financially disadvantageous investment, the risk that a competitor will make a better decision, etc. Taking risks can cause a business financial damage or some other inconvenience. From a management perspective, risk analysis has come to play an important role in decision-making and project planning.

A simple formula to calculate degree of risk is:

Risk = Probability x Consequence

Risk is then a function of the probability that an element of risk will occur and the consequences that will result if it occurs. Consequences can be estimated in monetary terms but are usually expressed in the form of an index.

Let us suppose that a management group has to choose between five different strategies, from A to E. For each strategy, there is an identified element of risk (F-J). The management group has evaluated for each element of risk:

1. the probability that it will happen; and

2. the consequence if it happens.

Probability is expressed as a percentage and consequences have been given a value of 1 to 10, where 1 = small consequences and 10 = disastrous consequences. The result can be seen in the following table (overleaf).

Alternative	Element of risk	Probability	Consequence	Risk
A	F	20 % (0,2)	10	2
B	G	80 % (0,8)	8	6.4
C	H	50 % (0,5)	4	2
D	I	90 % (0,9)	2	1.8
E	J	20 % (0,2)	4	0.8

An example might be an investment in new technology, where the element of risk is that this technology will not find favour with customers. Another might be acceptance of a customer's delivery requirements, with the element of risk being that we will not be able to make delivery in time with the agreed level of quality.

Looking at the results, element G should be an obvious candidate calling for action. But tolerance levels are commonly given for consequence values, for instance, action must be taken on all risks with a potential consequence of over 7. In that case element F should be prioritized, even if the risk here is quite small because of the slight probability. It is easier to appreciate the basis on which decisions are taken if the elements of risk are charted in a graph, with Consequence and Probability as the two axes. Based on the figures from the above table, an illustration can be seen overleaf.

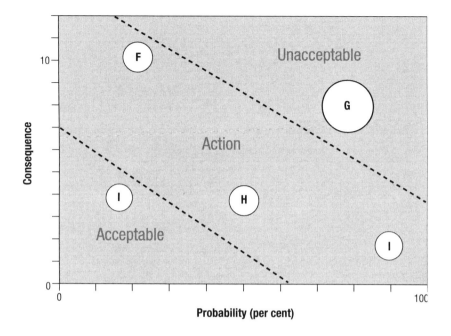

The size of the circles indicate the level (probability x consequence) of risk, while different fields in the graph are normally demarcated by lines. Elements of risk that come into the bottom left-hand corner are acceptable. Action should be taken on those that fall into the middle field, while those elements coming into the upper right-hand field are unacceptable and should be either avoided or eliminated. The graph can thus be used for making informed decisions on the risks presented by different alternatives. The same method can of course be used to deal with the risks involved in decisions that have already been made.

In this section we have chosen to give a fairly general model often used for risk analysis. This subject is not simple, however, and calls for considerable expertise. Company policy and stakeholder requirements will often help to decide what is an acceptable risk and what is not.

Other methods used for risk analysis include different kinds of simulation (for example the Monte Carlo simulation), scenario analysis (see *Scenario*) and different types of case study.

RECOMMENDED READING

1. Hugh Courntney et al, Harvard Business Review on Managing Uncertainty.

2. James Lam, Enterprise Risk Management: From Incentives to Controls.

3. Michel Crouhy, Dan Galai and Robert Mark, Risk Management.

4. Neil A Doherty, Integrated Risk Management: Techniques and Strategies for Managing Corporate Risk.

The S-Curve

The S-curve has become very popular mainly in technology-driven business development, and represents the relationship between resources available for improvement to production and the effect of action taken in this respect. The S-curve is shown below in its common form.

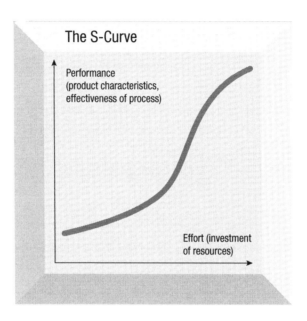

In technology-based business development the S-curve is usually used to illustrate the performance improvements of established technology in relation to new technology. A company which invests in new technology at an early stage often lacks a tradition in the industry where applications are developed. There are plenty of examples where a shift in technology has been initiated by actors outside the industry in question. For example, the first ice machines were developed by semi-conductor companies and not by companies in the ice-making industry. Companies in the semi-conductor industry developed the first electronic calculators and not companies in the traditional electro-mechanical calculator industry.

New technology has a revolutionary effect in an industry because technology in general is only capable of a certain level of performance determined by the laws of physics. The level of performance of a piston-engine is limited by forces resulting from friction and thermo-dynamics.

Advances in an area with existing demand are generally initially small when new technology is applied. Technology is then gradually improved so that returns in the form of better performance rise quickly, only to gradually fall off as the physical limits of the technology are approached. The law of diminishing returns enters into force and a performance ceiling is reached. A shift in technology occurs and a new performance ceiling is set. This can be seen in the illustration below.

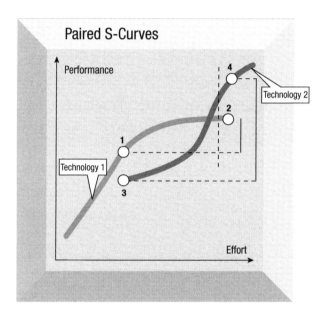

Two companies are in the market. Company A uses technology 1 and at point 1 can only marginally affect performance, reaching point 2. Company B begins to apply new technology with a higher technical performance ceiling; it puts its resources into technology 2. This technology is initially weaker than technology 1 from a performance perspective, but has much greater potential. Company B gradually comes to point 4.

At this point, Company B can take large market shares from Company A. The situation represented by the illustration can be exemplified by Boeing Group's decision to change to jet engines in its development work at the end of the 1940s, while McDonnell Douglas stubbornly stuck to Pratt & Whitney's piston engines which were then near to their performance ceiling. It is true that McDonnell Douglas was able to raise the stakes some-

324

what with the DC-7 but only with high operational costs and unreliable performance. The four-engine DC-7 was once called the world's fastest 3-engine aircraft, a reference to the fact that Douglas had instructed its pilots to run the engines at high power settings to achieve the promized performance. As a result, one of the engines often failed. The relationship between electro-mechanical calculators and electronic ones serves as another example of the illustration above.

Of course the model is a simplification of reality but this does not detract from the essential truth that when new technology takes hold in an area with existing demand that is based on old technology, the performance ceiling suddenly shoots up.

RECOMMENDED READING

David B Montgomery and George S Day, Experience Curves: Evidence, Empirical Methods and Applications.

Sales force

Nowadays a company's success depends more and more on the quality and performance of its sales force. Results from a comprehensive empirical study carried out by the HR Chally Group reveal that from 40 to 50 per cent of a company's growth is put down to the competence, organization and quality of its sales force. Two developments explain the increasing importance of an effective and high-performance sales force. These are:

1. Coordination of purchasing. Customers are coordinating their purchasing to a few preferred suppliers who cover a large part of their customer's needs. A salesperson's ability to understand the customer's business and skill in the development and management of long-term customer relations are therefore increasingly important.

2. The time given to product management through differentiation is decreasing because of shorter product life cycles and the speed of imitation, so that in many cases, the salesperson is given responsibility for the differentiated function. A study carried out by the HR Chally Group showed that customers in many cases thought that a sales force's effectiveness had a greater effect on their decision to buy than the qualities of the product they were selling.

A consequence of the above trends is that competition is becoming tougher and customers are becoming more powerful; it is a buyer's market. Given these conditions, it is vital for a business to have a focused and effective sales force.

Much of the literature on selling focuses on sales techniques (for example how questions are structured and sales are closed) and the personal development of a salesperson (for example, overcoming blocks such as the fear of calling a customer.) These things are naturally important, but should be supplemented by structural and cultural functions if a sales force is to be successful.

Some important factors in the development of a business's sales performance are:

- **Cultural factors**. Do we have a performance-oriented sales culture that focuses on developing and maintaining good customer relations? What is the status of the sales organization in the business? Is the sales director part of the management group?

- **Sales organization**. Do we have an effective sales organization unhindered by bureaucracy, for instance in the form of complicated decision procedures? How much of the sales force's time is spent on administration and other in-house work? Are salespeople given support (for instance technical support) to assist their work?

- **Sales planning**. Is there a simple sales process that everyone knows and adheres to? How are goals for the sales organization established? Do salespeople have personal development plans? How does the sales force get feedback on its performance?

- **Support system**. Are our support systems user-friendly? Are they constructed to creat minimal administration and maximum value?

Do customers have access to parts of the information in information systems? Is it possible to automate certain routine tasks?

- **Competence provision**. Do we have competence profiles for different categories of salesperson? Do local sales managers have the necessary competence for effective recruiting? How are new salespeople phased into their roles without this affecting customers adversely? How do we avoid losing our top salespeople? Are there procedures in respect of customer relations when a salesperson leaves?

- **Customer relations**. Do we know what customers think of our sales force? How much time does the sales force spend with customers? Are our customers loyal? How much of customers' total purchasing in a particular area do we have? What service do we provide for our customers apart from sales work?

- **Market**. Do we have a meaningful market segment? Do we know the profiles of customer need structures in the different segments? Have we thought of the possibility of differentiating reward models and competence requirements for different segments? Have we made an assessment of the products and segments we should focus on based on criteria such as growth potential, profitability and our own competence? Do the degrees of repurchase and customer satisfaction vary between segments and if so, why?

- **Adaptability**. Do we have a flexible sales organization that can adapt quickly to meet new customer needs and exploit new opportunities? Are decisions centralized or decentralized (i.e. taken locally)? Do we have open customer relationships and good communication with them? How, when and in which forums are trends and developments in the business's sales, both generally and in respect of specific customers or customer segments, assessed?

A sales organization's performance can be measured and followed up in different ways. Measurements are usually divided into outcome measurements (which describe results) and leading indicators (which indicate performance leading up to results). Greater focus is being placed on the latter category, as such measurements can be early warning signals that make it possible to influence actions before they have had time to affect income and cause possibly irreparable damage. Metrics common to each category (with examples) are:

- Outcome metrics.
- Costs/income metrics.
  - Sales costs (including cost allocation through, for instance, ABC – see this section).
  - Sales contribution to profitability.
  - Profitability contribution per salesperson.
  - Sales costs' portion of turnover.
- Growth metrics.
  - Sales growth.
  - Marginal growth (relationship between sales growth and cost trend).
- Leading indicators.
- Time metrics.
  - Portion of administrative time.
  - Portion of time with customer.
- Effectiveness metrics.
  - Cycle time (e.g. sales process) metrics.
  - Portion of revenue-contributing persons (number of salespeople divided by total number of people in the sales organization).
  - Number of customer visits per salesperson and month.
  - Number of offers per salesperson and month.
  - Number of offers leading to a deal ('win-ratio').
- Customer metrics.
  - Degree of repurchase.
  - Customer satisfaction.
  - Portion of customers' sales.
  - Market share.
  - Average sales per customer.

- Co-worker metrics.
  - Salesperson satisfaction.
  - Business/manager satisfaction with salespeople.
  - Staff turnover
  - Number of training days per year.

The most common metrics, apart from outcome metrics, are customer metrics such as customer satisfaction and degree of repurchase. The latter is often given as one of the very most important metrics, as it is roughly from five to seven times as expensive to replace a lost customer as it is to offer an existing customer an equivalent amount of value. Unfortunately, repurchase is often measured as, 'portion of sales from previous customers'. A high level of repurchase using this means of calculation really tells us nothing; it is just as likely to be because of a greater portion of customers who return as because the number of new customer sales has dropped. It is better to measure degree of repurchase as, 'the portion of customers who return', which will give a direct measure of customer satisfaction. We would also raise a finger of warning in connection with customer surveys that have not been properly prepared. Three of the most important things to note in this respect are:

1. What will we get from a customer survey? A 'satisfied customer index' in itself has no immediate value except perhaps as marketing material. It is vital to ask the right questions if the replies are to have a direct influence on improvement work. PDS (see the section under this term) is a useful method for this purpose.

2. How should the results of a survey be analyzed? It can often be useful to discuss results together with customers, or at least make a thorough internal analysis. There are many examples of surveys which reported extremely high customer satisfaction, when customers had meanwhile switched to the products of other companies. Analysis must aim to interpret results on the basis of the questions which have been formulated.

3. How are results dealt with in the organization? Perhaps the greatest danger in carrying out customer surveys is a failure to deal with results so that both customers and the sections of the sales organization working with customers benefit from the survey.

Nothing could be worse than customers registering their complaints then seeing nothing being done about them. Surveys can then have negative consequences for a business.

RECOMMENDED READING

1. David J Arnold, Sales Management (Business Fundamental Series).

2. Frank C Cespedes, Concurrent Marketing: Integrating Product, Sales and Service.

3. Neil Rackham and John R Devincentis, Rethinking the Sales Force: Redefining Selling to Create and Capture Customer Value.

4. Stephan Schiffman, The 25 Sales Habits of Highly Successful Salespeople.

Scenario

A scenario is defined as an assumed or possible course of events in a given area. The scenario form is used as an alternative to forecasts of an extrapolatory nature. Forecasts are predictions of the future based on known trends and known facts. The forecast method, however, is incapable of predicting discontinuities and is not conducive to the free thinking that is essential at times when there is a need to defend a situation instead of planning another one.

The terms scenario, prognosis and vision can be distinguished as follows:

- Forecast: what we think will happen.
- Scenario: what *can* happen.
- Vision: what we want to happen, based on belief (forecast) and possible situations (scenarios).

Forecasting was refined and played an important part in the age of technocratic planning (a technocrat is one who applies rational technical or economic criteria without regard for human values). During the period from World War II up to the mid-1970s when the future was predictable, forecasting methods of all kinds seemed to work admirably as a tool for determining strategy. As part of the radical reappraisal that had to be made after the crises of the 1970s, traditional forecasting methods were also critically reviewed. What struck heads of businesses most forcefully in those days was the tendency of forecasts to prolong existing trends, which pointed to investment in increased capacity and other forms of expansion. Such investments showed a very poor return when the demand curve flattened out, leading to overcapacity in many industries. There was a need to find other ways of assessing the future. The scenario form has proved to be effective in two ways:

1. In the first place, it is possible to state a probable line of development on the basis of predictions and assumptions.

2. In the second place, it is possible to visualize alternative courses of events, and use them for the basis of intelligent discussion.

The scenario, then, is a description of a future set of circumstances. It may refer to business or some other form of activity, and is based on a selection of assumptions and forecasts about future events.

In the field of strategy the scenario form is generally used to predict possible structural changes in an industry and probable competitive situations. Here the scenario generally serves as a platform for creative discussions, strategic thinking and, of course, the determination of a strategy.

The forecasts and assumptions on which a scenario is constructed must embrace all the factors that have a bearing on the future of a business. One of the most important advantages of the scenario is that both extremes and probable developments can be taken into account in an intelligent discussion, based on the assumptions and forecasts underlying the scenario.

We usually speak in terms of pessimistic, probable and optimistic scenarios. The probable scenario is the one on which decisions and strategy formulations are usually based, whereas the extreme cases help management to identify the factors that are relevant to the future of the business. However, these distinctions have been heavily criticized in that a normal scenario tends to be self-evident. It can be a useful exercise to work with several (let us say, four) scenarios, where the degree of probability of each one is not evaluated at first. A *scenario cross* can be produced in which the extremes of two different variables are placed opposite one another to form four scenarios.

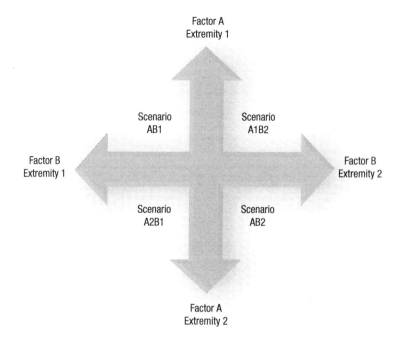

Factor A
Extremity 1

Scenario
AB1

Scenario
A1B2

Factor B
Extremity 1

Factor B
Extremity 2

Scenario
A2B1

Scenario
AB2

Factor A
Extremity 2

The emerging scenarios should meet the following criteria:

- Scenarios should be plausible, motivating, but not complete fiction.

- Scenarios and the variables on which they are founded should be relevant to both the organization as well as the issue at hand (perhaps a certain strategy with an uncertain future).

- Scenarios should differ from each other in essential aspects.

- Scenarios should be given a name and should be described so as to make them seem real and dynamic.

RECOMMENDED READING

1. Kees van der Heijden, Scenarios: The Art of Strategic Conversation.

2. Peter Schwartz, The Art of the Long View: Planning for the Future in an Uncertain World.

3. Mats Lindgren and Hans Bandhold, Scenario Planning: The Link Between Future and Strategy.

Segmentation and differentiation

These two terms can suitably be defined as follows:

1. Segmentation is the process of dividing a total market into distinct sub-sets of customers with similar demand.

2. Differentiation means a special formulation of a product (goods and services) and price to match the demand and cost structure respectively of the segment for which they are intended.

Segmentation and differentiation are linked terms, one having to do with demand and the other with supply.

A segment, then, is a subgroup characterized by shared evaluation of the utility functions of a product or service. The segmentation process can be separated into two phases:

1. Grouping individuals with the same evaluations of utility functions

2. Labelling or identifying the segments

Companies often begin by labelling segments, which sometimes leads to erroneous segmentation.

Segmentation has proved to be a much more intricate process than marketers originally thought. Traditional methods of market analysis do not give automatic answers to the problems of segmentation, for a segment is not the same thing as a statistical group, although it may be practical to work with such groups. We speak for example of large companies that need a particular kind of service, medium-sized ones that need another kind, and small companies that need a third kind of service.

The segmentation process can be viewed in two ways. Either we separate a homogenous market comprising a large number of individuals into segments, or else we group a large number of individuals into a smaller number of operative segments. This is shown in the illustration overleaf.

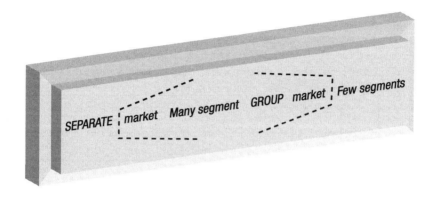

A homogenous market can be separated into a number of segments, and a market with many small segments can be grouped into a smaller number of operational segments.

Such a breakdown by size is only an approximation, or rough estimate, of something else that we are really looking for. What we are trying to identify in terms of size of company may, for example, be the level of knowledge of the management or degree of willingness to buy a particular service; perhaps large companies are less price sensitive when they pay for consultancy services than small companies, and so on.

Such differences in demand usually have nothing to do with the statistical groupings as such, but are often assumed to match those groupings reasonably well, or at any rate well enough for marketing purposes.

Another way to explain the use of statistical groupings is that willingness to buy simply cannot be ascertained without comprehensive polling, so estimates are used instead. Marketing aimed at private consumers often uses other statistical criteria such as age group, religion, sex, or place of residence. These, too, are approximations of actual market segments; the statistical groupings are assumed to correspond to types of buying behaviour. Intelligent segmentation requires a great measure of creative ability, a fact that is often neglected.

SAS's identification of the special needs of business travellers is an example of segmentation and consequent differentiation. The same thing was done a few years earlier by Linjeflyg (the Swedish domestic airline now merged with SAS), which managed to satisfy the demand of private passengers for low-price air travel by utilizing the great increase in carrying capacity afforded by its new fleet of Metropolitan aircraft in combination with off-peak flights that were little used by business passengers.

The re-segmentation undertaken by Swedish speciality car-makers offers a splendid example of how different segments of a market can be identified and the product differentiated accordingly:

Volvo has moved from the position of being a manufacturer of fairly ordinary family cars to another, more up-market, segment of family cars that are more comfortable to ride in, thus encroaching on the traditional territory of Mercedes-Benz. At the time of writing, Volvo is a part of Ford's luxury division of cars. Saab has taken a slightly different route and moved in the direction of a sporty type of family car that is fun to drive. It has entered the part of the market traditionally dominated by BMW.

By these exercises in differentiation, both companies have succeeded in attracting a clientele with higher purchasing power, and have been able to raise their prices and improve their margins.

Most people have a tendency to associate differentiation with upgrading, that is, a change in a product that makes it more advanced and expensive. Segmentation, however, does not necessarily mean upgrading. It is merely an orientation to a specific group with a homogenous need structure.

Examples of differentiation that have led to simplification of the product and lower prices are Linjeflyg's drive to attract private passengers, and the establishment of the People's Express airline in the USA. Both companies identified groups looking for a lower-priced product with a lower level of service.

RECOMMENDED READING

1. Jack Trout, Differentiate Or Die: Survival in Our Era of Killer Competition.

2. Michael E Porter, Competitive Strategy: Creating and Sustaining Superior Performance.

3. Michel Wedel and Wagner Kamakura, Market Segmentation: Conceptual and Methodological Foundations.

Service companies and knowledge companies

"Knowledge is power", as Francis Bacon wrote.

Production of services has grown in importance as the proportions of gross national product (the total value of a country's production) accounted for by agricultural and industrial production have declined. Not least in Scandinavia, theories have been formulated about companies that sell services and know-how.

The term 'service company' focuses interest on the value of what is delivered. Services may be unskilled and industrialized, or highly skilled and personalized.

The term 'service company' in itself gives no clue to the know-how content of the services delivered. Some services, like computerized systems, involve heavy capital investment. Others, like medical care, legal advice and management consultancy, require little or no capital, but an extremely high level of knowledge on the part of those who supply the services.

The service component of industrial products is growing proportionately larger in almost all industries. This can include equipment maintenance, after-sales service, financing and other services associated with the actual delivery of hardware.

It is for these reasons that the term 'knowledge company' has gradually gained currency (see also *Knowledge Management*). It is used to distinguish mass production of standard products with low information content from one-off production of goods or services with a high information content. The specific problem of knowledge companies is the difficulty of combining professional skills with management ability. In extreme cases the professional skill is synonymous with the corporate mission. High-profile knowledge companies have chronic difficulty in recruiting people willing and able to assume the role of chief executive.

The term knowledge company should be used advizedly, because many industrial products today have a high software content. There are no obvious generalizations that can be made from different industries with a high knowledge content, so other and more distinctive terms will undoubtedly be coined in the future.

Knowledge companies fall into four main types. The agency is a congenial workplace for professional people, but has low survival potential. The secretariat rates low on both professional and managerial skills. The factory does not have to depend on the problem-solving abilities of individuals. The professional organization is an ideal environment for the development of new skilled employees.

RECOMMENDED READING

1. Karl-Erik Sveiby, The New Organizational Wealth: Managing & Measuring Knowledge-Based Assets.

2. Richard A Normann, Service Management: Strategy and Leadership in Service Business.

Service management system

The idea of the Service Management System emerged gradually in the course of Richard Normann's work on service organizations. According to him, the aim of the theoretical base is to integrate, but also to extend to, the model or magic formula of the service system as developed by Pierre Eiglier and Eric Langeard, the marketing theorists, and to include the corporate mission as expounded in Normann's own book, Creative Management. In the service management model, we begin with *market segment* and proceed to *service concept, service delivery system* and *image. Culture* wraps up the whole concept.

Market segment refers to the special category of customer for whom the whole service system is devized.

Service concept comprises benefits offered to the customer. Experience shows that the service concept often includes highly complex combinations of values that are often difficult to analyze; some of them are tangible, others are psychological or emotional; some are more important than others and can be classed as core services, while others are of a more peripheral nature.

Service delivery system is equivalent to the production and distribution system of a manufacturing company, though often of a radically different kind. We shall consider the service delivery system in some depth because it is here, more often than in the formulation of the service concept, that we find a service company's unique and most innovative ideas. In analyzing the service delivery system, we can distinguish three components:

1. **Staff**: service organizations are usually personality-intensive and the most successful ones have devized highly creative and rigorous methods of discovering, developing and focusing human resources. They also strive to find ways to mobilize people not on their own payroll.

2. **Customers**: the customer plays an astonishingly complex part in a service organization, because s/he not only receives and consumes service but also acts as a component in its production and delivery. This is one of the reasons why customers must be selected and guided just as carefully as the company's own employees.

3. **Technology and physical support**: services, besides being generally personality-intensive, are often capital-intensive or equipment-intensive too. It is worth noting that modern technology, especially information technology, will come to play an important part in influencing social relations.

Image here is regarded as an instrument of information that management can use to influence staff, customers and other suppliers of resources whose function and whose perception of the company and its development affect its position on the market and its cost-effectiveness. In the long run, of course, a company's image depends on what it actually delivers and who its customers are, but in the short-term image can help to fashion a new reality.

Culture and philosophy are the over-riding principles according to which management controls, maintains and develops the social process that manifests itself as delivery of service and gives value to customers. Once a superior service delivery system and a realistic service concept have been established, there is no other component so crucial to the long-term efficiency of a service organization as its culture and philosophy.

RECOMMENDED READING

Richard A Normann, Service Management: Strategy and Leadership in Service Business.

Six Sigma

Six Sigma, as a measurement standard in product variation, goes back to the 1920s when Walter Shewhart showed that three sigma from the mean was the point where a process normally required correction. Credit for coining the term 'six sigma' must however be given to Bill Smith, an engineer at Motorola, where it was developed as a methodology for quality control and cost reduction. John ('Jack') F Welch, General Electric's legendary CEO, was the charismatic apostle for the methodology when it was implemented in the whole group. In 1996 General Electric staked a great deal of time and money on Six Sigma in their attempt to eradicate errors throughout the group by utilizing the statistical expertise acquired through training in Six Sigma.

The result was impressive. There was said to have been a reduction in costs amounting to some eight billion dollars in a three-year period.

Six Sigma is the application of a statistical methodology to business processes in order to improve effectiveness (i.e. value and productivity), thereby raising profitability.

Sigma is a letter in the Greek alphabet that is used to indicate standard deviation.

Six Sigma goes further than merely to reduce defects. It stresses improvements to business processes in general, including reduction in costs, shorter cycle times, greater customer satisfaction and other important metrics. Like many popular initiatives, Six Sigma has blossomed into a whole culture of strategies, tools and statistical methods to improve operating profit.

An essential goal of Six Sigma is to eliminate any suggestion of the waste often to be found in organizational processes. The highest possible productivity and the greatest possible customer value are demanded in today's competitive world. This can only be achieved through systematically working with costs and questions of quality.

Customers want high quality products at lower prices, faster. Six Sigma helps organizations to achieve this goal. Developed from the manufacturing industry, it is a disciplined, fact-based approach to performance that includes service production.

To achieve Six Sigma, a process must not produce more than 3.4 defects per million opportunities for non-conformance, where a defect is defined as everything that is outside customer specification.

The Six Sigma approach is a structured, data-driven method, which focuses on process improvements and the identification and elimination of defects. This is done by the application of two subsidiary initiatives, which go by the acronyms DMAIC and DMADV. DMAIC stands for Define, Measure, Analyze, Improve and Control. The aim of this method is to improve existing processes, which have not come up to specification in respect of quality.

The other method, DMADV, stands for Define, Measure, Analyze, Design and Verify and is an improvement system which focuses on new processes or products. This method can also be applied if an existing process or product needs more than just small improvements.

Both of these Six Sigma methods are carried out by Six Sigma Green Belts and Six Sigma Black Belts and are in turn monitored by Six Sigma Master Black Belts. A Six Sigma Academy has been formed consisting of Black Belts, with the boast that large companies can save a great deal of money per project. The Academy carries out from four to six projects per year.

Six Sigma can be a huge success or an expensive failure depending on how the system is applied. According to its proponents, a successful application of Six Sigma requires the methodology to be introduced into the organizational culture so that co-workers think in terms of Six Sigma techniques during their daily work.

Some of the most important steps in the process have been stated by Forrest W Breyfogle III, founder of the company Smarter Solutions:

Step 1.   *Executive level training.* It is not enough for executives to support Six Sigma, they must lead the process. Many of the less successful Total Quality Management (TQM) projects lacked senior management leadership.

Step 2.   *Establish a customer focus mindset.* The factors that are critical to our customers' success are necessary if a process improvement team is to have true success. Therefore, evaluating customer-perceived quality should be at the fore of the implementation process.

Step 3.   *Define strategic goals.* Six Sigma must be viewed as a method for reaching strategic goals, which in turn must be measurable and have the focus of senior executives. For more information see Goals.

Step 8.   *Mitigate the effect of cultural barriers on success.* Many companies which attempt to improve products or processes with numerous small changes neglect to measure or document results. Substantial improvements are seldom obtained in this way. Companies are embracing Six Sigma not only to improve quality, but also as a catalyst to change the culture of the organization. For more information see Culture.

Step 9.   *Determining strategic Six Sigma metrics.* Metrics must be appropriate to the situation. It is important for Six Sigma metrics to be applied wisely and used for 'fire prevention' rather than 'fire fighting'. According to proponents, there is much confusion in relation to Six Sigma metrics.

Step 16. *Project execution.* The importance of careful preparatory work before the beginning of projects is stressed, as well as the importance of the use of customer feedback in the organization.

Some judgments of Six Sigma

Those who began to work enthusiastically with Six Sigma in the early 1990s now sometimes adopt a more reserved attitude. Jack Welch and General Electric's enthusiasm for the methodology has lead to an almost sectarian development. The analogy with the martial arts, with its green and black belts, can cause many people to distance themselves from Six Sigma, while its proponents often seem to be somewhat fanatical. Nonetheless, there are large and mighty companies and organizations behind the methodology, which emerged at about the same time as Business Process Re-engineering (BPR) and could be said to be a more concrete version of BPR. In recent years, Six Sigma has also been applied to service-producing organizations such as banks, medical services, and so on. Articles on the methodology and its development pop up in the world press with relatively high frequency. Examples of companies which systematically use Six Sigma are Dow Chemical, Dell Computer, Wall Mart and 3M.

Its critics say that the time and resources necessary for training and preparatory work are too high. Then further costs are involved in the gathering and analyzing of data – costs which sometimes exceed any savings. This applies especially to processes that cannot be standardized. Even General Electric admits that it has been difficult to apply Six Sigma to problem-solving businesses, for example on the legal side.

RECOMMENDED READING

1. George Eckes, Making Six Sigma Last: Managing the Balance Between Cultural and Technical Change.

2. Peter S Pande, Robert P Neuman and Roland R Cavanagh, The Six Sigma Way: How GE, Motorola, and Other Top Companies Are Honing Their Performance.

Stakeholder analysis (stakeholder model)

Stakeholder analysis, whereby a comprehensive list of stakeholders is written down without reference to hierarchy or weighting, used to be very popular. During the 1990s there was unusually heavy emphasis on one stakeholder group in particular, namely, owners and deriving from this, shareholder value.

The most important stakeholder groups are normally customers, owners and employees. The illustration below shows how each principal stakeholder delivers value:

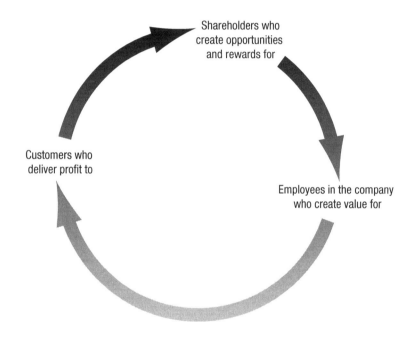

More stakeholders can usually be added to this list after a little thought. If an analysis is done with an internal department in mind (IT service, purchasing, a particular competence group, etc), countless internal stakeholders can usually be found on which the unit in question depends. In addition to the stakeholders listed above, those given below can be of interest in an analysis:

1.   Suppliers

2.   The local community

3. The media

4. Analysts/investors

5. Partners

6. Lenders

A stakeholder model normally looks like the illustration below.

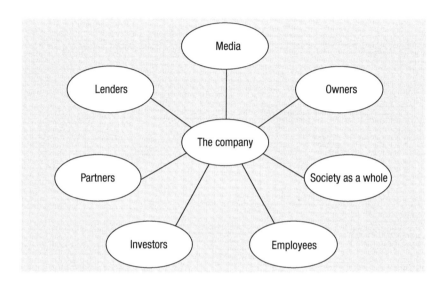

A common approach in analyzing stakeholder relationships is to answer the following questions (or a selection of them):

- What do we get from stakeholders? (This can be physical products, money, knowledge, ideas, image, etc.)

- What do stakeholders get from us? (See the above.)

- How well do these transactions function? Are there any areas that could be improved?

- How important is a stakeholder to us; how much time and energy do we devote to them?

- What are our strengths and weaknesses in relation to this stakeholder relationship?

- What potential for improvement is there?

- Do we have a unique relationship which we can use as a basis for investment?

Through discussion and by answering these questions, a plan of action can be drafted to develop – or terminate – each company stakeholder relationship. Alternatively, a *SWOT analysis* can be carried out (see this term) for every stakeholder relationship. Stakeholder models can be used to analyze an organization's financial flow. Here is a simplified model of how this can look:

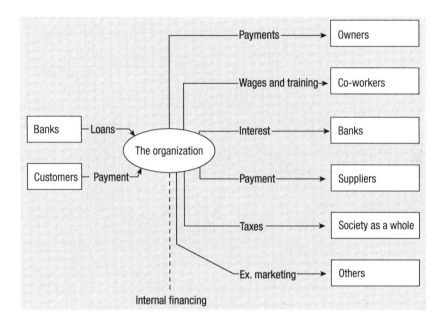

Inflow of financial funds to the organization (arrows in) must correspond to or exceed outflow (arrows out). A chart like this can be used as a basis for discussion in budgeting or other company initiatives.

Lars Bruzelius and Per-Hugo Skärvad, consultants in BSI and Partners, have divided main criticisms of the stakeholder model into five areas:

1. The stakeholder model is static. It only looks at stakeholder relationships at any one given time. Because organizations are constantly undergoing change it is important to review and update the stakeholder model regularly.

2. The stakeholder model gives a false impression of reality. Through the technique exemplified above we get the impression that all stakeholders are equally important. Moreover, the dependency

relationship between an organization and its stakeholders would appear to be the same in every case. Bruzelius and Skärvad suggest that factors like power, dependency, collaboration and conflict, should be included in the model.

3.   The stakeholder model favours a harmonious perspective. However, this is more likely to be because it is used incorrectly. In the procedure described above it seeks to reveal and resolve conflict.

4.   The stakeholder model is based on the idea of a balance between the power and influence of individual stakeholders. If one stakeholder gets more power or less influence, another one gets less power but then has to have more influence. The stakeholder model has come in for heavy criticism in this respect: equilibrium has become a goal in itself and created a kind of zero-sum game.

5.   Business leaders are often the people who interpret the stakeholder model. As they of course represent their company, the model has been criticized for attributing to them too important a role when they should be seen rather as representatives of the company's owners.

Six steps in strategic planning

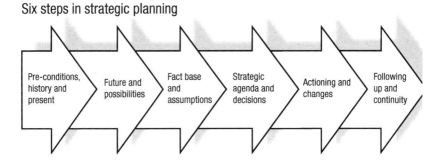

Pre-conditions, history and present

Future and possibilities

Fact base and assumptions

Strategic agenda and decisions

Actioning and changes

Following up and continuity

Tools and concepts connected to the steps

Business concept and owner expectations	Vision	Pre-conditions and assumptions	Agenda analysis	Management of strategic changes	Rolling agenda
Portfolio analysis	Scenario planning	Establishing factual basis	Decision methodology	SMART methodology	Working methods
Effectiveness	Zero-base initiative empty sheet	Customer value analysis	Return visit assumptions	Ends-means hierarchy	Following up and measurement
History	Strategic visioning	Capital investment appraisal	Return visit	Performance tree	
SWOT Analysis Product market matrix	Newspaper exercise Strategic type situations		Capital investment appraisal	Leading indicators and lagging indicators Obstacle analysis	
Stakeholder analysis	Benchmarking			Balanced Scorecard	
External environmental analysis				Organization	
Industry and competition analysis				Critical questions in strategy actioning	
Competence analysis					

RECOMMENDED READING

1. Ann Svendsen, The Stakeholder Strategy: Profiting from Collaborative Business Relationships.

2. James E Post et al, Redefining the Corporation: Stakeholder Management and Organizational Wealth.

3. Jeffrey W Marr and Steven F Walker, Stakeholder Power: A Winning Plan for Building Stakeholder Commitment and Driving Corporate Growth.

Strategic focus areas and type situations

The lack of an integrated theory of strategy can be a little embarrassing for researchers and consultants working in the field. For two years Karlöf Consulting have been working with a new approach that was originally called 'strategic type situations'. We decided that, for want of a suitable theory, we would introduce empirical elements from a large number of strategic situations that managers could encounter. We jokingly call this 'benchmarking in a tin', as the idea is related to benchmarking (building on others' experiences instead of having to re-live their experiences ourselves).

Focus areas and types of situation thus emerged from a need to come to terms with questions which could be included in a company's strategic agenda. In the dichotomy of content and process, focus areas and type situations can be included under content. As it is not for outsiders to shape strategic content, we have instead chosen to provide general information which ought to be considered, and either accepted or rejected within a framework of strategic thinking. We are convinced that the work of strategic planning should be a process owned and driven by top management possessing a thorough knowledge of the content. However, studies have shown that managers throughout their careers only come into contact with a limited number of strategic situations. If concepts such as insourcing, demand price elasticity or after sales have never been encountered in the course of their planning work, then it is unlikely that managers will introduce them as alternatives in any discussion on strategy.

Focus areas and type situations are thus a kind of smorgasbord for reminding us of the huge range of questions that can crop up. Focus areas can be compared to the side-table of herring, the selection of small, warm dishes, or the sweets, while the types of situation are the herring in mustard sauce, the Swedish meat balls, or the chocolate gateau.

The types of situation have been divided into five categories with a number of strategic focus areas within each category. Under these focus areas are listed a number of types of situation, which are ideas and issues that could be candidates for a strategic agenda. The categories we have chosen are not entirely mutually exclusive; some do overlap. For example, in the borderland between organic growth and structural change, there is something usually termed 'organic acquisitions', which are acquisitions of supplementary products or markets that have been added to the existing business.

Operations	Market and customers	Business development/ organic growth	Structural change	Enablers
A. Effectiveness in parts • Performance measuring • Benchmarking • Outsourcing • Process modelling	A. Marketing • Market communication • Marketing audit • Segmentation • Trademark	A. Market development • Take market shares • Redefinition served market • Globalizing • Penetration of fast-growing market • New channels	A. Acquisitions • Synergies • Diversification • Position with capital strength • Size – economies of scale	A. Human resources • Culture and values • Competence provision • Learning • Sustainable development • Reward system
B. Procurement • Roles in the value chain • The supply chain • Sourcing • E-business	B. Customers • Repurchase – loyalty • Customer value – quality • CRM	B. Products and services • Innovation – product development • From special commodity to staple • Differentiation – segmentation • Needs – new demand • Optimal delivery capacity • Supply pressure	B. Cooperation • Alliances • Co-ownership • Insourcing	B. Technology and IT • New technology for needs satisfaction • IT for greater productivity • IT for higher customer value • Internet as channel creator
C. Organization • Flow and dependencies • Work distribution and working methods • Control and measuring • Centralized – decentralized	C. Sales • Measuring • Rewards • Choice of channels • After sales • Sales management	C. New playground • Deregulation • Business displacement • New technology	C. Disposals and divisions • Parts of the whole • More attractive ownership structure • Fission – concentration	C. Ownership and management • Owner expectations • Board work • Group management's role • Business or Group responsibility
D. Production • Productivity • Quality • Lean production • Capital intensity, JIT	D. Pricing • Relative brand • Elasticity of demand • Relative segment • Yield Management		D. Contraction and unfair competition • The industry shrinks • Capital base, price squeeze, overcapacity • Unfair play, subsidies • Ownership-financed bubble	D. Economy and finances • Financing • Control and measuring • Effectiveness – (see operations) • Cash flow

The category called 'market and customers' can be partly assigned to operations, while more expansive actions in this category should be assigned to business development and organic growth.

A commentary on the content of the tabulation now follows, while we refer the reader to *Strategic Tools and Processes* (Strategins processer och verktyg) by Bengt Karlöf.

Operations

By 'operations' we mean all activities resulting from a given demand. The creation of a demand belongs to the category of market and customers, which follows below:

1. *Effectiveness in parts.* All parts of a company or organization operate under the conditions of a planned economy in the sense that the receiver of goods and services does not have a free choice between different alternatives, while the supplier has a monopoly and receives revenue from the company as a whole.

   Effectiveness in all parts of a company is a major challenge for managers. The fundamental question for all practicing managers is: "How effective can my organization be?" For future management, the answer to this question will probably be a priority in all their operational work.

2. *Procurement.* The terminology here is not clear. Other terms often used are purchasing, supply chain, etc. However this may be, we generally use procurement as an umbrella term that includes the supply of goods and services externally, as well as decisions on whether to make or buy.

3. *Organization.* Organizational questions are always sensitive, involving as they do both effectiveness and personal aspects of work. The more complex an organization is, the more complex will be the inter-dependent relationship between business units and co-workers.

   A sensible division of labour should aim to achieve work specialization while creating forms of work that bridge the boundaries resulting from such specialization. Identification of the most important specializations and inter-dependent relationships, together with the creation of forms of work to bridge boundaries, are crucial questions for organizations today. The question of what should be kept centralized and what is better off in a decentralized small-scale structure, is also an important one.

4. *Production.* Production comprises both goods and services and thus covers a large area. It includes questions of competence, work organization in production, outsourcing, bench-marking, design and logistics, etc. In general, productivity aims at achieving the lowest possible cost per unit for a given level of quality.

Market and customers

This category is based on an existing offering of goods and services which is to be brought to a market. The aim is to spread information about the offering and to create as high a customer-perceived value as possible in order to optimize pricing per segment.

1. *Marketing.* Studies in the USA show that the marketing function can all too easily become routine. A critical examination of marketing, creative segmentation, care of the brand and so on, are sensible moves for reaching out to customers.

2. *Customers.* A knowledge of how customers value a service in different segments is essential when looking for optimal pricing. Re-purchase is an indicator of customer loyalty and is a parameter of great importance in evaluations of competitiveness and profitability.

3. *Sales.* Apart from the elimination of all costs of a long-term nature, an investment in sales is the best and quickest way to improve results in a business. Amazingly enough, sales are still neglected in many business environments. This is especially true of after sales, which often has lower status in an organization than new selling.

4. *Pricing.* Customer-perceived value, market communication, sales effectiveness and brand all have effects on pricing. The effect on demand of raising or lowering prices is unfortunately rarely investigated. Another important factor that tends to affect pricing is the capital base of an organization. The concept of yield management has been developed in the airline and hotel industries. Both are characterized by high fixed costs at an early stage in their operations, as well as a great dependence on capacity utilization.

Business development/organic growth

We define business development as that part of strategy which is oriented to commercial risk-taking and expansion. The concept of business development sometimes also covers structural changes, which is why we have chosen to confine ourselves to organic growth – that is, expansion on the basis of existing customers and products. However, we do realize that the boundaries of market and customer, as well as those of structural change, can vary.

1. *Market development.* The concept of a market can refer to both existing customers and potential ones in the form of new customer groups or new territories. The served market is that part of the market in which market share is calculated and questions related to it (e.g. should we also sell to Russia and calculate our market share in this market?) should always be given careful consideration.

2. *Products and services.* Innovation is based on an understanding of customer needs; then ingenuity takes over. This is an alternative to asking customers what they want, something that often is not possible as customers do not always know what they want. Products and services which used to have a special attraction become staples with time; then other advantages have to be found.

   Differentiating delivery capacity so as to adapt to certain segments falls into this category. Innovative product development seeks to focus demand on the offering in question, so that customer needs can be better satisfied.

3. *New playground.* Conditions in many businesses are more or less changing radically. In Europe, low-price players like Ryanair and Easy.Jet are making an overhaul of cost structures in the more traditional airlines a necessity. Industry displacement is bringing unthinkable constellations, for instance in banking and insurance, in its wake. New technology is creating substitutes which threaten traditional industries. For example, video conferences are likely to interfere significantly with traditional business travel.

Structural change

There is a big difference between being a managing director of a company and the managing director of a group. Organic growth usually accounts for the rise through the ranks of, say, the manager for saloon cars of a large auto group. If he is chosen to be the group's chairman, he can show his paces only by buying and selling companies, something that drives group management to structural deals even when they should not happen. Caution is advized where deals of this kind are concerned, especially when there is a temptation to exploit financial strength and existing businesses are not particularly successful.

1. *Acquisitions.* Acquiring other businesses is the classic way for a group chairman to show drive. Acquisitions can be synergic and supplement existing businesses. The term synergy is frequently used to motivate structural deals that often do not result in the synergies that were supposed to happen.

2. *Cooperation.* In the 1980s and 1990s, a wave of alliances swept the world, especially in airlines and telecommunications industries. Many of these alliances lacked commercial viability and have therefore ceased to exist. At the same time, a need is growing for different structures where organizational forms, other than the traditional one of a limited company, can be used to bind businesses together.

3. *Disposals and divisions.* Changes in the value chain have effects in both directions and give rise to new constellations and the search for optimal structures. A basic rule is that low competitive pressure in certain markets gives rise to diversification mania which in turn speaks of the need to focus on core businesses.

4. *Contraction and unfair competition.* Changes are required in a number of unsatisfactory aspects of certain industries. One thinks of those with diminishing markets, or of the IT industry, where managements turned with scarcely concealed expectation to the financial markets instead of to its market and customers.

Enablers

There are a number of support processes, stakeholders and conditions that exist to encourage successful long-term effectiveness in business. We have bundled them together under the term 'enablers': the people, the technology and the funds that will support a company's strategic development.

1. Staff

The increasingly important role played by people in the success of a business becomes more apparent as repetitive work is phased out and businesses become more knowledge-intensive. Culture and values are becoming the lynchpins that hold businesses together and develop them. New skills, lifelong experience that can be motivating and a source of pride, sustainable development – these are increasingly becoming essential to a business in addition to work motivation and a sensible rewards system.

2. Technology and IT

New ideas are constantly being developed to satisfy needs more effectively, whether these are related to IT or to some other branch of technology such as 3G or DVD. From being something rather exotic, IT has become systematized and integrated into everything we do so that it affects the two parameters of effectiveness, customer value and productivity.

3. Ownership and management

During the last decade there has been a marked trend towards shareholder value that has led to a degree of short-sightedness. In future, it will be essential for owner expectations to be formulated, not only on the basis of a 'quarterly capitalistic' perspective, but also on a broader, long-term basis. In this connection, the role played by the board of directors is becoming increasingly important. The difference between running a business unit and running a portfolio, together with the role played by group management, must be considered carefully by boards.

4. Economy and finances

Basically, a sound business should be financed by the market. However, there can be many ups and downs on the way there, which makes the financing, management and measurement of both the use of capital and the results for parts of organizations of the utmost importance.

Observanda and pitfalls

There are a number of pitfalls of which we should be aware. One of these is the modernity trap, which refers to our natural inclination to be up-to-

354

date and always in possession of the latest technology. Crazy sums have been invested in IT because of this most human of instincts.

Synergy is often an illusion. Research comparing the expected returns from synergies with the actual sums involved indicates dramatic differences that can be put down to wishful thinking or self-delusion. Look out when you hear the word synergy. Ask awkward questions!

In recent years, CRM (Customer Relations Management) has been annexed by IT and has led to the construction of extensive systems for mechanized customer relations. This sort of thing has often led to alienation and defeated the aim of creating loyal customers. The *way markets develop and mature* continues to be poorly understood.

A contemporary example has been the feverish investment in Internet business in many countries. But it has always been the case that enthusiasts fail to correctly assess how fast and to what extent customers will adapt to new circumstances. The motto, 'bigger is better' seems to dominate in many situations. The result can be unfortunate. We should remember what Gary Hart said in the 1984 American presidential election: "Bigger is not better – better is better". Otherwise rational people have a tendency to sing the praises of economies of scale while questioning the advantages of small-scale operations. The latter are often of a behavioural nature, which makes them more elusive than the certainties of mathematical equations.

Strategy – historical perspective

Our concept of strategy has been formed relatively recently. Naturally, a history of strategy could be taken right back to the Ancient Greeks, but we have chosen instead to anchor ours in the modern business world, and in so doing will look at some of the major influences on strategy work.

In the middle of the 1920s a commanding officer at Wright Patterson Air Force Base just outside Dayton in Ohio discovered that unit costs fell by about 20 per cent every time he doubled the volume of an aircraft component. This ostensibly commonplace revelation was exploited in American aircraft production in the 1930s and 1940s so that any component produced for one type of aircraft, for example the landing gear, could also be produced for others and lead to a fall in production costs. This connection came to be called the experience curve. It later spawned a number of different models, among them the Boston Matrix, which has two parameters: market growth and relative market share. The matrix is shown below with the cheerful figures which usually feature in it.

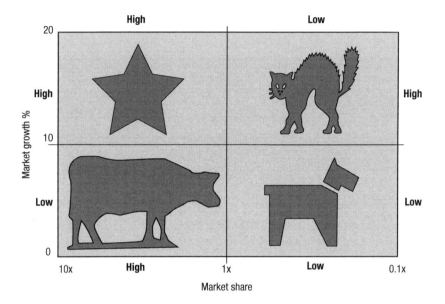

The theory underlying the Boston Matrix is that high relative market share (relative to the competition) should be pursued in order to attain high accumulated volume; we would then have lower production costs (through the experience curve). This can be utilized in one of two ways: either prices remain the same and margins are increased, or prices are lowered and market share is captured. This logic works best in an industrial context but is of limited value in the production of services, which is constantly growing. However, effects of the experience curve are not sufficiently observed and taken into account, especially in connection with company mergers, etc.

World War II had great importance for the development of strategy, mainly because of a whole range of mathematical methods that were used to control complicated war-time logistics. These methods were summarized by the term *operational analysis*, the aim of which is to optimize flows. Operational analysis was inducted into the business world after the end of the war with some success. Business operations were then largely seen as a question of optimization. There was a general shortage of goods and demand could be taken for granted, which meant that production, administration and distribution were the areas where know-how was most needed.

Operation-analytical initiatives were tempered by influences from the Soviet planned economy, which led to a period dominated by long-term planning when extrapolations and trend predictions became the order of the day. Companies such as General Electric and International Harvester, which promoted strategic thinking in large think-tanks, set the general fashion.

This outlook on strategy came to an end as a result of a number of discontinuities (occasioned principally by wildly fluctuating oil prices) in the 1970s and was symbolized by the arrival of Jack Welch, General Electric's CEO. At the beginning of the 1980s the emphasis moved from thinking to action. Peters and Waterman's well-known book, *In Search of Excellence*, was one source of inspiration. Thought and reflection suddenly became two very old-fashioned words. Action ('try it, fix it, do it') was preferred to thinking and strategy questions were out of fashion.

At the beginning of the 1990s the world was suddenly hit by a recession and strategy ceased to feature in the conversation of executives. Instead, rationalization and other synonyms for cutbacks such as 'rightsizing', 'business process re-engineering', and so on, came to dominate in large sections of the corporate world.

Since the stock market and IT comeback at the end of the 1990s, strategy questions have again returned but partly in a difficult guise, as a source of learning and innovation. Some of the thinkers currently in fashion are Gary Hamel, Henry Mintzberg and Michael Porter.

Gary Hamel, Visiting Professor in Strategic and International Management at the London Business School, has wittily said that we in the strategy industry – researchers, academics and consultants – share a dirty little secret: strategy theory does not exist. Researchers and academics can describe a successful event and like butterfly collectors stick a pin through it and frame it for the world to admire as a beautiful example. We all then pretend that we could have predicted the outcome of the event – but we cannot. According to Hamel, we do not have a comprehensive theory of strategy.

Henry Mintzberg, Cleghorn Professor of Management Studies at McGill University in Montreal, expresses similar thoughts when he likens the search for a strategy theory to three blind men trying to describe an elephant. They do their best according to which part of the body they happen to get hold of – a foot, an ear, the trunk, or the tail. In the same way, researchers in questions of strategy have tried to explain success on the basis of corporate culture, the process perspective, or the experience curve. These initiatives are however, only part of the truth.

RECOMMENDED READING

1. Gary Hamel with C K Prahalad, Competing for the Future.

2. Henry Mintzberg, The Rise and Fall of Strategic Planning.

3. Jeffrey A Krames, The Jack Welch Lexicon of Leadership: Over 250 Terms, Concepts, Strategies & Initiatives of the Legendary Leader.

Strategy – three types

The tabulation below lists three strategic archetypes: portfolio strategy, business strategy and what we will call functional strategy.

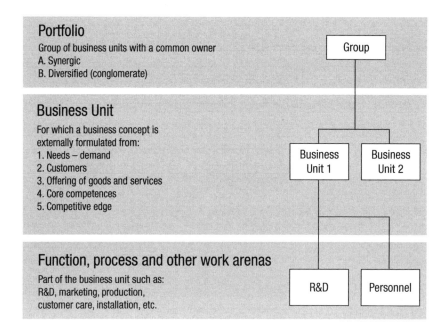

Portfolio strategy

The concept of a *portfolio* has been borrowed from the stock market to indicate a diversity of companies owned by the same entity. As can be seen below, a portfolio can be both diversified and synergic, depending on the kind of connection between the companies in the portfolio.

A *diversified portfolio* is also called a conglomerate, and is made up of a financially or politically unified group of units usually without any real internal connection. The activities within a municipality could be called a diversified portfolio.

Synergic portfolios are very common. The word synergy represents one of the more ambiguous and misused concepts in business. It is often used to motivate company mergers and takeovers with hidden agendas. When the word 'synergy' is used, therefore, we should be very cautious until we are quite sure where the reported synergies lie. For more information see *Portfolio*.

Business Strategy (Competitive Strategy)

A business unit is defined by the five components of the business concept.

1. Needs/demand
2. Customers
3. Offering of goods and services
4. Core competences
5. Competitive edge

It is often important to separate *need* and *demand*. This is especially true in situations where development has been rapid and customers have to be made aware that new ways exist of satisfying their needs.

We define 'customer' as 'the physical person who makes the decision to buy'. A legal entity is seldom a customer, but individuals within an organization can be customers. For more about this see *Customers*.

The offering of goods and services is the means of satisfying the needs of customers and end-users. The key to a successful business operation (or its equivalent in other sectors) lies in understanding the customer's needs and applying creativity to offers.

By defining our *core skills*, we gain the advantage of defining what is not a core skill and what can therefore be outsourced. See also *Competence*.

The concept of a competitive advantage seems to pertain only to the business world. However, this is not the case in a society increasingly without boundaries, where pupils can choose their schools, patients the suppliers of their treatment, and companies the location of a new venture – Prague or a Dublin suburb. For more on this, see *Competitive edge*.

Functional Strategy

Functions, processes, and all other work arenas are lumped together in relation to the concept of a *functional strategy*. This also applies to the various denominations of departments in an organization, for example, Human Resources, Southern Region, IT, etc. Where such departments are concerned, strategy involves a pattern of decisions and actions in the present to ensure future success – *given an orientation for the whole organization*. In the 'strategy industry', there is a phenomenon that is seldom observed: the number of strategic situations involving parts of a business that go completely haywire. This is why functional strategy is work of fundamental importance if parts of the whole – and hence the whole – are to be effective.

According to our definition, parts of company's function within a framework of a planned economy, i.e. delivery takes place internally to a recipient who lacks a free choice between different suppliers while the supplier enjoys a monopoly. This means that the concept of effectiveness is essential within the framework of functional strategy. (For more on this see *Effectiveness*.) Effectiveness is defined as a function of value and productivity, where value is the relation between utility and price and productivity is the cost per whatever is produced and delivered. For more on this, see *Functional strategy*.

RECOMMENDED READING

Michael E Porter, Competitive Strategy: Creating and Sustaining Superior Performance.

Strategy

The long-term survival and success of a business enterprise is closely connected to its strategy. This is a complex subject due to the many factors that can affect a business, factors which may differ considerably and affect development in an almost infinite number of ways.

 The word 'strategy' comes from the Greek *strategos*, which is a combination of the words *stratos*, 'army', and *ago*, which means 'to lead'. Strategos is an ancient Greek word for commander and features in our knowledge of the ancient city of Athens, where from the end of the 6th century B.C. ten such commanders were chosen annually.

The activities of these strategists involved the use of military theory and other resources to reach political goals through battle with an opponent. Of course there were goals other than the purely military, such as keeping the peace, maintaining neutrality, or preserving or changing the balance of power.

In modern business economics, the term is used to express a nexus of ambition and goals together with the orientation to achieve them. Strategy in business may best be described as eminently businesslike and long-term, being thus an activity that goes beyond the operative management or operations of a company.

We define strategy here as, 'a pattern of decisions and actions in the present, undertaken to make the most of opportunities and secure future success'. One of the big problems with strategy work is the difficulty of separating it from daily operations with their daily crises and quick solutions. It is essential to work, not only with the content of strategy, but also with the strategic process, that is, not only with *what* but also with *how*.

People generally have a notion of strategy as being something very grand, demanding abstract thought and reserves of intelligence. They associate the subject with complex questions debated in the boardrooms of powerful conglomerates – what companies are to be bought or sold; how a big, new market, such as the Chinese market, can be penetrated.

With delegation of responsibility constantly increasing, there is a growing need for know-how in strategy work, and methods must be adapted to all arenas in which strategic thinking is expected. Strategy includes long-term development work on activities which call for a management responsibility, whether these are projects, processes, functions or departments. Our definition can be applied in the context of all organizational work.

Strategy, then, is far from being a subject reserved for group management. It can be applied to any organizational unit whatsoever.

Strategy has become a vital component in the larger concept of management. Greater strategic expertise is needed now that responsibility is being decentralized and more employees are being given a management responsibility for some part of their organization.

It can be useful to define the organizational unit for which a strategy is required, its relation to the whole organization and external environment, as well as the fundamental concepts that are often involved.

Sustainable development

The term *sustainable development* was minted by Gro Harlem Bruntland, the former Director General of the WHO, and has since been generally accepted in both business and political circles. A number of conventions on global sustainable development have been held under the auspices of the UN, while many large companies have staff to deal with questions on sustainability. Many organizations have even begun to publish sustainability reports to highlight their work in this area.

It is generally accepted that sustainable development (SD) comprises three main areas: finances, social responsibility and ecology (the environment).

These three areas are interdependent and are mutually supportive, as illustrated in the figure below.

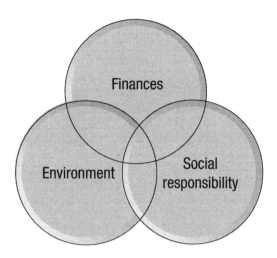

Most people agree about what the areas of social responsibility and the environment refer to. Environmental issues cover the effect of a business on the environment, both directly, for instance in the form of business trips and energy consumption, and indirectly when, for example, the business places demands on suppliers and other stakeholders. By social responsibility we mean the ethical side of an enterprise's social questions, including the working environment, sexual harassment, kickbacks, bio-diversity, equal opportunity, bullying and whatever affects the company's standing in society as a whole. The last point includes, for example, a refusal to exploit the work of children and young persons and the application of good business ethics.

Social responsibility is sometimes designated by the acronym CSR (Corporate Social Responsibility) or Corporate Citizenship. The European Commission's definition of CSR reads: "the integration of social and environmental concerns on a voluntary basis beyond compliance with the law."

Finances

Environment Social

Roger Crow, in an article in *FT Management* defines a number of fundamental indicators for CSR work:

In the market	In the environment	At the workplace	In society at large
1. Number of customer complaints 2. Number of complaints per advertisement 3. Customer satisfaction 4. Solutions for customers with special needs 5. Established cases of breaking anti-trust legislation (unlawful trusts, etc.)	1. Energy consumption 2. Water consumption 3. Waste disposal 4. Discharge of carbon-dioxide 5. Successful environmental lawsuits	1. Profile of the work force (ethnicity, sex, age, functional disabilities, etc.) 2. Sick absence 3. Number of departures from current legislation 4. Established cases of corruption and other corporate misdemeanours 5. Number of recorded security incidents 6. Staff turnover 7. Education and training (value and time per employee) 8. Co-worker satisfaction metrics 9. Existence of procedures to deal with complaints	1. Financial contribution to the community as a percentage of profits 2. Time spent on socially beneficial actions

At the time of writing, opinions are divided where the financial perspective is concerned. Some people think that it is all about profitability, in that a good environmental and social programme contributes to a positive financial development for a business (*Balanced Scorecard*). Others argue that it is about focusing on long-term financial growth to the detriment of quarterly capitalism which in turn will make it possible to focus on questions in the two other areas. When the 'triple bottom line' is applied to nations (and this was the original intention), the financial perspective deals with such questions as foreign aid and income distribution politics. It is when this model is applied to businesses that the ramifications become uncertain.

There are many signs that from a commercial standpoint, sustainable development and related matters are becoming increasingly important for companies and organizations. One clear sign of this is the interest shown by the public and media in these questions. Businesses which neglect their responsibilities in one area of the triple bottom line risk attracting negative publicity that can have a deleterious effect on brands.

Co-worker studies have shown that an organization's ethical standards are important to its employees: high standards go hand in hand with a pride in management and the overall organization. A good reputation can also improve a company's chances of attracting the right people. On the downside is the danger that profitability-conscious companies will use sustainable development purely as a marketing tool. Codes of ethics and other corporate policy documents may just give lip service while organizations forget their promises.

It should be remembered that a policy on, say, equal opportunities or biodiversity which has been announced through the media is nothing less than an invitation to journalists and others to find out how the land actually lies. If corporate statements are not well substantiated, any intended marketing spin-offs grind to a halt. A success factor in working with questions of sustainable development is a real desire for a company to have a good reputation internally, regionally, nationally and globally.

RECOMMENDED READING

1. Chad Holliday et al, Walking the Talk: The Business Case for Sustainable Development.

2. Harvard Business School, Harvard Business Review on Corporate Responsibility.

3. Jennifer A Elliot, Introduction to Sustainable Development.

Taylorism – Scientific management

The theories promoted by Fredrik Winslow Taylor at the beginning of the 1900s and grouped under the concept of *scientific management*, were seen to represent the working man as a machine motivated only by monetary considerations, a picture that was not entirely fair. Taylor did not really imagine that workers should be used like machines, although he did believe that wages should vary directly with, and motivate, performance. The theories on which Taylor based scientific management came to be exaggerated and brought *taylorism* into disrepute.

F W Taylor in fact had two careers. The lesser-known first career, evolved around the machining process. Taylor came from a very wealthy Philadelphia family but broke off law studies at Harvard and began as an apprentice in an engineering workshop, eventually becoming foreman at the Midvale Steel Company, where his brother-in-law was Managing Director. The company was owned by a friend of the family.

What is not generally known is that Taylor, through machine and tool design, developed theories on chip formation in steel cutting. He carried out tens of thousands of experiments to establish the right data for a certain kind of machining procedure. In 1898 he established, together with a colleague, that high-speed steel had superior cutting characteristics which allowed double the amount of steel to be cut per unit of time. F W Taylor became world-famous for this contribution to industry and was presented with a gold medal at the 1900 World Fair in Paris. He wrote a mammoth paper entitled *On the Art of Cutting Metal* that was published in 1906, the fame of which spread over much of the industrialized world. His theories on the machining process were extensive, with parameters such as cutting speeds, tool wear, tool materials and work piece materials. On the basis of these parameters Taylor was able to calculate feed speeds, cutting angle, depth of cut, etc, in order to optimize manufacturing.

However, he found that skilled workers were unwilling to apply the knowledge that he had developed. Workers in those days had a tendency to continue working with the methods they were familiar with. Taylor therefore became interested in questions of labour organization, which led to his second career, the one which has attracted greater attention from posterity.

The workmen who Taylor worked with would hold conservatively to their own work rate. As soon as someone new joined a team he was shown by the rest of the group how much work he had to do per unit of time. Better performance was not rewarded with an increase in wages, so there was no reason to work harder than was necessary.

Taylor saw all of this as a colossal waste of human resources that was deleterious to productivity. He therefore decided to study, by means of systematic analysis, how workers ought to carry out their work, as well as the suitability of the human physiology for certain work tasks. Taylor also believed that both employer and employee should profit from higher productivity through lower production costs and higher wages, respectively.

Implicit therefore in scientific management was the idea that co-workers should develop as much effectiveness as possible. Scientific management did lead to certain excesses for which Taylor was not entirely responsible. He drew a line between intellectual and manual labour. The underlying purpose of scientific management was of course to exploit economies of scale, the experience curve and work specialization and thereby increase productivity. Taylor went beyond this, forbidding workers to think for themselves. He maintained that worker skills which profited from experience were more a hindrance than a help for increasing productivity.

We should add in this connection that the USA is one of the few large, unified and barrier-free markets in the industrialized West. Production techniques there have developed differently to those in Europe. The experience curve, economies of scale and price as a means of competition have existed in North America for much longer than in Europe, for example. In Western Europe we may have a tendency to belittle Taylor and his work but we should not forget that Europe has a tradition of segmentation, differentiation, and short production series which make it difficult to appreciate Taylor's work as it deserves to be.

In 1911 F W Taylor published his well-known work, *Scientific Management*. It is a book very much of its time, one in which people did not have a free choice between different employers but were forced, to a much greater extent than is the case today, to submit to authoritarian systems characterized by direct management. In spite of this fact, Taylor was subjected to a degree of reprobation. He was ordered to appear before the House of Representatives, where his theories were criticized as being incompatible with human rights.

However Taylor is criticized, the fact cannot be hidden that scientific management leads to low production costs, greater added value, higher wages, lower prices and faster capital growth. On the other hand, his theories are difficult to apply to knowledge-intensive environments.

Taylor's research and experiments were revolutionary in their time.

Scientific management should be judged on the basis of a knowledge of the period in which it emerged, a period in which a predominant section of the working population were carrying out routine, repetitive work, and work tasks were based on the skills of an intellectual minority. This can be contrasted with the situation today, when most of the work done involves some form of problem-solving. Taylorism has much in common with the experience curve and the concept of effectiveness.

RECOMMENDED READING

1. Frederick Winslow Taylor, The Principles of Scientific Management (a classic).

2. Robert Kanigel, The One Best Way: Frederick Winslow Taylor and the Enigma of Efficiency.

Teambuilding

Teambuilding has become a popular term in organizational development (OD). A survey of 179 of Fortune 500 companies revealed that teambuilding was the method most commonly used in human resources development. Sixty-one per cent of the companies taking part worked with teambuilding.

As the word implies, teambuilding is about establishing and developing well-functioning teams in organizations. A team is a formal group of two or more individuals brought together by a common purpose.

If a team is to work effectively and develop an ability to learn together, its members must have confidence in each other. Another aspect of team-building is the importance of having a heterogeneous team. If the members of a working group all have similar personalities and back-grounds, the conditions for creativity and improvement will not be as favourable as when personalities and experiences are different. Dr R Meredith Belbin is a researcher who has studied the building blocks of high-performing teams and won general acceptance for his ideas. Through his research, Belbin has identified nine useful team roles that can be included in a framework for his Team Skills™ concept. Each team role has its strengths and weaknesses, so it is important to find the right combination for particular assignments. An individual's strengths can lie in one or more ream roles, while weaker roles can be accepted if the situation requires.

The nine team roles are:

1. Plant™ – Creative, imaginative, unorthodox.

2. Monitor Evaluator™ – Reflective, critical and discerning.

3. Coordinator™ – Ability to get others to work together towards common goals.

4. Shaper™ – Dynamic leader who spurs others on to action.

5. Resource Investigator™ – Relationship-oriented, curious and communicative.

6. Team Worker™ – Flexible, diplomatic, averts friction.

7. Implementer™ – Systematic, disciplined and practical.

8. Completer™ – Goal-oriented, delivers on time.

9. Specialist™ – Dedicated, single-minded expert.

Belbin's research has generated a number of very important success factors in creating high-performing teams, among them:

1. Coordinator as chairman.

2. The presence of a clever Plant.

3. Good intellectual abilities of team members

4. A good spread of team roles.

Other researchers and practicing managers have supplemented the list of success factors:

1. Clear goals for the team.

2. Access to necessary competence and skills.

3. Confidence of team members in each other.

4. Good communicative atmosphere in the group.

5. Effective leadership.

6. Right support and conditions in relation to the organization.

Many people have also stressed the importance of a diversity of experiences and ethnicity, as well as the presence of both the sexes, in a group's ability to overcome problems.

Once a team is well established, it will generally go through a number of more or less predictable phases. Perhaps the most useful model to describe these phases is FIRO (Fundamental Interpersonal Relationship Orientation), which has been based on Will Shutz's in-depth studies of the US marines. FIRO describes three main phases in a team's development:

1. Inclusion

2. Control

3. Openness

Inclusion

This phase is characterized by uncertainty about our presence in the group, what rules are to apply and how much of ourselves we dare to show. Sometimes it can be difficult to take the plunge. But before the next phase is reached we begin to show our commitment to the group, and at the same time take a few risks and show that we are not entirely held to ransom by our initial fears.

Control

Groups which do not break up at Inclusion sooner or later reach the Control phase. Members suddenly begin to question the formal leader, sub-groups are started and conflict increases. This can be a trying time for many people, and some groups do not survive this phase.

Openness

On the way to Openness, many participants show themselves prepared to engage in conflict, clear the air and try to find constructive solutions. Groups which reach the Openness phase show that they perceive conflicts as problems that must be solved if they are to make progress. The members of the group share ideas, opinions and feedback openly, and ask for suggestions. Communication is open, direct and honest, 'We have confidence in the other members and give the group our active support', this phase is often arrived at more quickly if group members can openly discuss how confident they are.

A way of preventing problems and conflict in a group is by clarifying the 'rules of play' at the outset. This can be done in different ways. One is to get each participant to tell the others about earlier experiences of teamwork, including what went well and what did not work as well, giving opinions as to why this was the case. When everyone has finished doing this a discussion can be held on the same theme. The point of this exercise is to see whether the group can function as a team and at the same time get a comprehensive picture of good and bad group experiences; members will then be on their guard for problems that could affect the team's results.

Bill Isaacs of the MIT Dialogue Project stresses the importance of learning together. The idea is that discussion is the first step in a team's learning process, which has to do with working openly and being able to solve problems together. A team's ability to work successfully on projects often depends on whether it has been given the opportunity to develop effective communication at the preparatory stage.

RECOMMENDED READING

1. Naomi L Quenk, *Essentials of Myers-Briggs Type Indicators® Assessment.*

2. Patric M Lencioni, *The Five Dysfunctions of a Team: A Leadership Fable.*

3. R Meredith Belbin, *Team Roles at Work.*

4. Will Schutz, *The Human Element: Productivity, Self-Esteem, and the Bottom Line.*

The strategic process

Executives in companies and organizations often have a bad conscience because questions of strategy are not given the time, the resources and the attention that they deserve. This can be because of three important circumstances:

- *First,* questions of strategy are never acute in the way that operative questions often are. The latter tend to make themselves known immediately.

- *Second,* in many cases the leadership does not really know how to carry out effective strategic work, i.e. economizing with resources and creating value without having costs that are sky high.

- The *third* reason why questions of strategy are sometimes poorly handled, is the difficulty of paying for work which looks so far into the future. In many cases, people are rewarded when they have not done anything.

People who have devoted themselves to strategy work have for far too long concerned themselves only with the content, that is, 'what'. Content in strategy work is of course extremely important. However, if it is allowed to expand at the expense of learning and the whole process, an emphasis on content could affect the strategic outcome, especially if the content is of poor quality and lacks validation.

At the strategic level, a familiarity with content will not suffice. In fact, a too-perfect knowledge of content can be a hindrance to strategic thinking, which is process-based rather than content-based. Management of an operation requires analysis, while strategic leadership in addition, demands the ability to achieve a synthesis. By this we mean the ability to make rational decisions based on subjective, sometimes contradictory or incomplete information. Synthesis in this context is therefore qualitative by nature, and this aspect is very characteristic of strategic thinking.

The strategic process is therefore exceedingly important as a supplement to strategic content, which is often industry-related.

A great deal of consideration must of course be given to content in all strategic planning. However, undue focus on content can easily lead to a distorted picture where strategies have not been given due consideration within a framework of what is known as a fair process.

Recently there have been indications that too great an emphasis has been given to content, and too little to the strategic process. Strategy as a process also includes how work is done. All too often, strategy work is plagued by a lack of continuity. In some situations, the work is allowed to become routine, and filling in figures becomes more important than strategic thinking. Strategic planning and the management of daily operations do not go well together. Since operative problems tend to be acute, strategic questions get pushed aside. This is a good reason to reserve an annual excursion to a mountain-top or an island for strategic thinking. Once people are there they may feel impelled to make strategic decisions in spite of the fact that they might not have the ideal documentation or enough time for reflection. Strategy questions usually require information that may not be readily accessible through the normal channels, information such as re-purchase frequencies, customer value analyzes, etc.

Logical thinkers would typically describe a strategic process as a sequence of thoughts and actions leading to the determination of a strategy. However, the subject's complexity would suggest that strategic planning has rather more in common with a kind of mind-map, the tracing of associations with a myriad of possibilities, which like a fox's burrow has any number of entrances and exits.

A strategy process always begins with a history, the present, the external environment and various forecasts. A crucial factor in strategy work is the ability to throw out certain questions while focusing on others; it is these 'others' which will constitute the strategic agenda. Karlöf Consulting has successfully used the following six steps in strategy work. They are accompanied by a menu of tools that can be used in the work of strategic planning.

The strategic success factors of Collins and Porras

James C Collins and Jerry I Porras, researchers of the business environment, asked themselves the question: what is it that distinguishes really successful companies from others? They, together with their team of researchers, carried out wide-ranging studies in which very successful companies, or *visionary companies,* with a long history of success, were compared with average companies in the same industry. The results were published in their book, Built to Last – Successful Habits of Visionary Companies. The most important conclusions of this research were:

1. Companies founded on the basis of a brilliant corporate mission were not any more successful in the long-term. Collins and Porras compare successful companies to the tortoise in the fable of the hare and the tortoise. They are often slow to start but they win in the long run.

2. There is no connection between charismatic, visionary leadership and long-term success.

3. Maximizing profit margins has not been the most important aim for successful companies. They have had aims and core values that commanded greater attention than market capitalization or profits.

4. Co-workers in successful companies share many aspects of their company's culture, which has more to do with a common ideology than having the right values.

5. Successful companies do not make changes based on short-term trends or current fashion. When there are changes to be made they are carried out without jeopardizing the company's core values.

6. Successful companies set themselves challenges and a high ambition level. Collins and Porras use the slogan 'Big Hairy Audacious Goals' (BHAG) to sum up this attitude.

7. The working environment in successful companies is stimulating and enjoyable for those people who share the company's core values. For those who do not share these values the workplace

is an absolute hell. "It's okay" is not a phrase its employees will use to describe the environment in the visionary company. More often we hear something like, "it's great" or "it's lousy" in a binary relation.

8. Visionary companies are not slaves of the planning chart but rather, opportunist and entrepreneurial. They try a great many things and keep those things that work. Collins and Porras have made the comparison with Charles Darwin and the survival of the fittest.

9. The managing director or group chief executive of visionary companies is nearly always recruited internally. Managers recruited internally were six times more common in visionary companies than in other companies.

10. Visionary companies compete with themselves rather than their competitors in their industry. They never feel dominated by the market; instead they want to continually develop and be better.

11. Visionary companies think in terms of 'and' rather than 'or'. They do not confine themselves to being stable or progressive, to satisfying shareholders or surviving internal evaluations, etc. They want the best of both worlds. They can, as Collins and Porras have shown, have their cake and eat it.

12. Visionary companies concentrated on *living* success rather than thinking about it. Documented visions were certainly to be found more in visionary companies than in others, but only in retrospect, as it were, amidst much else.

We should remember that the research done by Collins and Porras was based on large, multinational companies, the majority of which were American. But in the field of management strategy there is a striking lack of research to tell us what makes some companies more successful than others. The studies that do exist are only case studies where a successful development is described in retrospect. The lessons of Collins and Porras's studies cannot then be taken too literally for companies all over the world, but they can still inspire and provide interesting food for thought for executives and company planners.

RECOMMENDED READING

1. Jim Collins, Good to Great: Why Some Companies Make the Leap… and Others Don't.

2. Jim Collins and Jerry I Porras, Built to Last: Successful Habits of Visionary Companies.

Time-based competition

Time-based competition focuses on the time required for the completion of important work processes. This has often been seen as a strategy leading to competitive strength based on minimal completion times. It is said that top companies can deliver whatever the customer wants, anytime, anywhere. Tightening up a company's procedures makes for quicker decisions and faster lead times while making companies more sensitive to customers' wishes.

Time-based competition can be said to lead to greater effectiveness, i.e. a combination of greater efficiency in production and an eagerness to serve the customer. Experience shows that it is hard to introduce market-oriented processes into manufacturing companies; time-based competition could be a useful way of achieving this.

Research carried out on time-based competition has surprisingly revealed that:

1. Costs are reduced when production series are shortened.

2. Investment in quality lowers production costs.

3. Costs are reduced instead of raized with shorter answering times.

4. Demand is not only affected through margins but also to an amazing extent by greater choice and customer sensitivity.

In this there is the paradox that large stock buffers and longer preparation times do not lead to work precision, just the opposite in fact. Furthermore, compressing the time element leads to greater motivation and work satisfaction in spite of the fact that work rates increase. The simple explanation is that work feels more meaningful when it is done under pressure.

A fast work rate places demands on the concentration and creates variation, which in turn stimulates learning. The total effect is to create a more dynamic environment, which raises effectiveness and the level of job satisfaction.

What many people have not realized is that similar paradoxes exist in knowledge companies. Some ten years ago a consultancy firm was faced with what seemed to be the reasonable proposition of reducing the time available to its co-workers, i.e. to reduce production in order to drive the firm's own development of concepts and methods.

The logic has turned out to work back-to-front. The people with the highest productivity in terms of generation of revenue also seem to be the ones with the most innovative ideas per unit of time, and they are also best at running the firm's marketing. In other words, the competition in developing concepts and methods that was expected to result, was only there to a limited degree.

Effectiveness means to deliver more, better, cheaper and faster. Time-based competition seeks to improve effectiveness, initially through a focus on timescales – a very relevant factor in many situations.

RECOMMENDED READING

1. Christopher Myer, Fast Cycle Time: How to Align Purpose, Strategy and Structure for Speed.

2. George Stalk Jr and Thomas M Hout, Competing Against Time: How Time-Based Competition is Reshaping Global Markets.

Value

As the term value is of prime importance in all organized activity, we will deal with it under the following headings: value theory, customer-perceived value and value analysis. The semantics in connection with the term 'value' are extraordinarily vague, but as it has come into general use, it is important to use the term with a degree of accuracy. We will be using it primarily in respect of three stakeholder groups:

1. Customers
2. Employees
3. Owners or other principals

In addition to these three main groups, others are increasingly gaining our attention; among them, suppliers and local communities.

An important statement made in the introduction to this section involved the definition of value as a function of utility and price or, in other words, quality and the price required to get it. Value is thus an algorithm with a numerator – utility – and a denominator – price. This means that value can be created either through working progressively with utility, or through rationalization in respect of the costs which in the end control price.

Value theory

Thinking on the subject of value goes a long way back. Aristotle's drew attention to a problem with ethical overtones which has bemused economists for a very long time: why should the most useful things in existence have the lowest market value, while some of the least useful command the highest prices?

Until well into the 19th century, many economists were preoccupied with the distinction between usage value and exchange value. Bread and portable water are useful and relatively cheap, whereas silks and diamonds have little practical use but are far more expensive.

Adam Smith, father of all economists, got stuck on the same question. The riddle of usage value and exchange value was not to be solved for another century or more until the discovery of marginal utility. This term refers to the fact that it is the most desirable usage or need that determines value.

The utility value of water is marginal because of its abundance, and the value of diamonds is high because of their rarity. One could conceive a situation in an arid desert where the brightest and most splendid of gems would gladly be exchanged for a glass of water. Scarcity creates value.

Adam Smith solved this by what he called the labour theory of value, by which he simply meant that the value of an asset is measured by the amount of labour and materials for which it can be exchanged.

The classical economists approached the problem of value from the cost side, proposing costs of labour as the explanation of the value of anything. The neo-classicists, on the other hand, held that it was utility that determined value quantitatively and was actually the key factor in explaining the system of micro-economic relations.

The theory of marginal utility, like many conceptual breakthroughs, arose at about the same time in a large number of places when the time was ripe for its acceptance. The economist to whom the theory of development was attributed was Herman Heinrich Gossen (1810–1858). Gossen expounded his theory in a book which, unfortunately, did not sell very well. So he himself collected the remaindered copies, made a bonfire of them and died a disappointed and embittered man, totally unaware of his posthumous fame.

The essence of marginal utility theory can be expressed thus: "The marginal utility of an article is the increment to total utility or satisfaction generated by the most recently purchased unit of the article in question" (Richard T Gill, *Modern Economics*).

There are also two important corollaries to the theory:

1. The law of diminishing marginal utility states that marginal utility to the customer diminishes with increasing consumption of a given product.

2. The customer tends to maximise the total utility of his/her consumption by distributing purchases of goods in such a way that the marginal utility of buying one type of goods is equal to the marginal utility of buying any other type of goods.

This theory of value thus has much in common with the general law of supply and demand.

Customer value

One of the old-fashioned terms that has been given a new lease of life by the hardening climate of competition is customer-perceived value. Other terms are used for the same thing but it is the very foundation of the idea of business development when it is united with productivity.

Value is a function of utility and price, or if you like, of quality and cost. From the point of view of the customer therefore, value constitutes a judgment of the utility (quality) that is added in relation to the sacrifice the customer has to make in the form of a price to obtain this utility. This is demonstrated in the diagram, below.

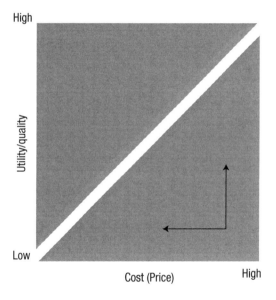

The vertical axis of the graph represents the value offered and the horizontal axis represents the price paid. On the diagonal, the customer feels s/he is getting value for money. Customers at the lower left end of the diagonal get relatively little value but also pay a relatively small price. Here we find the customer who buys one of the cheap models produced by Ford, Fiat or Volkswagen. The customer at the top right end of the diagram gets a lot of value, but pays a lot of money for it. S/he buys a Mercedes, a Saab or a Rolls Royce. Any industry with a variety of competing goods and services can be classified in this way.

Customers in the upper left triangle of the graph get more value than they pay for. They reckon they have got a bargain. Companies in this zone usually increase their market share. In actual fact the value graph for any given industry must show a fairly uniform spread of products from different companies. Some must be regarded as better value for money than others.

A company whose products are in the bottom right triangle of the graph is not so happily situated. Its product (goods and/or services) is not regarded as worth the asking price and the customer reckons s/he is paying over the odds for what s/he is getting in return.

In the bottom right triangle we have drawn a point with two arrows pointing away from it. The classical strategy for a company finding itself in this position is to move leftward in the graph by rationalizing its costs and capital (managing its resources) to be able to cut its prices, and thus be regarded as competitive.

There is however another possible way to get your product accepted as worth its price, and that is to move upward on the graph, to get your product back into the competitive diagonal by increasing its customer-perceived value. The trouble with using the value variable is that it involves taking commercial risks and is difficult to model mathematically. The thinking needed to understand what customers perceive as valuable is also different from that needed for resource management.

Customer value can be expressed in different ways. A common phenomenon is revealed by attitude surveys, on customer satisfaction, which seldom reveal information that can be used for concrete improvements. It hardly matters if an indicator falls from 68 to 65 per cent – we are none the wiser as regards what needs to be changed in order to make us more competitive or whatever. We should therefore make more use of methods based on action.

RECOMMENDED READING

1. John D Martin and J William Petty, Value Based Management: The Corporate Response to the Shareholder Revolution.

2. Richard J Park, Value Engineering: A Plan for Invention.

3. Bradley Gale: Managing Customer Value.

Values

We define values as the fundamental principles and behaviour that give an *organization its form and character and pervades its performance.* Values pervade organizations. They survive managements, new strategies and technological breakthroughs. Values could be said to be the glue that holds organizations together when operations have been decentralized, diversified, developed or expanded.

By definition, values are not discovered by some management group; they are already part of the organization. Values are a function of history, strong leaders, customers, competitive pressure and much more besides. It is as though they are in the very bricks and mortar.

Attitudes and even patterns of behaviour can be changed relatively quickly. Values take time to change. It has been recognized that it takes at least four years to change a corporate culture. To draw a parallel with individuals, research has shown that very few people change their fundamental attitudes after the age of 17.

Experiences can be positive as well as negative: a readiness to change, openness, curiosity, conservatism, self-absorption and a nasty attitude to women are all examples of values that can be present in organizations. Working on values generally seeks to stress the positive ones and make them part of the corporate culture. Negative values are harmful to a company.

Values may be somewhat intangible but they can be extremely effective in guiding and unifying a business. In strategy work, values often provide a framework for principles that must be observed on the journey to the desired future.

Concepts normally connected to a company's values are its policies, business practices and guidelines. All of these seek to establish fundamental values, and describe what they mean for the business in practical terms. An analysis of values can result in a code of behaviour or an ethical code that documents how a business stands on various questions, as well as how co-workers are expected to act.

Values can be worked on in different ways, depending on ambition level and preferences. A number of approaches are given here:

- **Employee surveys**. Co-workers are asked to take a position on a number of statements. These can be based on a standardized list of loaded words or identified through in-depth interviews. Out of 50 statements, co-workers have to mark which agree best with their organization. On this basis, a discussion is held about the values of the organization.

- **Creative exercises**. There are a number of creative exercises which can be useful to perform in seminars. For example, people could be asked to describe the business as a physical person. What characteristics and interests does this person have? What job does s/he do? What does s/he think about various questions? This exercise is often combined with one where the group has to draw the person and describe him/her. A variation of this is for participants to describe how a new employee should behave in order to like, and be successful in, the organization. The advantage of these kinds of exercise is that participants approach delicate subjects which otherwise they might not. What opinion for instance does the illustrated person have on equality of the sexes?

- **History**. We mentioned earlier that organizations were imbued with values which seemed to live in their physical structure. How then did they get there? The answer is often to be found in the company history. How was the organization affected by being owned by the county council during the 1980s? What legacy did that dynamic manager leave in the 1990s?

- **The dilemma exercise**. Another way of approaching a discussion of values is to imagine that your company faces a terrible dilemma. This should be of such a character as to put company values to the test. What for example would you do if a supplier sent you a couple of theatre tickets with his quotation?

- **Organizational-psychological diagnosis**. A skilful organizational psychologist makes a qualified diagnosis of a business's values by taking part in company meetings and group meetings and by carrying out interviews with co-workers and executives. This approach is most common in connection with conflicts or when working on negative values.

We would like to raise a finger of warning in respect of the most common kind of exercise with values, and this is where management on the basis of a vision, brand or something else, identifies a number of key words which they think should represent their organization. This can often result in clichés such as 'customer-oriented', 'businessmanship', etc. Of course these are genuine values, but if they do not truly represent an organization's real values they will never be anything but empty rhetoric. Even what Professor Evert Gummesson, of the Stockholm University School of Business, calls *legalistic values*, should be profiled (and worked on) if they characterize an organization. Gummesson gives examples of these values: rigidity, legal mumbo-jumbo, the application of inadequate laws and regulations, a focus on internal procedures, blind faith in the infallibility of experts and the ignorance of customers, and a greater interest in rituals than in the end result.

RECOMMENDED READING

Edgar H Schein, Organizational Culture and Leadership.

Value analysis

Value analysis has been with us since the beginning of the 1950s. It is known by a number of other names, such as:

1. Axiology
2. Function analysis
3. Value engineering

Value analysis emerged from the manufacturing industry and basically means that all company functions are optimized in order to deliver more value to the customer. Value analysis was developed at the end of the 1940s in the General Electric Group. The Director of Purchasing, H L Erricher, had the idea of improving the cost-function relationship of a product, that is, to give better value. Lawrence D Miles was asked by GE in Baltimore to develop a methodology for what gradually came to be called value analysis. Miles went on to become its spiritual father.

The method can be briefly described as a means of developing a product or service so that utility functions are provided at the lowest cost.

Value, on the one hand, is the relationship between the customer's utility of functions or attributes of a product or service, and on the other, the financial sacrifice in the form of a price that must be paid to have access to these functions or attributes.

This can be expressed algebraically as:

$$V = \frac{U\,(f)}{C\,(f)}$$

U (f) is the utility of functions and C (f) is the cost of these functions. The numerator and denominator are expressed in the same unit of measurement, for example, euros.

If utility increases, so too does value; if costs increase (and thus price), value decreases. Utility is usually divided into functions that correspond to attributes in a product or service.

We might divide utility into useful functions and attractiveness functions. By useful functions we mean that part of utility that promotes use. By attractiveness functions we mean such attributes of the product or service as only aim to make it desirable to acquire, use or own.

Shareholder value

For about 15 years, shareholder value has been a mantra (a hollow slogan) among mainly American consultancy firms. Value for shareholders is important, yes, but in what timeframe? Reward systems based on short-term shareholder value have unfortunately been devized that have tempted managements to balance costs, discount revenue streams and otherwise cook the books with a view to creating short-term value at the cost of long-term value.

Co-worker value

Employees are responsible for an increasing share of value added in most industries, not only in straightforward knowledge companies, but in other companies where success is founded on creative thinking. Value for employees has in many cases gone too far and people have been rewarded for their company's financial success without having participated in the innovation that was the basis for that success. Insurance clerks and pharmaceutical directors have been rewarded for what was created before their time by other people. It can be a delicate matter to reward the right people where value has been created over a period of time.

We could simply say that value is in the eye of the beholder, namely, the customer's, co-worker's or the buyer's eye. The question is how value should be distributed between the main stakeholders, who comprise employees, customers and shareholders. Suppliers are becoming an important factor in a world where more and more functions are being outsourced. Apart from all of this, the political sector and local communities are placing demands on organizations and the creation of value.

RECOMMENDED READING

1. Archie J Brahm, Axiology: The Science of Values.

2. H M Joshi, Recent Approaches to Axiology.

3. Richard J Park, Value Engineering: A Plan for Invention.

Value-based management

The concept of value-based management (VBM) has developed over the last 20 years. It started with the development of performance metrics and has gradually matured into a whole management system based on the creation of value. A number of well-known companies, among them Coca Cola, Cadbury and Du Pont, have apparently achieved good results by implementing VBM into their organizations. Proponents of VBM maintain that companies which have taken it on board perform better, but nothing is said about causality, i.e. do they take on VBM because they are successful, or are they successful because they take on VBM?

Inherent in the VBM concept is the thesis that value-based management leads to a management style which guarantees that companies and organizations will base their activities on the creation of value.

There are three important building blocks for value-based management:

1. The creation of value, meaning that there is a focus on increasing, or creating maximum value.

2. Managing for value – including shared values, corporate culture, external relations, organization and, not least, management style.

3. Measuring the creation of value: finding effective indicators for progress.

Value-based management has the ambition of creating a coherent system consisting of:

1. Corporate mission – business philosophy and business model.

2. Strategy – guidelines for achieving goals.

3. Corporate government as an expression of owners' ambitions and orientation.

4. Corporate culture.

5. Internal communication.

6. Organization.

7. Decision processes and systems.

8. Performance management.

9. Reward systems.

According to its adherents, the success of VBM depends on a company's aims, corporate mission and values. Goals can either be financial in the form of shareholder value or be oriented to a broader spectrum of stakeholders. Many people believe that in the last decade VBM has been too focused on short-term shareholder value to the detriment of both other stakeholders and the long-term perspective.

VBM is essentially an approach wrapped around an attitude. It does not really possess a systematic methodology. According to its proponents, success in the use of VBM depends on how well it has been integrated into the corporate culture, while reports would suggest that it is the converse, i.e. how well the corporate culture has been integrated into the creation of value in the organization.

VBM is all about organizing the company's main processes (performance measurement, strategic planning, budgeting, training and communication) on the basis of value creation. This approach is necessary to create a culture in which individuals and groups at all levels make decisions that are oriented to creating value for shareholders who make profits to compensate them for their financial contribution, and the risks they take by investing in the first place.

In short, we could say that VBM deliberately factors in a calculation for the use of capital with all decision-making in order to be sure that value is created. There are three questions that we should be asking ourselves within the framework of VBM:

1. How much do I need to invest in this project?
2. What profit can I expect from the project?
3. Is this profit sufficient to compensate for my risk?

VBM developed, as part of a trend where there was a deviation from traditional accounting figures, to include what were called value-based metrics representing profitability. This approach has been developed in a similar way to EVA (Economic Value Added) which came to include not only capital expenditure activated in the balance sheet but also the cost of generating profit.

RECOMMENDED READING

1. John D Martin and J William Petty, Value Based Management: The Corporate Response to the Shareholder Revolution.
2. Randolph A Pohlman and Gareth S Gardiner, Value Driven Management: How to Create and Maximize Value Over Time for Organizational Success.

Value chain

The *value chain* developed by Michael Porter represents one of the first serious attempts in the field of strategy to analyze customer need structures. Porter presented the value chain in his book *Competitive Advantage*, published in 1985.

Value is defined in this context as what buyers are willing to pay for what they get from suppliers. A company is profitable if the value it generates exceeds the cost it has to pay for generating that value. Analysis of the competitive situation must therefore be based not on cost, but on value.

According to Porter, a company's competitive edge cannot be understood simply by studying the company as a whole. A competitive advantage arises out of the manifold activities which a company pursues in its design, production, marketing, delivery and supporting functions. Each of these activities can contribute to the company's relative cost position and create a basis for differentiation.

Porter places the corporate value chain in a greater stream of activities, which he calls the value system; it is illustrated below.

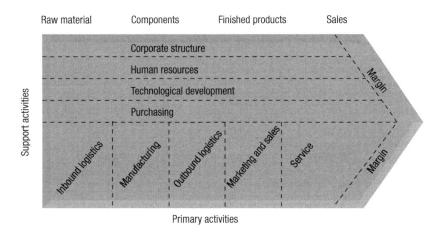

Professor Michael Porter has drawn these two diagrams to illustrate the value chain (also called the added value chain). It describes the addition of value to a product from raw material and purchasing to the finished article. By analyzing the process step by step, we can identify links in the chain where we are competitive or vulnerable.

Porter's value system

Porter's definition of value in a competitive context is the sum a buyer is willing to pay for what a supplier delivers. Value is measured as total revenue, which is a function of the price a company's product fetches and the number of units the company can sell.

Every value-generating activity involves:

- bought-in components.
- human resources.
- some form of technology.
- information flows of various kinds.

Value-generating activities can be divided into two classes:

1. Primary activities
2. Support activities

Primary activities are shown under the large arrow. They are the activities that result in the physical creation of a product and its sale, delivery to the buyer, and the after-sales market.

1. Inbound logistics comprises reception, warehousing, sorting, handling, buffer storage, stocktaking, transportation and back deliveries.

2. Manufacturing comprises all activities that convert the inflow into end products, such as machining, packaging, assembly, plant maintenance and testing.

3. Outbound logistics comprises activities concerned with shipment, warehousing and physical distribution of products to buyers. This includes order processing, scheduling, deliveries, transportation, and so on.

4. Marketing and sales comprises all activities designed to persuade buyers to accept and pay for the product. This includes advertising, sales promotion, personal selling, quotation writing, choice of distribution channels and pricing.

5. Service comprises all activities designed to maintain or enhance the value of the product delivered. This includes installation, repairs, training, spare parts and product modification.

Support activities are shown on the top four lines of the figure. They are:

1. Corporate structure, which embraces a number of activities including management, planning, finance, accounting, legal business, relations with the public sector and quality management.

2. Human resource management, which includes the recruitment, training, development and remuneration of all categories of personnel.

3. Technological development, which affects every value-generating activity in the areas of know-how, procedures and processes.

4. Purchasing, which has to do with procurement of materials, that is, the actual function of buying supplies, not the logistic flow of materials.

RECOMMENDED READING

1. Kim B Clark et al, Harvard Business Review on Managing the Value Chain.

2. Michael E Porter, Competitive Strategy: Creating and Sustaining Superior Performance.

Vertical integration

Vertical integration is an expression for the portion of value added that is produced within the framework of common ownership. If a product is sold, its price probably comprises the input costs of materials, components and systems. If the price of buying this input is high, integration is low. But if the major share of sales value is produced internally in one's organization, integration is high. The term horizontal integration is used considerably less often nowadays. It expresses the utilization of a wide range of products to achieve maximum customer satisfaction.

Vertical integration is the process of replacing market transactions by internal transactions, resulting in a planned economy in which suppliers enjoy a monopoly and consumers lack alternative choices. Vertical integration, like diversification, was at one time the height of fashion in business management, although it passed its peak of popularity several decades ago. A classic example is Singer, the American sewing machine company, which at one time integrated its total operations from primary raw material sources (forests and iron mines) to finished sewing machines.

Vertical integration in a company is closely related to the *concepts of outsourcing and make-or-buy analysis* and touches on such philosophical points as the question of whether Ronald Coase got the Nobel prize for 1992, or, where does a company begin and end and why?

Experience shows that low competitive pressure leads to a high level of integration, i.e. diversification. Those parts of the world where competitive pressure has proved to be low have thus seen too much planned economy for them to be competitive in the modern, globalized world. This has led to a discreet review of the entire business chain and consequent deliberations on outsourcing. As a result, traditional value chains are broken up and new companies are created, while at the same time the old ones have to reduce delivery capacity. Manufacture of components and supply of subsystems in the telecommunications industry have been farmed out to specialized companies with their core business in electronic production.

Most industries have now been through a phase of diminishing integration in that they are making less of the end product themselves and buying more components from outside suppliers.

In theory, all functions can be operated as separate companies. We can hive off a computer department, a factory, a sales company and other parts of the administrative apparatus. A decision on vertical integration is essentially a decision whether to make products and provide services oneself or buy them from somebody else.

The disadvantages of advanced vertical integration have become increasingly apparent with time. Advanced vertical integration was the problem that Mikhail Gorbachev wrestled with in the Soviet Union, much in the same way that traditional airline companies do. Flagship companies in Europe have traditionally been relatively free of competitive pressure and therefore have advanced levels of integration. In competition with new companies such as Ryanair or Easy.Jet such companies have problems with their cost structures but with advanced integration levels as well. These companies operate their own engine maintenance, clean their own aircraft, run their own ground support and cargo operations, etc., which of course gives rise to a whole range of intermediate transactions.

Organizations of a centralistic nature tend to have a misplaced faith in their own abilities, which is expressed in a desire to do everything themselves. Organizations tending more to the entrepreneurial, on the other hand, show the reverse tendency, making the whole chain more efficient by buying what they need from other companies. The disadvantages of advanced vertical integration are these:

1. It eliminates market forces, and with them their corrective effect on accumulation of deadwood.

2. It makes it tempting to introduce subsidies which distort the competitive picture and obscure the question of *raison d'être*.

3. It gives an artificial negotiating strength, which does not correspond to the reality of negotiations on a free market.

4. It creates mutual dependence, which can be a handicap to any of the functions involved if one of them runs into trouble.

5. The captive market (guaranteed outlet) which it creates lulls the organization into a false sense of security.

6. This false sense of security blunts the willingness and ability of the organization to compete.

Misapprehensions or a high degree of self-deception underlie many cases of vertical integration. The most usual fallacy is to believe that we can eliminate competition in a given step in the production chain by controlling this step. Some of the illusions prevalent in the world of vertical integration are:

- *Illusion 1: A strong market position at one stage of production is transferable to another stage.*

    This belief has often led to bad investment decisions in the Swedish Consumer Co-operative movement and other conglomerates, which have subsequently been affected by all the disadvantages listed above.

- *Illusion 2: In-house trading cuts out salesmen, simplifies administration and therefore makes transactions cheaper.*

  This of course, is nothing but the classic creed of adherents of the planned economy, for whom central control is dogma and free market forces anathema.

- *Illusion 3: We can rescue a strategically weak unit by buying up the link before or after it in the production chain.*

  This may be feasible in exceptional cases, but they are rare. The logic of every industry must be judged on its own merits and that applies here too, unless it is a case of diversification to spread risks.

- *Illusion 4: Knowledge of the industry can be utilized to gain a competitive edge in an upstream or downstream operation.*

  This may be true, but it is advisable to scrutinize the alleged advantages closely to be sure that the logic is not fallacious.

There are plenty of examples of spectacular improvements in profitability achieved by breaking up vertically integrated structures. This is probably the reason why business as a whole is moving in the direction of less integration. Car manufacturers with their own shipping lines do not deliver their cars to export markets more cheaply than those who use the services of independent shipping companies. Nor can they make their own gearboxes at lower cost than specialist gearbox manufacturers. The list of examples could be considerably extended.

One of the reasons why vertical integration was so popular during the technocratic era was, we believe, the evident economies of scale, which were tangible and computable, as opposed to the advantages of small scale, such as entrepreneurial spirit and competitive drive, which cannot be reduced to numbers.

There are also some definite advantages to vertical integration in certain special cases, especially where control of a key resource gives a competitive edge. Some of the advantages are:

- better co-ordination of operations with better possibilities for control.

- closer contact with end-users through forward integration.

- attainment of stable relations.

- access to technological know-how of crucial importance in a particular industry.

- assured supply of essential products and services.

The integration of Vingresor, a travel agency, into the hotel business by establishing holiday villages at tourist resorts, is an example of expansion from selling package holidays to providing holiday accommodation, a step that was reckoned to offer a strategic advantage.

SAS's investment in hotels is another example, and yet another is IKEA's backward integration from selling furniture into design and production planning, balanced by forward de-integration by leaving the last step in production, assembly of the furniture, to the customers themselves.

Vertical integration is often prompted by motives of self-aggrandisement or over-inflated pride, so it is advisable to examine our own motives if we are contemplating it.

RECOMMENDED READING

Kathryn Rudie Harrigan, Vertical Integration, Oursourcing and Corporate Strategy.

Vision

Vision in the sense of something seen in a dream is the term used to describe a picture of a company's situation in a relatively remote and desirable future. Willi Railo, the sports psychologist, defines vision as a "barrier-breaking mental picture of a desired situation". The words 'barrier-breaking' are important in Railo's description. The most important aspect of a vision is that it challenges the comfortable present, calling for action and change.

Vision plays an important role in strategic work, as it defines what future success will mean for a business. A vision should:

1. portray the long-term aspirations of a business.
2. set an ambition level for strategy work.

If a company's vision includes a plan that in five years it will go from being a local player to a leading global one, then decisions, actions and the appropriate investment will be necessary in the present to make this possible. If the vision instead aims at achieving technical supremacy in a particular area, the series of decisions and actions involved will naturally be different.

It is important to remember that there are two main types of vision. The first kind is based on a visionary or entrepreneur with strong convictions about where the business has to go. Examples of visionaries are Ingvar Kamprad (IKEA), Erling Persson (H&M) and Lars Magnus Ericsson (Ericsson).

The other kind of vision, which is by far the most common, is developed rather than suddenly discovered: a group of managers work their way to a long-term projection of a goal based on conditions in the company, trends in the business environment and intuition. This kind of vision builds on the strategic ability of a group rather than on strong entrepreneurial convictions.

It could be argued that only the first type is a real vision, while the second should really be called a long-term projection or desired future position. However, our experience is that it can be misleading rather than helpful to make such distinctions. In practice, visions are often a combination of these two main types. As we have said, intuition is an important element in the emergence of a vision. It is therefore important to have people with an insight into the business and the ability to think creatively. It may even help to call in an outsider who, by questioning and motivating, can challenge established assumptions in the business.

Inspiration may often be triggered by a consultant, someone from a trade organization, a researcher with new ideas from a particular discipline, or a role model from another industry. Apart from the right person, it is important to have the right documentation when working with a vision.

- **Owner expectations**, or the expectations of someone at a more senior organizational level, must be clear. The realization of a vision should lead to the fulfilment of owner expectations, so a good idea is to hold a seminar with the company board to discuss the vision in question.

- **The business concept** (or operations concept in non-commercial environments) will form a framework for the process, although it may be challenged by a vision.

- **The business environment**, with its trends and developments, either in the form of an analysis, or through the involvement of people with the required expertise. A business vision must be in harmony with the expected development of the industry or business environment in general.

- **Current strengths and weaknesses** of the organization, in particular those of its co-workers and customers. It is to the advantage of a business if a vision indicates a direction that makes it possible to use its strengths, while at the same time steering clear of its most serious weaknesses. Here we would like to point out that it is crucial for personnel working with a vision not to be unduly hampered by conditions around them. With this in mind, time spent on a vision will be time well spent.

We have seen examples of the vision of a business as a powerful tool for motivation and impelling progress. There have also been examples of visions being put to the wrong use.

Towards the end of the 1990s especially, visions were used to communicate with shareholders rather than to motivate co-workers. Visions ('we want') were often mixed up with forecasts ('we believe'), contributing to the creation of the proverbial bubble that burst.

The business of formulating a vision should not be overly formalized. In one organization, a memo went out to managers in which visions were referred to in more or less the following way:

"Departmental visions must be handed in to central administration by 24 April, at the latest, to be listed for the Spring Planning Conference on 4 May."

Some visions are justifiably seen as vague or overstated. One-liners on the theme of "biggest, best, loveliest", which could be used for any company at all, come to mind. In our experience, there are two reasons for this. One is that a vision may have been produced to satisfy some requirement from a head of planning or the owners, instead of being the guiding star for the development of the business as a whole. The other has to do with how a vision is communicated.

We have seen company management who have been through a painstaking process to arrive at a vision. Different aspects of the business have been clarified, trends analyzed and scenarios elaborated.

For management that has been through an intellectual journey, a vision can have deep significance and intensity. However, when this vision is then communicated to personnel who have not gone through the same journey, it can run the risk of seeming woolly and devoid of meaning. Desirable as it may be to find a vision that can be expressed pithily, it can be very dangerous to summarize without explaining the content or the reasoning behind it.

One of the challenges we face when we work on a vision, is to raise our sights and leave behind acute, operative daily tasks. It can be difficult to think five or ten years ahead when customers arrive with their enquiries and staff are knocking on the door.

As with strategy work in general, the task of formulating a vision must be pursued with extra energy and in parallel with operative work. Having a role model can be a powerful tool for raising ambition levels in strategy work.

Suppose you are a high jumper and you think that the best you can do in a five-year period is 2.41m. You then see a fellow athlete jump 2.45m. You will most probably try to raise your target. If your fellow athlete jumps 2.45m, your barrier-breaking mental picture of a desired future might be to jump 2.50m! The same idea holds for businesses in general.

Some companies base their visions on competition with role models:

- The cycle industry's Nike (Giro Sport Design, 1986).

- To get the same respect in 20 years as Hewlett Packard has today (Watkins-Johnson, 1996).

- The Harvard of the West (Stanford University, 1940s).

For more on role model learning, see *Benchlearning and Benchmarking*.

RECOMMENDED READING

1. Jim Collins and Jerry I Porras, Built to Last: Successful Habits of Visionary Companies.

3. Ken Blanchard and Jesse Stoner, Full Steam Ahead! Unleash the Power of Vision in Your Company and Your Life.

Yield management

Yield, as in the term 'yield management', refers to the starting capital of companies with a heavy capital base and fluctuating capitalization rate.

The concept of yield management has mainly emerged in service companies like hotels, airlines, rail companies, etc, which are characterized by high capital intensity, variable willingness to pay, fixed capacity, low variable costs and real-time demand. The crisis experienced by airlines all over the world in 2003 is a measure of the crucial importance of capacity utilization in connection with high fixed costs.

There are a number of factors in yield management that interact to optimize finances. The main ones are the following:

1. A division of the customer base into distinct market segments based on price, i.e. willingness to pay, as the differentiation element.

2. A detailed knowledge of sales and booking data in order to forecast demand.

3. An important factor is overbooking, which is based on detailed analysis of past customer behaviour and how this will affect future bookings.

4. Whether it be manual or computerized, it is vital to have an efficient information system. Yield management is based on comprehensive selection and handling of data.

5. Yield management is really a form of discrimination that manages to maximise profit by weighing together the elements of price, product, buyer and willingness to pay, and thereby increasing net returns.

Information technology has made it possible to do what they do so well in oriental bazaars, that is, estimate the price that each potential customer is willing to pay, then sell to those customers who are ready to pay the highest price. Yield management, then, is the essence of what good businessmanship should be; it is based on some of the most complicated resources in management, such as segmentation, price elasticity evaluation, and detailed forecasting based on comprehensive statistics and access to IT.

To begin with, the reader might wonder why some customers are willing to pay more for goods and services than others. Why, for example, can a hairdresser charge a higher price on Saturdays and offer discounts to students on Tuesday afternoons? Why can passengers flying tourist class pay a much lower price than the business class passenger who booked her flight just before take-off? The problem in many service industries with a large capital base is to adapt probable demand of a limited resource and in so doing maximise capacity utilization, prices and profit. Yield management is mainly based on market segmentation and helps marketing organizations to optimize the efficient use of available fixed resources, thereby contributing to financial success.

Or to put it even more simply, we could say that yield management is a technique whereby the right kind of capacity is allocated to the right customer at the right price in order to maximise revenue (i.e. profit). There are still many areas in which yield management has not been generally applied, for example in the operation of ski lifts, golf courses, theatres, museums or public attractions.

One of the best-known examples of yield management to date is that of the Ford Motor Co. During a period which saw falling prices and markets in decline in the USA, Ford was able to raise their prices by 0.2 per cent. During one quarter, yield management was responsible for 260 million dollars out of 896 million dollars in profits. Clever pricing has been an important link in the development of the Ford Group and Bill Ford, Chairman and now CEO, has appointed their revenue strategist Lloyd E Hansen as Vice-President Controller in charge of revenue management.

Now, after a number of years, we are witnessing a paradox: some companies are applying intelligent yield management through segmentation, price elasticity, etc, while others are achieving success by simply operating without frills at the lowest possible costand offering their customers, "one price for everyone, always".

Yield management is closely related to the marketing function in businesses and other organizations, and its implementation calls for a number of marketing principles, for example:

1. Identification of customer base using segmentation techniques. Ideally, we should be able to connect certain customer groups to certain times or other purchasing factors.

2. Communicate changes in customer needs and expectations to the whole organization.

3. Pay attention to price elasticity of demand (i.e. how volumes change with price levels) for different segments.

4. Produce historical analyzes of demand that can be combined with the best possible forecasting methods.

5. Educate the organization to think in terms of yield management.

The Chartered Institute of Marketing, based in the United States, has defined marketing as follows:

"Marketing is the management process responsible for identifying, anticipating and satisfying customer requirements profitably."

We can apply the same definition to yield management by simply exchanging the word marketing for yield management. The reader may well appreciate the close connection between yield management and relationship marketing. The leading principle in relationship marketing is that every customer transaction should not be seen as an isolated case but in the context of transactions past and transactions yet to come.

RECOMMENDED READING

1. Anthony Ingold et al (ed), Yield Management: Strategies for the Service Industries.

2. Sylvain Daudel, Barry K. Humphreys and George Vialle, Yield Management: Applications to Air Transport and Other Service Industries.

Zero-base planning

Zero-base analysis is founded on existential grounds. It is a great deal more radical than continuous improvement methods. In its purest form, zero-base planning begins with a clean sheet of paper. Every step of a company's operations, beginning with the most important, is called into question.

The method has two essential functions:

1. A diagnostic function, in that it begins by questioning the very existence of work tasks.

2. A procedural function, in that other frames of reference, such as benchmarking exercises or internal demand, can be transformed in practice through zero-base planning.

The method is said to have had its origins among president Jimmy Carter's staff. Since then it has been taken up generally and is popular with a number of consultancy firms.

Many business leaders have been attracted to the method's uncompromising and radical approach. It is often difficult to improve effectiveness because of an inability to get to the roots of problems. The zero-base method can therefore be extremely useful because it calls for a radical and creative approach (creative in the sense of re-integrating known elements in completely new ways).

The method's stages can be briefly described as follows:

1. Break down every function into a number of activities that can be handled easily and establish the purpose of each function.

2. Where relevant, establish why an activity is not performed at all and take appropriate action.

3. Look at different ways of carrying out activities, each way with a different level of service. This should include a *make/buy analysis* (see this term).

4. Determine the risks of large-scale change in the organization or in a process.

5. Act on your analysis through renewals and cost reduction.

Through the use of zero-base planning we can find more efficient ways of utilizing resources and at the same time abandon unnecessary work tasks; we can then apply ourselves to the 'right things'. We can see if things are being done 'in the right way' by applying the make/buy methodology or an alternative approach. The steps in this approach can of course be adapted to the actual situation. In this respect, R&D departments and other special cases should be handled rather differently.

Zero-base planning should be used with one caveat: the tough, radical approach can be overdone. We sometimes see this in companies at diagnostic meetings. People tend to exaggerate when they are invited to be openly critical. In the same way, the opportunities of saving costs through zero-base planning tend to be exaggerated.

Against this should be set the very common circumstance that a business bases its existence mainly on what it has to offer, rather than on what people want to buy. As in most things, it is a question of maintaining a balance.

Our experience is that the zero-base process is most useful when, instead of contemplating its navel (i.e. the very grounds for its existence), a business looks more objectively at how its processes can be improved. In other words, we prefer zero-base planning as a procedural instrument to reduce costs rather than as a diagnostic instrument to find the correct basis for a company's cost reductions. This is in no way to detract from the methodology; we are only indicating where the system can be best applied. Zero-base planning on a more general level is common in connection with visions and organizational change. What we do is to imagine that there are no problems or structures that get in our way and then find the right way to make a completely new beginning. The radically new picture is then contrasted with reality and used as a template for prioritizing the long-term work of change.

RECOMMENDED READING

Paul J Stonich, Zero-base Planning and Budgeting: Improved Case Control and Resource Allocation.

Index

D

E

H

I

J

K

P

418

S

Z

Other titles from Thorogood

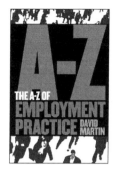

THE A-Z OF EMPLOYMENT PRACTICE

David Martin
£19.99 paperback, £42.00 hardback
Published November 2004

This book provides comprehensive, practical guidance on personnel law and practice at a time when employers are faced with a maze of legislation, obligations and potential penalties. It provides detailed and practical advice on what to do and how to do it.

The A to Z format ensures that sections appear under individual headings for instant ease of reference. The emphasis is not so much on the law as on its implications; the advice is expert, clear and practical, with a minimum of legal references. Checklists, procedures and examples are all given as well as warnings on specific pitfalls.

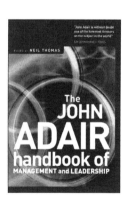

THE JOHN ADAIR HANDBOOK OF MANAGEMENT AND LEADERSHIP

John Adair • Edited by Neil Thomas
£12.99 paperback, £24.99 hardback
Published April 2004

"A book for constant reference … A great achievement …ought to be found on every manager's bookshelf."
JOURNAL OF THE INSTITUTE OF PUBLIC SECTOR MANAGEMENT

"… without doubt one of the foremost thinkers on the subject in the world." SIR JOHN HARVEY-JONES

A master-class in managing yourself and others, it combines in one volume all of Adair's thought and writing on leadership, teambuilding, creativity and innovation, problem solving, motivation and communication.

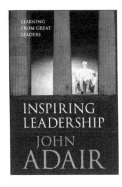

INSPIRING LEADERSHIP

Learning from great leaders

John Adair

£15.99 paperback, £24.99 hardback

Published January 2003

'I discovered once again how rare it is to come upon a book about leaders with depth, conceptual bite and historical context. It was a relief and joy'.

WARREN BENNIS, US MAJOR LEADERSHIP GURU

'I believe it is a 'must read' book... He is without doubt one of the foremost thinkers on the subject in the world.'

SIR JOHN HARVEY-JONES, PREVIOUSLY CEO OF ICI

Great leaders from Lao Tzu, Machiavelli and Washington to Thatcher, Mandela and Reagan are not only great leaders in history, they also have much to teach us today about the nature and practice of leadership. Adair uncovers their different facets of leadership in this heavily illustrated book.

COMPANY DIRECTOR'S DESKTOP GUIDE

David Martin

£16.99 paperback

Published June 2004

The role of the company director is fundamental to the success of any business, yet the tasks, responsibilities and liabilities that directors' face become more demanding with every change to the law.

Written in a clear, jargon-free style, this is a comprehensive guide to the complex legislation and procedures governing all aspects of the company director's role. The author's wide experience as a Director and Secretary of a plc and consultant and author provides a manual that is expert, practical and easy to access.

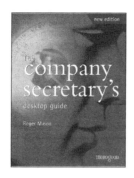

THE COMPANY SECRETARY'S DESKTOP GUIDE

Roger Mason
£16.99 paperback
Published April 2004

Written in a clear, jargon-free style, this is a comprehensive guide to the complex legislation and procedures governing all aspects of the company secretary's work. The Company Secretary's role becomes more demanding with every change to the law and practice. The author's considerable experience as both Company Secretary and lecturer and author has ensured a manual that is expert, practical and easy to access.

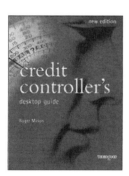

THE CREDIT CONTROLLER'S DESKTOP GUIDE
Proven procedures and techniques for getting paid on time and preserving cash

Roger Mason
£16.99 paperback
Published September 2004

Clear and jargon-free, this is an expert and practical guide to the techniques of effective credit control. This book takes account of all the recent changes to the law and practice, including: winding up, bankruptcy, receivership and administration, following implementation of The Enterprise Act 2002; statutory interest; obtaining judgment for unpaid debts; the abolition of Crown Preference and the effect on ordinary creditors; new rules concerning the recovery of VAT when there is a bad debt; what is available from Companies House; the latest thinking on retention of title clauses in conditions of sale.

SUCCESSFUL BUSINESS PLANNING

Norton Paley
£14.99 paperback, £29.99 hardback
Published June 2004

"Growth firms with a written business plan have increased their revenues 69 per cent faster over the past five years than those without a written plan."

FROM A SURVEY BY PRICEWATERHOUSECOOPERS

We know the value of planning – in theory. But either we fail to spend the time required to go through the thinking process properly, or we fail to use the plan effectively. Paley uses examples from real companies to turn theory into practice.

THE SHORTER MBA

A practical approach to the key business skills

Barrie Pearson and Neil Thomas
£35.00 Hardback • Published July 2004

A succinct distillation of the skills that you need to be successful in business. Most people can't afford to give up two years to study for an MBA. This pithy, practical book presents all the essential theory, practiced and techniques taught to MBA students – ideal for the busy practising executive. It is divided into three parts:

- Personal development
- Management skills
- Business development

HIGH-PERFORMANCE CONSULTING SKILLS

The internal consultant's guide to value-added performance

Mark Thomas

£14.99 paperback, £24.99 hardback

Published November 2003

This book provides a practical understanding of the skills required to become a high-performance internal consultant, whatever ones own area of expertise. It will help you to: market your services and build powerful internal networks; secure greater internal client commitment to initiatives and change projects; enhance your own worth and value to the organization; develop stronger more productive working relationships with internal clients.

MANAGE TO WIN

Norton Paley

£15.99 paperback, £29.99 hardback

Published April 2005

Learn how to reshape and reposition your company to meet tougher challenges and competitors, when to confront and when to retreat, how to assess risk and opportunity and how to move to seize opportunities and knock-out the competition. Real-life case-studies and examples throughout the text. Extensive appendix of practical guidelines, numerous management tools and usable checklists.

Thorogood also has an extensive range of reports and special briefings which are written specifically for professionals wanting expert information.

For a full listing of all Thorogood publications, or to order any title, please call Thorogood Customer Services on 020 7749 4748 or fax on 020 7729 6110. Alternatively view our website at **www.thorogood.ws**.

BUSINESS SEMINARS

Focused on developing your potential

Falconbury, the sister company to Thorogood publishing, brings together the leading experts from all areas of management and strategic development to provide you with a comprehensive portfolio of action-centred training and learning.

We understand everything managers and leaders need to be, know and do to succeed in today's commercial environment. Each product addresses a different technical or personal development need that will encourage growth and increase your potential for success.

- Practical public training programmes
- Tailored in-company training
- Coaching
- Mentoring
- Topical business seminars
- Trainer bureau/bank
- Adair Leadership Foundation

The most valuable resource in any organization is its people; it is essential that you invest in the development of your management and leadership skills to ensure your team fulfil their potential. Investment into both personal and professional development has been proven to provide an outstanding ROI through increased productivity in both you and your team. Ultimately leading to a dramatic impact on the bottom line.

With this in mind Falconbury have developed a comprehensive portfolio of training programmes to enable managers of all levels to develop their skills in leadership, communications, finance, people management, change management and all areas vital to achieving success in today's commercial environment.

What Falconbury can offer you?

- Practical applied methodology with a proven results
- Extensive bank of experienced trainers
- Limited attendees to ensure one-to-one guidance
- Up to the minute thinking on management and leadership techniques
- Interactive training
- Balanced mix of theoretical and practical learning
- Learner-centred training
- Excellent cost/quality ratio

Falconbury In-Company Training

Falconbury are aware that a public programme may not be the solution to leadership and management issues arising in your firm. Involving only attendees from your organization and tailoring the programme to focus on the current challenges you face individually and as a business may be more appropriate. With this in mind we have brought together our most motivated and forward thinking trainers to deliver tailored in-company programmes developed specifically around the needs within your organization.

All our trainers have a practical commercial background and highly refined people skills. During the course of the programme they act as facilitator, trainer and mentor, adapting their style to ensure that each individual benefits equally from their knowledge to develop new skills.

Falconbury works with each organization to develop a programme of training that fits your needs.

Mentoring and coaching

Developing and achieving your personal objectives in the workplace is becoming increasingly difficult in today's constantly changing environment. Additionally, as a manager or leader, you are responsible for guiding colleagues towards the realization of their goals. Sometimes it is easy to lose focus on your short and long-term aims.

Falconbury's one-to-one coaching draws out individual potential by raising self-awareness and understanding, facilitating the learning and performance development that creates excellent managers and leaders. It builds renewed self-confidence and a strong sense of 'can-do' competence, contributing significant benefit to the organization. Enabling you to focus your energy on developing your potential and that of your colleagues.

Mentoring involves formulating winning strategies, setting goals, monitoring achievements and motivating the whole team whilst achieving a much improved work life balance.

Falconbury – Business Legal Seminars

Falconbury Business Legal Seminars specializes in the provision of high quality training for legal professionals from both in-house and private practice internationally.

The focus of these events is to provide comprehensive and practical training on current international legal thinking and practice in a clear and informative format.

Event subjects include, drafting commercial agreements, employment law, competition law, intellectual property, managing an in-house legal department and international acquisitions.

For more information on all our services please contact Falconbury on +44 (0) 20 7729 6677 or visit the website at: www.falconbury.co.uk.